Adventures at the Auction

D1401182

Adventures at the Auction

THE ULTIMATE GUIDE
TO BUYING AND SELLING AT AUCTION—
IN PERSON AND ONLINE

Leslie Hindman
with Dan Santow

THREE RIVERS PRESS • NEW YORK

Published by Three Rivers Press, New York, New York. Member of the Crown Publishing Group.

Random House, Inc. New York, Toronto, London, Sydney, Auckland
www.randomhouse.com

Three Rivers Press and the Tugboat design are registered trademarks of Random House, Inc.
Originally published in hardcover by Clarkson Potter in 2001.

Printed in the United States of America

Design by Maggie Hinders

Hindman, Leslie.
Adventures at the auction: The ultimate guide to buying and selling at
auction—in person and online / Leslie Hindman.—1st ed.
1. Auctions—Computer network resources.   I. Title.
HF5478.H56   2001
025.06'38117—dc21
00-055073

ISBN 0-609-80819-2

10   9   8   7   6   5   4   3   2   1

First Paperback Edition

Acknowledgments

In many ways, this book took a lifetime to write and is the product of many more voices and experiences than merely my own. I am fortunate to have been involved in the auction business, one that I love and one that is constantly challenging and changing, and I've been blessed to have worked with an incredibly talented group of people through the years. We at Leslie Hindman Auctioneers might have dreamt of success together, but ultimately it was built by each person individually, one at a time. It's these people—my mentors, my colleagues, my friends—to whom I dedicate this book.

I am indebted to the entire staff at Eppraisals.com, the online appraisal service I founded in 1999. My thanks especially go out to Gary Piattoni, Andrew Decker, Michael Tirrell, Ann Gaughan, Sam Stott, Jerramie Glover, Sarah Gordon, Wendy Fleske, Tania Ralli, Tim Douglas, Derek Sheaks, Elizabeth Rossi, Joe Crump, and Tom Finke, without whose help and assistance the writing and researching of this book would have been impossible. In addition, I'd like to especially thank my colleague Dan Santow, without whom this book simply could not have been written.

Also, from the Eppraisals.com Experts Network, I'd be remiss in not pointing out the assistance given to me by Susan Bagdade, Al Bagdade, Elizabeth Kurella, Ellie Thompson, Reyne Haines, Sarah Shinn Pratt, Paul O. Phillips, Maury Bynum, Chris Coy, Robert Reichner, Roseann Ettinger, Richard Norton, Dan Weinberg, and Michael FitzSimmons.

Of my many friends and colleagues who throughout my career have been an inspiration, I would like to thank in particular Nate Berkus, Robin Kimball Eisenbeis, Scot Campbell, Manya Sheehan Basile, Lita Solis-Cohen, Maron Hindman, Terry Dunning, Tom Porter, Tom Weschler, and Virginia Weschler, for their knowledge of our industry, their kind words, and their sage advice.

The staff at Butterfields, both in San Francisco and here in Chicago, was a constant source of aid, in particular Patrick Meade, Leslie Wright, Steven Zick, Levi Morgan, and Alice Kaufman. Thank you all.

Others whose input, help, and experience were indispensable to me include Alan Wintermute, Bill Goldstein, Bill van Stratten, Amy Campbell, and Susan Brown.

To Lauren Shakely, my editor, and to Maggie Hinders, Joy Sikorski, Mark McCauslin, and all the others at Clarkson Potter with whom I've been fortunate to work, thank you for giving me this opportunity.

Special thanks to my colleagues at Thea Flaum Productions, including Thea, of course, and our director Bill Heitz, as well as to the entire staff at HGTV, including Burton Jablin, Channing Dawson, and Ken Love, all of whom provided valuable assistance. In addition, this book could never have been written without the love and support of my mother and father, Don and Pat Hindman, and that of Blair Hull.

Finally, I would never have founded Leslie Hindman Auctioneers or Eppraisals.com, let alone have been so fortunate, had it not been for two of my dearest friends who just so happen to also be my most respected mentors, Fred Krehbiel and Richard "Buzz" Norton. To them I owe so much yet all I can say is thank you from the bottom of my heart.

Contents

Appendixes

Introduction

Many people are afraid of auctions! And no wonder.

They move *this* fast.

The language can seem as confusing as hearing Shakespeare for the first time. And at first it's hard to tell who's bidding and how much they're bidding.

To make matters worse, everyone seems to know exactly what's going on—everyone, that is, but you.

If it is any comfort, you are not alone in thinking that auctions can be a tricky, confusing business. I founded one of the largest auction houses in the country, which Sotheby's acquired in 1997, so I know firsthand just how intimidating auctions can be for newcomers.

The simple truth is that even confident, highly competent people who are interested buyers can walk into an auction house and find themselves at a loss. Depending on their personality, some newcomers sit mute, afraid to jump into the bidding. Others, the competitive ones that auction houses covet, succumb to auction fever, start bidding, and sometimes can't stop.

For those who want to sell their belongings, auction houses can be even more intimidating. Some auction houses are filled with snobs who will laugh at your grandmother's treasures. Or an object will fail to sell and you will be stuck with it. Just the question of how to get that chest of drawers you inherited across town to the auction house can be daunting enough.

To end the mystery for buyers and sellers alike, I host two television shows on the Home and Garden Network (HGTV): *At the Auction with Leslie Hindman* and *The Appraisal Fair*. In *At the Auction* I walk you through the process, familiarizing you with what you might encounter along the way. For *The Appraisal Fair* a team of art and antiques experts and I set up shop at Navy Pier in Chicago. Hundreds of people line up in advance, clutching their prized possessions, hoping to be one of the lucky few whose flea market or garage sale find or inherited Victorian silver tea service will turn out to be the key to early retirement.

Sometimes those possessions turn out to be beautiful but of more sentimental than monetary value. Sometimes, however, family treasures are truly treasures, worth much more than the person ever expected. Bowls that for years were used to mix cookie dough are suddenly insured and displayed in curio cabinets. Paintings emerge from attics to achieve prominence above the mantel.

You can buy almost anything at auction, including real estate, Arabian horses, fish by the ton, and used washing machines, but my goal on television—and in this book—is simply to demystify the world of auctions that sell primarily works of art, antiques, and collectibles at brick-and-mortar auction houses like Christie's and Sotheby's and on Internet sites such as eBay, Yahoo!, eHammer, and Auction Universe—to name just a few of hundreds of sites.

Auctions have changed dramatically just in the past five years. Through the mid-1990s going to an auction meant *going* to an auction. Traditional auctions are still popular, but going to an auction today might also mean sitting in your bathrobe at 2:00 A.M. while drinking hot chocolate and logging on to the Internet. There you'll find over two million auctions going on simultaneously—*two million auctions!* There are auctions for hobnail glass cake stands and auctions for first edition Noël Coward songbooks. There are auctions for vintage Barbie doll floral print dresses and auctions for Sheffield plated candlesticks. If you can name it, someone is auctioning it.

Internet auctions have revolutionized the way we think about auctions, but they have also underscored how very similar the process of selling and buying at auction is, whether in real space or cyberspace. Pierre Omidyar founded eBay in 1995 so that his wife could sell and build her Pez dispenser collection. It proceeded to grow in leaps and bounds, but it had no relationship to any brick-and-mortar auction house.

Today the established auction houses are fully aware of the power and potential of the Internet—and vice versa. In 1999 Internet eBay bought brick-and-mortar Butterfields for $260 million in eBay stock. That same year, brick-and-mortar Sotheby's joined with Internet Amazon to form Sothebys.Amazon to sell higher-end arts and collectibles over the Internet. Increasingly, auction houses themselves are creating online auction sites as adjuncts to their brick-and-mortar business operations.

In this newly united auction world the rules, the do's and don'ts, and the how-to's, are in many cases different. As a consigner at a live auction you merely drop off your goods, sign a contract, and take care of a few other minor details, all of which I'll discuss later, and that's pretty much it.

As a consigner at an Internet auction, however, you are not only the seller, you are the auction house, too. Whether you like it or not, by choosing to sell online, you identify yourself as a business, with all of the attendant responsibilities. So even if you think you are just trying to unload a pair of silver candlesticks your great-aunt gave you last Christmas, potential buyers—or bidders, in this case—assume you have considered all the details, just as anyone else in business would: What kind of payment will you accept? How will you ship the candlesticks once they are sold? How will you charge for shipping? Will you charge for handling?

You not only have to ask yourself these and many other questions beforehand, but you have to have answered them all as well, to your own satisfaction and to that of your potential customer.

Selling objects through a brick-and-mortar auction house is easy, but it's a service you pay for with a commission; selling online is a responsibility, but you share none of the profits, except, of course, with the IRS.

In these pages, you will find advice on how to navigate the online sites, but the technical details on how to upload your images, use a digital camera, and post information can be found in online tutorials available on most auction sites. In today's fast-paced world, where technological change moves at the speed of light, if not faster, the most up-to-date information about these things will always be found on the Internet itself.

I want you to discover that buying and selling at auction—no matter if you are wearing a pinstripe suit and bidding at Christie's or are in shorts and a T-shirt at the computer in your home office—is far from the nerve-racking process that many people imagine. Instead, it is a lot of fun.

You don't need to be an expert to understand this wonderful world. I'm going to take you by the hand throughout this book and help you beat back the fear—and realize the excitement—by learning how to buy and sell at auction.

I fell in love with auctions in 1978. One of my first jobs after college was as an administrative assistant in the Chicago office of Sotheby's. Every day as I toiled away in the office with Catharine Hamilton, an elegant Sotheby's Midwest representative who at the time managed the Chicago office, I would secretly eye the wonderful art and antiques that came in through the front door but left through the back door, heading for New York to be sold in the Sotheby's salesroom.

In 1980, after much pleading, Catharine persuaded Sotheby's to hold an auction in Chicago. We worked feverishly on securing consignments, calling dealers, and using our connections to gather what I thought—and still think, in retrospect—was an impressive array of works of art to be sold. Since Sotheby's had no Chicago salesroom, we contracted with the Drake Hotel, on Michigan Avenue, to use their gilded and aptly named Grand Ballroom.

The auction, Sotheby's first in Chicago, was a great success, but even so the auction house hesitated to invest the time and resources needed to establish a permanent branch in the Midwest.

When Sotheby's decided not to pursue Chicago auctions in 1981, I decided to open my own auction house, called Leslie Hindman Auctioneers. I was twenty-seven years old, hardworking, determined, and as it turned out, lucky. It didn't hurt that I had nothing to lose and everything to gain.

Few people realize that the key to a successful auction business isn't how good you are at *selling* property but how good you are at *obtaining* good property to sell in the first place. I can stand at the lectern all day, gavel in hand, trying to sell what people have consigned, but if the quality of that merchandise is poor, no one will bother to attend my sales. Searching for the right mix of objects to sell at an auction is one of the auctioneer's most important skills.

Fortunately, I soon discovered that I had a certain flair for marketing and for creating a friendly and welcoming atmosphere that encouraged people not only to come to our auctions but also to trust us to sell their antique silver collections, their household estates, their libraries, and anything else of value—real or imagined.

Leslie Hindman Auctioneers was a full-service auction house, willing to take all the property from an estate, from vacuum cleaners to fine French porcelain. (I once really did sell a vacuum cleaner, from the estate of Mrs. Robert R. McCormick, the *Chicago Tribune* family matriarch.) Though we were competing against firms like Christie's and Sotheby's for consignments, our "we'll take it all" business philosophy won us some plum assignments.

We sold the estates not only of Mrs. McCormick but of many other socially prominent Chicagoans and their families: Elizabeth Cheney, of the Dole pineapple family; the Potter Palmer family; and Mrs. Ruth K. Flower, whose estate on Chicago's North Shore included more than 10,000 objects. We sold off the old Comiskey Park as well, along with lockers, seats, bricks, uniforms, and signs. Within a few years, we had built the number one auction house in the entire Midwest.

Then luck stepped in and gave us the opportunity to make news around the world.

One day in 1990 we sent one of our representatives to a modest home outside Milwaukee to appraise some Victorian furniture. While he was there he noticed a small oil painting, a still life with flowers, hanging in a hallway. It was not included among the objects he was there to see, but any good auction house employee keeps his eyes open.

"We've always called it our little van Gogh," said the owner, almost embarrassed at her presumption. She explained that her husband had inherited it from an uncle, a banker in Zurich, Switzerland, who had purchased it sometime between 1910 and 1930. "It's our favorite painting, even though we know it's worthless."

Little it was. But if it *was* a van Gogh—and the unlikelihood of finding an original van Gogh hanging in the hallway of a ranch house in Wisconsin wasn't lost on our representative—it was, to put it mildly, hardly worthless. He looked at it once, then twice, and finally he couldn't take his eyes off it. He asked if he could take it back to Chicago with him for further investigation. After receiving the owner's approval, he took the precaution of having the "little painting" insured for $25,000, then loaded the picture into his car and drove carefully back to Chicago.

Although we all looked at it immediately upon his return to the auction house, the painting sat around the auction house for nearly three weeks before we took it to a professional. After all, it wasn't unusual for people to bring us a work of art thinking that it might be an undiscovered Picasso or Rembrandt or even a van Gogh. To be honest, we were pretty skeptical about the "van Gogh" and didn't think it required our immediate attention.

Finally, though, we took the picture to Robert Henry Adams, a dealer in fine art whose gallery was right around the corner, and he surprised us by saying that it might actually—maybe, who knows?—be a van Gogh. In fact, he bet me that it was. He urged us to keep investigating. We then began the long process of getting the painting authenticated. We sent transparencies to Impressionist painting experts in Chicago and New York. They all agreed that the possibility that it might be for real could not be ruled out.

We finally sent the photographs to the ultimate authority, the van Gogh Museum in Amsterdam. There, a panel of the world's top van Gogh experts examined the photographs. Their decision came through by fax right after New Year's 1991. The brushstrokes, they concluded, were typically van Gogh. The coloring and composition were similar to those in other still lifes the artist did during the summer of 1886, when he was in Paris.

It was, they concluded, an authentic work by Vincent van Gogh!

Before 1991 we had sold many fabulous artworks and antiques, but uncovering the van Gogh gave us an international reputation. Two months later the auction took place amid a torrent of worldwide publicity. We were covered by *Good Morning America, Le Figaro,* CNN, and *Time* magazine. Even *Late Night with David Letterman* called, trying to book the Milwaukee couple as guests. On a sunny fall afternoon I stood at the podium with my favorite good-luck gavel in hand and sold "our" van

Gogh to a Japanese businessman for $1.43 million. It was, to put it plainly, one of the most exciting moments of my life.

I have often thought that my van Gogh story is a good illustration of why people fall in love with auctions. It's the thrill of coming across the unexpected, of discovering something new (even though it's old), that keeps them coming back again and again.

1

Starting Out

1

Types of Auctions

Virtually every auction house and the companies that run auctions have their own personalities and cultures. The most prestigious auction houses appear, at first glance, to be hush-toned galleries rather than bustling marketplaces. Walking into Christie's at Rockefeller Center in New York City is like walking into a high-class yet rather bland-looking law firm. Everyone struts around exuding efficiency. Fit young men in well-tailored suits and preppy-looking women crisscross the lobby carrying catalogs, escorting rich collectors and hoping-to-be-rich consignors through the premises. Gold-framed portraits line the walls, a landscape perches on a nearby easel, and in the distance, in one of the many exhibition galleries, an assortment of American furniture and silver presents as fine a display as you would see in the museums of many cities. No one speaks above a whisper.

And yet, denim-clad customers still appear, a collector might occasionally lie on his back inspecting a chest-on-chest at a presale exhibition, and huge crowds can sometimes overflow into hallways and beyond during the actual auction.

Auction houses, by their very nature—that is, the kind of business they're in—have to be somewhat relaxed. After all, they are, in a way, stores.

In the United States, by far the most common type of auction is the English, or open outcry, auction. Here, the bidding starts at or below what the consignor is willing to sell an object for and increases as interested bidders vie to outbid one another. The bidding stops when the last person standing, so to speak, is the only person remaining who thinks the object is worth the price, whether it is $50, $100, $1,000, $1,000,000, or more. Bidders usually raise numbered paddles or cards to indicate their bids. At country auctions, bidders sometimes still shout out their bids for all to hear.

Dutch auctions are far less common today than in the past. Dutch auctions are the opposite of the English auction: instead of starting with the low bid and working up, the auctioneer starts the bidding at a high price and keeps dropping it until some-one bites—that is, until someone in the audience is willing to pay. In a Dutch auction, the winner is the only actual bidder, which makes the process especially tricky. You absolutely have to know what you are willing to pay for an object in order to partic-ipate. There are no second chances as there are in ascending-price auctions.

The other types of auctions are rarely practiced today. There is the Japanese hand-sign auction, in which hand signals, similar to American Sign Language, but indicating prices not words or letters, are placed simultaneously. In the ancient Chi-nese handshake-auction bidders shake the hand of the auctioneer, indicating a bid by squeezing the auctioneer's fingers in such a way as to indicate the amount. The winner's name is subsequently called out by the auctioneer. By far my favorite type of exotic auction is the charming lighted-candle type. This is an old English way to conduct a sale in which the auctioneer lights a small candle just as the bidding begins. The bidding continues as the candle burns and the flame flickers. Whatever bid stands the moment the flame gutters out is the winning bid.

Auction House Types

At the high end of the auction house world are Christie's and Sotheby's, both of which are huge international corporations with branches in New York, Los Ange-les, and Chicago and salesrooms or offices in many other cities around the world, from places you would expect—Paris and London, for instance—to some you might not, such as Reykjavik, Tel Aviv, and Shanghai. Actually, this shouldn't nec-essarily be that surprising. In my travels, I've attended auctions in Vietnam, Zan-zibar, and Tanzania, among other places, which just proves that where there is property to be sold, auctions will be found.

Christie's and Sotheby's hold regular, well-publicized sales of fine art and antiques, publish glossy catalogs, host lavish parties to which the city's elite are invited, and are covered in such glossy magazines as *Art & Auction* and *Town & Coun-try*. Although they appear fancy compared to country auction houses these firms do not limit themselves to Louis this and Louis that and paintings by Picasso and Renoir. They sell fine collectibles of any type, including posters, the belongings of long-gone celebrities, and almost any other object of great value.

Serving a broader range of customers are smaller auction houses, mostly regional. Some are fairly well known outside their immediate area, like Butterfield & Butterfield (now called Butterfields), a house founded in San Francisco in 1865, which today has a salesroom in Los Angeles, as well, and Sloan's, which opened in

Washington, D.C., in 1853 and expanded to Miami in 1997. Most cities and towns have their own similar homegrown auction houses—Skinner in Boston; Garth's in Ohio; Selkirk's, now known as Phillips-Selkirk's, in St. Louis; Dargate in Pittsburgh; and so on. These auction houses are smaller versions of the big leaguers, with a regular schedule of auctions and catalogs. Even smaller enterprises in smaller towns sell the estates of the local gentry; good-quality art, antiques, and furniture from the local population; and the belongings of local celebrities and institutions.

Regional auction houses are often the best places to begin to increase the quality of a collection. Here can be found the antique porcelain and silver, beautiful furniture, and fine jewelry, for example, that is too valuable for a simple country auction. These houses are honorable professionally run businesses, well respected in their communities. (See Appendix D.)

Country auctions, while far from Christie's and Sotheby's in style, are often fun and exciting—the last remaining bastions of bargains, sleepers, and deals in the auction world. The atmosphere is lively, and these houses never take themselves too seriously. If magazine and newspaper advertising can be believed, their numbers are growing quickly despite the Internet. Often held in barns, outside, or in the community room of a VFW hall, country auctions are the best place to get started, especially if the ambience and offerings of the sophisticated houses seem intimidating.

As far as production values go, however, don't expect too much. The seating at country auctions may consist of folding chairs, the presale exhibition may take place for just a few hours on the morning of the auction itself, and the party may be a man selling sodas out of a cooler and a bake sale to benefit the high school choir. The presale exhibit might be just stacks of lots around the periphery of the salesroom or an adjoining area. A country auction requires more preparation on the part of the auctiongoer, even including a tool kit of rulers, black lights, and flashlights, not to mention rags. (Cleanliness at these enterprises may be next to godliness, but not necessarily in a temporal way.) Numbered bid paddles, absentee bidding forms, and phone bidding—commonplace features of more upscale auctions—will probably not be available.

The merchandise at country auctions can be diverse. Works of art and furnishings may commingle with box lots of old clothes, a couple of used cars, and the type of belongings most people reserve for garage sales. Pickers—experts who scour the countryside buying antiques just to sell at auctions and to dealers or on the Internet—frequently haul in furniture and other objects by the truckload. The variety might be wide, but unlike more refined auctions, the contents will not be "deep." If you are looking for a number of silver tea services from which to choose, the country auction might disappoint. All of this is good, though. Country auctions appeal to a great number of buyers, and there's usually something for everyone. It is highly unlikely you will find an unknown painting by Monet, falsely attributed to someone else, for ten dollars, but then again, you never know.

Finding an Auction House

With the proliferation of auction houses across the country, it's hard to believe that not too long ago the average person's awareness of them was negligible. That's because for the most part the auction houses advertised only in trade publications read by collectors and dealers and others in the art world, not in consumer publications such as newspapers or general interest magazines. Today, however, it's a very different situation.

Finding an auction house in your area only takes a little work and is mostly common sense. First, of course, try the Yellow Pages for listings and ads. Then, turn to the Arts and Entertainment section of your local newspaper, especially on Thursdays or Fridays when there are often lists of weekend events. Advertisements and listings for antiques shows, gallery exhibits, and auctions often itemize, down to the last andiron, just what lots will be offered.

Another excellent source of information is the plethora of publications that specialize in art, antiques, and collectibles. Among the best of these publications are *Maine Antiques Digest, Antique Trader, Antique Week, Antiques and the Arts Weekly* (commonly called the Newtown Bee), and *Art & Auction.* These periodicals report the news and results of recent auctions across the country and list upcoming auctions as well.

A recent issue of the *Antique Trader,* for example, contained ads for dozens of auctions, including one at Meslers Auction House in Scottsdale, Arizona, that listed literally hundreds of the objects it was selling, from a signed lithograph by Marc Chagall to a late-nineteenth-century pump organ to a 1999 Grand Marquis with only 2,700 miles on it. Every weekend in nearly every town in the country, an auction is taking place.

The ads themselves, aside from being informative, can be a charming invitation to a new experience. An ad for an auction being held in the Great Plains Gallery in Lone Jack, Missouri, for example, declared that "statements made day of sale take precedence." At the 4-H Fairgrounds in Madison, Indiana, "food is available." An auction at the Champaign County Fairgrounds in Urbana, Ohio, offered "the early collection of the late Mrs. Marie Brown," and the auction on Clay Street in Niles, Michigan, included a "prize for best Halloween costume." Who could resist?

Another way to locate an auction house is to ask at local art galleries or antique stores. Since so many of the people who frequent auctions are dealers, they will be especially knowledgeable about local happenings. And don't discount word-of-mouth. Collectors and dealers you meet at an exhibit or an auction often know of another event just down the road and will gladly share their information.

Finding an auction house at which to buy traditional furniture, art, and decorative objects is one thing. Finding an auction that specializes in selling collectibles such as dolls or pinball machines can be a bit of a challenge.

I mention pinball machines because I know of a collector in a small town in southern California. Over the years, he built up a modest but fun collection of pinball machines by scanning the ads in the newspaper and by going to flea markets. As his collection grew, so too did his appreciation of their quirky history and their even quirkier interior workings. The more he learned, the more he wanted to become a more serious collector. He wanted to meet other collectors and attend auctions in search of rarer and better-quality machines, but the only auctions he knew of in his area sold farm animals and used cars. Eventually he found the information he needed in a publications guide in the local library. With a little effort on his part, he has a gleaming collection of pinball machines, his pride and joy.

Specialty auctions are actually quite common if you know where to look. A recent issue of *Antique Week* had advertisements for an auction of folk art in Buford, Georgia; Hummel figurines in Eaton, Ohio; vintage clothing in Springfield, Illinois; and dolls in Marshall, Michigan. That same week in the *Maine Antiques Digest* there were announcements for a gun auction in Findlay, Ohio; a sale of Native American arts and artifacts in Vancouver, British Columbia; and, in San Francisco, an auction of antique cars that included a rare 1941 Indian Sport Scout motorcycle with an estimated value of $35,000 to $45,000 and a 1958 Porsche 1600 Speedster for which they hoped to get between $40,000 and $60,000.

Once you find the auction houses in which you are interested, be sure to put your name on their mailing lists for upcoming sales so that you never again miss an opportunity to add to your collection. Some auction houses—like Christie's and Sotheby's, among others—accept subscribers (for a price) to their catalogs. Most major auction houses have Web sites as well, and these are always worth checking periodically.

ON THE INTERNET . . .

TYPES OF AUCTIONS

Just as each brick-and-mortar auction house has its own idiosyncrasies, so do Internet sites have their own peculiarities, rules, regulations, and personalities. Unlike brick-and-mortar auction houses, however, no matter where you are in the world, as long as you have a computer and a modem, you have seven-day-a-week, twenty-four-hour-a-day access to every one of the Internet sites. With hundreds—maybe thousands—of auction sites instantly available, and then possibly millions of auctions on a site in progress simultaneously, choosing where to log on, peek in, and bid is daunting.

Whether you are better off buying and selling on the less-visited sites or at one of the Big Three—eBay, Yahoo, and Amazon—is debatable. The specialized sites claim to meet the needs of their audience in a uniquely qualified way. There are fewer buyers and sellers, but the group overall is more targeted and motivated. On the other hand, eBay has thousands more auctions going on at any one time, with hundreds of thousands, if not millions, of potential buyers surfing its site around the clock. As a seller or buyer, you should visit both types of sites—the mega everything-to-everybody sites and the small, focused sites that concentrate in your area of interest. If you find yourself more comfortable on one type or another, you will know what is the best site for you.

Finding these and other online auctions can take some work—but not much. It makes sense to research these auctions in their home territory—the Net. You can go to one of the popular search engines, like Yahoo! or Google, and type in key words such as "online," "auction," and "list," and pull up the results. When I did that on Google, my search came up with 94,600 possibilities!

No matter the sites on which you ultimately choose to buy or sell, you should do a bit of research to make sure they are worth your while. As noted above, bigger doesn't necessarily mean better. You might find a narrower but better-quality choice of decorative objects more appealing. For instance, eBay sells everything from the authentic to the unproven, and as a company it makes no judgment. Caveat emptor is the rule at the big sites. However, some vertical sites, sites offering only one sort of object, do make promises—to sell only original objects, for example.

For serious collectors, such assurances can be an important time-saver as well. My friend Jeff is an avid collector of milk glass, an opaque white glass popular from about the 1830s through the 1980s. Recently, he could have found four auctions of milk glass objects on justglass.com or 2,806 auctions of milk glass on eBay. For a lawyer on a tight schedule, justglass.com is more convenient.

No matter the size of the site, read its terms of service, the equivalent of the conditions of sale at a traditional auction house. If you have questions or if some stipulation just doesn't seem kosher, either do more research into the site or find another one. With the vast number of sites, you should never feel pressured to participate.

If you do have questions, ask. How quickly and fully the site answers will be a good test of its commitment to customer service. In addition to asking questions, surf the site in search of online help. Are there tutorials to ease buying and selling? If so, are they clear and easily accessible? Even the most seasoned Internet auction user still occasionally needs assistance. After all, to their credit, the online auction sites embrace new technology as it becomes available. That means you too have to keep pace to stay competitive. To make sure you return again and again, a good site will want to make your experience on its site as trouble-free as possible.

All online auction sites have a user agreement, and by accepting its terms you also accept that site's rules, regulations, and its policy regarding privacy. Because sites vary in their policies, it's worth slogging through both the user agreement and the privacy policy (eBay's privacy policy is more than 3,500 words).

Be prepared, however, to give up some privacy in order to participate in online auctions. Many sites use the information you provide to target advertising or other services; some may sell or rent your personal information to third parties unless you ask them not to, while others collect information on your bidding and buying habits for marketing purposes, as well as collect the feedback others leave about you (that's public information anyhow).

So, don't think that because it's two A.M. and you're sitting in your fleece sweatpants sipping a cup of oolong tea in the privacy of your family room, bidding on that perfect pair of gilded wall sconces, that you're doing so in true privacy. You're not, and it's important to understand in what ways a site might use the information you provide about yourself.

In addition to the large number of auctions, the big sites provide chat rooms and cyber cafés in which users can exchange tips, finds, and other information. Some people find these useful as well as just plain fun.

Another feature to consider is how a site guarantees against fraud and misbehavior by its users. Some sites provide what's basically an honor system, called feedback. This feature allows buyers and sellers to report to the world both the positive and negative aspects of their interaction so that other users can decide whether or not they want to deal with one another. (See chapter 13, pages 137–141, for details on how this system works.)

Finally, it is important to like the look and feel of the site. It is supposed to be enjoyable as well as profitable. Just as you wouldn't enter a store that didn't appeal to you at first glance, you shouldn't patronize a site that seems unfriendly, unattractive, or poorly designed. Remember, however, that even though Internet auctions are a multibillion-dollar-a-year industry, they are still less than a decade old, and even the most established sites can have an experimental feeling.

Despite the differences in their details, almost all online auction sites offer pretty much the same services. They act as middlemen between seller and buyer. The sites offer several different auction formats, however, and depending on the merchandise up for bidding, one may be more appropriate than another. As a seller, you choose whichever format promises to yield the best returns at the least inconvenience to you. As a buyer, you can choose to participate in the type of auction in which you feel most comfortable.

The most common online formats are the minimum-bid auction, or English auction, (see page 2 for its real-world ancestor), and what eBay calls a reserve price auction, but what I simply call a reserve auction. Keep in mind that different auction sites sometimes use different terms to mean the same thing.

In a minimum-bid auction the seller lists the opening bid and will not sell the object for less than that. Often the figure is as low as a dollar, even on objects that eventually sell for much more, but the highest bid received, even if it only matches the opening bid, is the successful bid.

In the reserve auction, there is a minimum opening bid, but in addition the seller sets a secret reserve, below which he is not obligated to sell the object. In traditional auction houses the reserve is generally decided by the in-house experts in consultation with the consignor. Online, the consignor and the auction house are, so to speak, one and the same—that is, you, the seller.

Some online buyers hate reserve auctions, believing they are unfair and secretive, and that reserves imply the seller isn't sure about the true value of the object and is setting a reserve to protect his investment. In other words, that he's not concerned with selling the object for market value so much as he is with getting the buyer's money.

The people who feel this way—and this attitude is endemic in the online auction world—are probably new to auctions. In the traditional auction world, reserves are common, and they don't raise an eyebrow. How in the short time that online auctions have been in existence reserve auctions have come to be so reviled is an indication that cyberspace is a new world and to some extent has its own culture and norms.

In truth, reserve auctions make little sense when the object being sold is relatively inexpensive. For higher-priced antiques and decorative arts, however, a reserve can ease the fear a seller might have about selling way below market value. After all, auctions are quirky and the online seller has no way to sniff out the tenor of the community in advance. Even though I believe most things really do reach and sell at their true value out there in the world at the moment they are sold, just the opposite does sometimes happen.

Just as in traditional auctions, if you are the high bidder in a reserve auction but your bid is below the reserve, the seller is under no obligation to sell. Recently I bid on eBay in a reserve auction for a book. By the closing of the auction the reserve was not met. A day later I received an e-mail from the seller asking me if I was interested in buying the book for my high bid, which was $24. Although the reserve was not met, my bid must have been close enough for him to feel he would still earn a reasonable profit. I wanted the book, so I agreed, and even though the auction wasn't concluded on eBay itself, I chose to abide by all the rules the seller put forth in his sales policy in his auction listing.

Just as in the traditional auction world, there is something online called a Dutch auction. The name, however, is all that these two auctions have in common. Online, Dutch auctions are used when a seller wants to auction more than one—usually several—of the same thing, such as prints or Beanie Babies.

In a Dutch auction online, the seller lists a minimum opening bid, not for the entire lot but for each object in the lot. He also says how many of the objects he is selling. You bid not only the amount you want to spend but on the number of objects in the lot that you want to buy. The amount you bid is per object, so if there are twelve prints and you bid $20 each on four of them, you've actually bid $80. Bids with a total value less than the current bid are rejected.

Ultimately, the winning bid is the one whose total, calculated by multiplying the price per object times the number of objects desired, is the highest. The best way to understand Dutch auctions is to participate in them.

Come to think of it, that goes for all auctions, online and off.

2

The Top Ten Auction Bargains

The concept of a bargain is relative. An eighteenth-century writing desk selling at auction for $10,000 can be considered a bargain if most eighteenth-century writing desks are selling retail for $60,000. And yet some works of art, decorative objects, and home furnishings that sell at auction are what I like to call enduring, not to mention endearing, bargains. These are things that, as a group and in general, consistently sell for so much less at auction than they would at retail that their value as bargains holds true year after year and auction after auction.

These things are not always inexpensive, but they are almost always a good value. Mostly their value, like that of anything else at auction, is a direct result of supply and demand, but these objects usually have a limited market, and that translates into a bargain for whoever is interested in buying them. In some cases—when objects are monogrammed, for example—potential buyers can disappear quickly!

Here are my top ten best bargains:

1. Upholstered Furniture

Some house hunters look at houses that need to be painted and spruced up a bit as great deals. After all, cosmetic changes aren't so hard to make if good bones hold the place together. Likewise, with furniture, it's all about good bones. Anyone who has visited shops specializing in late-nineteenth- and twentieth-century furniture has seen the surprising sight of a classic wing chair stripped to its nail-punctured frame, offered for sale even though it will require a trip to the upholstery shop before anyone can take a seat on it. A well-constructed sofa's feathers may be in bad condition or the fabric may be stained, but if the construction is high-quality, the sofa can be restuffed and reupholstered. Old-fashioned shapes can be updated with camelbacks or scrolled arms.

Such cosmetic changes are at your discretion. Upholstered furniture at auction may be battered, but you should only really worry about the underlying structure—the springs and frame. Just like the crazy-colored house that sits on the market because most home buyers can't see beyond the paint, homely sofas and chairs in need of repair sell at reasonable prices at auction. But, since most things can be upholstered relatively inexpensively, sofas and chairs are frequently huge bargains.

Terry Dunning of Butterfields told me about a magnificent Victorian parlor set he once sold. Incredibly, it had fourteen pieces, including a sofa, rocker, and chairs, all of which were in good condition. Almost as incredibly, it was upholstered in a high-quality fabric that was, unfortunately, Barney-the-dinosaur purple, or, as Terry put it, "a god-awful color," which must have cost the owner many thousands of dollars. "It would have cost new owners at least that much to change it," Terry lamented. "No one wanted it. We had a hell of a time even getting $1,500 for it."

Once at Leslie Hindman Auctioneers we offered as separate lots a pair of very fine, quite small down-filled sofas. The previous owner, at great expense, had slip-covered them both in a floral chintz from Brunschwig & Fils, a company founded in 1880 in Aubusson, France. Those slipcovers had been very costly. Because the sofas were small—no more than two people could comfortably sit on each—they were estimated to sell for between $350 and $450 each. One sold to a young woman in the audience, the other, coincidentally, to my friend Eric, for only $300 each. At the time Eric had just finished graduate school and could barely afford one of the sofas, let alone both. But it was both, he confided in me, that he really wanted. "Together they seemed so Charlotte Ford in Southampton," he said.

Here's the best part. About two years later a friend of Eric's went to a party, and there, in the hostess's house, was the twin of Eric's sofa. The woman who had bought it at the same auction as Eric was getting married and moving to Seattle. Better yet, she was hoping to sell her furniture. Eric immediately called her, offered her the exact amount of money, in cash, that they had paid at auction for the sofas, and the deal was done. Eric eventually had new slipcovers made in another Brunschwig & Fils chintz, and I have no doubt that in today's retail environment, his sofas would easily cost well over $3,000 each.

Leather-topped tables, like upholstered pieces of furniture, are frequently passed by because of wear and tear. Remember that worn, beat-up, damaged leather can easily be replaced at very little cost. We sold a small but elegant drum table with a badly stained inset leather top for only $250. The new owner replaced the leather for $75 and had a great-looking, not to mention terribly chic, table.

2. Chandeliers

Chandeliers stump auction houses. That's because they can't easily and beautifully display them at the presale exhibition. Sofas are easy, and so are chairs and tables. Books get lined up on a shelf, figurines, as well. But chandeliers? In most auction house settings there is just no way to take advantage of their beauty. Either they are suspended from a high beam so that their condition and detail are invisible to the potential buyer or they are plunked on a chair. As many times as I have seen a chandelier displayed like that, it never fails to depress me. It just looks so sad. No matter how chandeliers are displayed, however, they are almost never connected to an electrical outlet to show off their beauty when illuminated.

Indeed, although a lot of auction house activity comes from dealers, most dealers aren't interested in chandeliers, and most other customers just don't think about buying a chandelier at auction. People worry that the wiring will be faulty or that missing pieces will be hard to replace. To buy chandeliers at auction, the buyer must study them carefully and have a good imagination, in order to envision them hanging in the dining room or foyer. These disadvantages are advantages to the creative person. Having a chandelier rewired doesn't cost much. Likewise, missing prisms or crystal teardrops can be replaced easily and relatively inexpensively.

3. Dinner Services and Stemware

When you think of Wedgwood, you probably think of jasperware, a type of teapot or dish or other object in blue or brown or various other colors with raised white neoclassical designs. But Wedgwood is also famous for its cream-colored earthenware, called creamware, which has a lustrous, glossy surface and is strong, durable, and lightweight. Recently, Sotheby's sold a set that contained enough pieces to serve a dinner party for twelve for just $500, which, if you know china prices at all, you will recognize as an incredible bargain.

It's actually simple. No matter what all the home entertaining magazines say, people just don't entertain in their homes the way they used to. People today entertain in restaurants, and when they do invite people into their homes, it's either in small groups or done in as casual a manner as possible. Also, as far as both dinner services and stemware go, the department stores pretty much have, as someone I know at an auction house delicately put it, "a stranglehold on brides." When a couple gets married, their registry is as likely to list a lawnmower as fine china, and if they do want one service, Grandma's may be available—or they direct their wedding guests to a new one at the department store. In any case, one set is enough. In other words, there is no great demand for an elaborate set of Wedgwood for twelve.

For those who do want such a set, Wedgwood or not, the choice of pattern is often a very personal decision. "I've sold literally thousands of sets of dishes, and my wife has seen almost every one of them," said one auctioneer I know, "and through the years there haven't been more than two she really liked." China is highly dependent on personal taste and as everyone knows, personal taste can be unpredictable.

Auctions are also great places to find crystal stemware. You can often find sets of glasses for a fraction of what you would pay for new ones. One recent grouping contained thirty-two glasses, including white and red wine glasses, water goblets, and a pitcher. Made in the 1930s, the glasses had a geometric Art Deco design. They sold for just $110, which is only about $3.50 a glass, with the water pitcher thrown in for good measure. Try finding a deal like that today at retail—even at Target!

Dinner services and stemware are relatively cheap at auction because many sets come from estates, which means they've been used and used and *used* over the years and in many cases there are chipped pieces or missing pieces. A dinner service for twelve that really has eleven dinner plates, nine salad plates, twelve soup bowls, ten cups, and eleven saucers can be hard to sell. But if you only want eight of everything, you're in luck.

4. Silver Flatware

Like china and stemware, silver flatware is an overlooked bargain at auction, partly because most people—including engaged couples—just don't think of an auction house as the place to buy it. "Blushing brides should be forced to take an accounting class," says that same friend of mine.

He recently cataloged an auction in which a silver-plated service for eight had a few missing pieces. It was in good condition, however, and in a classic contemporary pattern that would easily sell for at least $75 a place setting at any of the major department stores. The entire service—that's right, the *entire* service—sold for $70.

5. Monogrammed Objects

In a culture like ours, where Ralph Lauren's logo is emblazoned on everything from his cashmere sweaters to baseball caps and where Louis Vuitton's initials grace bags hanging from the shoulders of some of the most chic ladies who lunch, to many people owning an antique object with someone else's monogram doesn't seem all that unusual. Yet some people still would find it quite bizarre to be named Mary O. Smith and have a silver Revere cup beside her bed monogrammed DRS, or to use a linen handkerchief embroidered with an *X*, *Y*, or *Z*, no matter how elegant. Those of you in the former category, however, won't believe the bargains you can find.

If you still feel funny about owning something etched with TRC when your initials are LSH, think about it this way: you would cherish a monogrammed silver cigarette case or set of linen sheets inherited from your great-aunt, and chances are her initials wouldn't match yours, either. Sure an heirloom passed down in your own family has more meaning, but an heirloom of any sort, aged with time and memories and monogrammed in faded cotton, can be perfect as an object for you to start imbuing with your own memories and heritage. And remember that if you see a metal object with someone else's monogram but you really want it, you can always have the letters buffed away and replaced with your own initials.

A sterling silver service for twelve by the International Silver Company came with knives, forks, salad forks, butter knives, oyster forks, teaspoons, ice-cream spoons, and even something called bouillon spoons—ninety-six pieces in all. It was on the block not too long ago. It was in the Minuet pattern, introduced in 1925 and no longer in production. This extraordinary set, which had my family surname initial—*H*—on it, sold for just $500, which is about one-tenth of its retail value today.

6. Old Books

Books, almost more than any other kind of object, really make a house a home. They lend a sense of warmth and hospitality; stacks of them can give a room a jaunty air. And best yet, unless they are rare first editions or leather-bound volumes of exceptional quality, they're a huge bargain at most auctions.

Think about it for a minute. Before television and radio, people read books for entertainment and to pass the time. And there was a lot of time to pass! As demonstrations of a person's rank, occupation, and education, as well as useful references for information, books were preserved. This means that *a lot* of old books have survived. Most of them, frankly, are pretty boring, too, so at auction they just aren't hugely popular.

In addition, when an auction house sells an estate, unless the books included in it are of unusual condition and value, they are usually grouped together either by subject or, more often, merely in boxes in sets of ten to twenty, with estimates attached that would depress most of their authors—though it would not surprise their publishers. The books are priced to sell, in other words. And sell they do—box lots of books are always popular.

A recent auction had a group of seven wonderful art books, including one with photographs by Ansel Adams, whose photographs of Yosemite still haunt the popular imagination, one called *Asian Art Treasures,* another on collectibles, and four monographs of individual artists. In a bookstore—even a used-book outlet—they would easily have cost at least $20 each. At retail they'd have gone for twice as much. And at auction? The entire lot fetched $30.

Another auction I attended recently had an absolutely gorgeous leather-bound gold-edged fifteen-volume set of the works of Oscar Wilde, published in 1909, including the popular titles *The Ideal Husband, The Picture of Dorian Gray,* and *The Importance of Being Earnest,* among others. Each book was priceless to me—Wilde is one of my favorite writers—but the set sold at the bargain price of $125 to the auction's successful bidder. That's less than $9 a book! Even paperback books exceed this figure today.

7. Jewelry

Jewelry is more personal than virtually anything else sold at auction. Rings that are engraved with "Sally, be forever mine" are attractive to very few buyers. Except for pieces of the finest quality or jewelry previously owned by hyperglamorous celebrities like Elizabeth Taylor or the Duchess of Windsor, jewelry tends to be a buyer's paradise at auction. Gold, which is most often sold at auction for its own weight, or what is referred to in the trade as its "meltdown value," continues to be an incredible bargain. We once sold a gold necklace made of beautiful crescent-shaped links with beaded borders. A necklace like that would sell at retail for about $2,000. At auction it fetched $750, an amazing bargain.

But by far the biggest jewelry bargain at auction is on engagement and wedding rings. If jewelry in general is personal, then these rings are almost embarrassingly intimate. At auction, says auctioneer Terry Dunning, wedding and engagement rings are "a real loser." The average couple wants to shop for an engagement ring together and make the experience of choosing it and buying it an important memory. A platinum wedding band that might cost $500 at a retail jewelry store usually doesn't go for more than $100 at auction. You could take the difference and spend it on your honeymoon!

Once again, bad news for the auction house, great news for you.

8. Minor Contemporary Works of Art

"Minor" doesn't mean Mark Rothko or Jackson Pollock, of course. For works by major, internationally known artists such as these, you will pay top dollar. But some artists who are well known in the art world may not be old enough to have established a secondary market, may not yet have a large following in the general population, or may be known only in their immediate region, town, or even family.

The auction estimates for works of art are always based on previous auction records of the artist's work. If there are no (or few) previous records, the works of fine contemporary artists often sell for far less than you would pay in a gallery.

Speaking of galleries, they charge a lot for contemporary works of art because they not only have to deal with practical matters like rent, but they are committed to launching the artist's career, hoping the effort will pay off in the long run. The art world is tough, however, and often it doesn't. At auction, these works frequently sell for no more than the price of the canvas itself.

In addition to that, unfortunately many people who buy contemporary works of art do so not for the picture's intrinsic artistic value but because the colors match the sofa or because it will fit right into that spot above the buffet and between the windows in the dining room.

Roberto Juarez is an American painter in his early forties whose work is rarely sold at auction. His acrylic-and-oil painting, *Waikiki Irises and Oranges,* was completed in 1994, and if it had been sold at the prestigious gallery in New York that represents Juarez, it would have carried a price tag of about $25,000. At 5 feet by 6 feet 6 inches, it was large enough to command attention, and before the auction there was a lot of comment about how attractive it was. Still, it sold for only $3,000—an astounding buy.

9. Large-scale Furniture

It used to be said that anything over 8 feet high or 8 feet long would never sell. Lots of people still say that's true. But I believe that while there may still be some truth to that, it is less true today than it used to be. Why? Just look at all the neomansions being constructed in subdivisions across the country. Forget their silly names— Cranberry Cove, Sunflower Gardens—just look at their size! They're huge. Thousands and thousands and thousands of square feet with soaring double-height "great rooms" with 12-foot ceilings, and more. Maybe the auction houses and dealers who insist that you can't sell anything over 8 feet high or 8 feet long have an untapped market to exploit. But until they do, large-scale home furnishings will, I guess, continue to be a relative bargain at auction.

I'll never forget a brightly painted one-of-a-kind Scandinavian pine cabinet that I thought would add a touch of whimsy to the right room. The front had been painted with colorful flowers, and vines and flowers had been carved into it. After years of use, the colors had mellowed, giving it a pretty country look. The dimensions, 84 by 55 by 20 inches, were considerable, not an easy fit into most rooms. That cabinet sold for just $650. The buyer has another family's heirloom that will become one of his own, with many more years of use in it.

Another memorable oversize piece was a huge sofa—over 9 feet long! This classic camelback has never really gone out of style, and the mahogany frame is as sturdy today as it was the day it was built, about forty years ago in this country. Curved cabriole legs and hairy feet were nicely carved and characteristic of the George III style, popular in the mid-nineteenth century. We expected it to sell for at least $1,000, which would have been a fabulous bargain, since a sofa like this would easily bring five times that much in a retail store. At auction, several bidders loved the sofa, but the hammer eventually came down at only $900. Even with the cost of reupholstery it was an unbelievable bargain.

10. Box Lots

These are among the most interesting things available at auction—a unique contrivance, really, for auction houses to sell a number of objects that individually would have relatively little value but that, taken together, might be worth a great deal.

Box lots are often found at auctions comprising the entire contents of various estates, when the auction house has agreed to sell everything from the furniture to the paintings to the knickknacks, which may be books, candlesticks, or odd assortments of bowls, figurines, vases, and photographs. Just look around your own house, at the windowsills where you display your bric-a-brac, or your shelves, with their books and bowls and travel souvenirs—those are the sort of things that end up in box lots. "After the auction house has finished cataloging the Georgian furniture and Limoges," one auction house specialist told me, "the rest of it just gets gathered into box lots. It can be pretty haphazard."

Examining box lots takes a bit of patience, because the lot cannot be broken down into individual objects. Even if there is only one thing in it that an auctiongoer truly wants, the successful bidder is obliged to take home—or resell in the parking lot—everything else in the box. In an auction that features many box lots—and it has been my experience that where there are box lots at all, there are a lot of them—some unscrupulous auctiongoers will try to switch objects from one box to another to create lots that satisfy their wants. It pays to check back with the box often during the presale exhibit to make sure the box lot you want still contains the objects that interest you. Another possibility is that in their haste to assemble the lots, the auctioneers may have separated a matching set of bookends, forcing you to bid on both lots in order to own the pair.

All that said, however, box lots can be a terrific bargain. Because their contents are of mainly sentimental value—sentimental, that is, to the consignor, and probably to the future owner as well, after he or she lives with them for a while—the monetary value is small. Their contents strike a chord with the bidder. Perhaps something reminded him or her of something else, or maybe an object fulfilled a specific need or rounded out a collection of figurines or books.

At a recent country auction I attended, vintage linens filled several boxes. On top of one box were several pairs of unattractive kitchen curtains. But buried deep in the box was what looked like someone's unused hope-chest linen. Those sheets and pillowcases of fine linen decorated with wide bands of hand-tatted lace—some bride's labor of love—would sell for hundreds of dollars in an antique linen store, but the entire box sold for just twelve dollars.

At one of Sotheby's auctions, a box of woodenware included a huge, 1950s-style walnut salad bowl at least 18 inches across, a dozen rosewood plates, and eight small, richly grained mahogany plates that would have been perfect for an after-dinner cheese course. The entire box lot sold for only a few dollars. Those pieces looked as though they had never been taken out of their boxes until we packed them all into one box. Maybe they were wedding gifts for someone who never liked woodenware, but whoever bought that lot got a great deal.

These home furnishings, objects, and works of art are good bargains. You can usually depend on them. But there are others as well, including bedsteads, which people don't replace very often (they are afraid that pieces will be missing or that they will have to buy a custom-made mattress), linens (they don't have the patience to go through boxes or bags of it), and old mantels and fireplace tools (people just don't think of buying them at auction).

The only thing you ever really need to buy in a retail store is clothing—if that. I try to buy everything else at auction, including pens!

3

Common Myths and Misperceptions

Walking into an auction house for the first time, especially one of the fine big-city auction houses, can be intimidating. So many beautiful things are for sale, so many beautiful people are milling about. Buyers and sellers alike, not to mention members of the auction house staff, rush around looking busy and concerned, speak as quietly as if they are at the library, and show a knowing reverence for the works of art. Sometimes it can seem as if you're entering a foreign land or a party to which you haven't been invited. No wonder there are so many myths and misperceptions! After all, if merely asking a question is intimidating, imagine trying to ask two questions, or five, or ten. To put an end to mishaps, untruths, and fabrications, here are the realities that shatter the auction world's top ten myths.

MYTH #1

"I can't afford auctions."

REALITY

There are objects, and auctions, for every price range.

> **Many people believe** that auctions sell only rare and expensive arts and antiques that only the very rich can afford. People read about celebrity auctions—Sting's guitars, Diana's dresses, Marilyn's furniture—and see TV reports about blockbuster sales that include multimillion-dollar paintings, such as Renoir's *Le Moulin de la Galette,* which sold with the buyer's premium at Sotheby's in 1990 for $78,100,000; extraordinary antiques, like a pair of Louis XV ormolu-mounted Chinese lacquer commodes by Mathieu Cri-

aerd, which set a record price in 1997 by selling at auction for $1,157,500; and spectacular jewelry, such as the 274.40-carat platinum-and-diamond necklace featuring oval, marquise-cut, and pear-shaped diamonds, which fetched $1,927,500. But the average price per lot of everything sold at auction houses, including the million-dollar decorative objects and works of art, is much lower than those high-stakes auction sales figures indicate.

The average lot price at Sotheby's, for example, in all the sales of a recent year, was $10,200—and that's for more than 180,000 lots. At its lower-priced sales, which Sotheby's calls Arcade Auctions in New York and Marketplace Sales in Chicago, the average lot price was far less. Similarly, at Christie's in Rockefeller Center, its main salesroom had an average price of $29,300. At its sales of less expensive goods at Christie's East, the average price per lot was $3,726. Chances are that the prices at your local auction house are a lot lower than even that. Some country auctions sell goods for an average lot price of only $50 to $75.

Here's another way to look at it: the goods that auction houses offer come as estates—entire households of goods made available when someone dies and the heirs want to turn the property into cash. Most people have two sets of dishes—fine china for holidays and special occasions, and less costly everyday dishes. You may be in the market for a fine set of dishes. Or you may want the more casual set. Both will be sold at bargain prices. Every price is relative to market value, and to the buyer's desire to own a particular object.

MYTH #2
"You have to be a real expert to buy at auction."

REALITY
Amateurs, in the original sense of "those who love," can educate themselves to know as much as they need to know in order to bid intelligently.

Every auctiongoer has to be willing to do a bit of homework in order to be knowledgeable about the value of the merchandise on the retail market. As a buyer, you usually have an advantage over a dealer, since the dealer has to buy objects wholesale, so to speak, in order to resell them for retail prices and make a profit. You, on the other hand, pay just a little more than wholesale and it's yours. For you it's an object to look at and love; for the dealer it's merely something to sell.

A decade ago I would have been comfortable saying that auction prices for many things are generally about half of what you would pay in a retail store. I wish I still could say that, but I can't. The auction business—like anything else that involves coveted commodities, a combination of traditional selling practices and high technology, and a global dollop of glitz and glamour—has changed immensely. While there are still values to be found, the hunt has become more complicated, the capture more elusive.

But no matter the degree of deal, bargain, or value—and no matter how much or in what ways these things change in the future—your success at ferreting out any of them will depend on your bidding wisely. And that means you will have to be informed. You don't have to be an expert, of course; you just have to be savvy enough to know what you know, smart enough to ask others about what you don't know, and interested enough to do your homework.

MYTH #3

"Auctions move so fast that you can't keep track of what's going on."

REALITY

Don't worry about it. Every auction has its rhythm, and everyone can catch on.

If you follow the action you'll quickly understand that auctions are *supposed* to move fast. Most auctioneers sell at a rate of 80 to 100 lots an hour. The fast pace isn't meant to confuse you, to take advantage of you, or to whip up a frenzied competition amongst the bidders (although, inadvertently, it sometimes does do that), but simply to set a rhythm. After all, auctions are like theater, with moments of high drama, emotion, and even the occasional laugh. Good auctioneers are performers who know the value of what they're selling—and the value of a good time.

Once you become accustomed to the pace and the auctioneer's style, auctions are actually quite easy to follow. You will need to know who in the room is bidding and how much is being bid at any given moment. Seeing the paddles go up is important, but watching the auctioneer and listening to the bid increments are even more vital.

And forget about the fast pace. In reality, if you are sitting around waiting for the lot in which you are interested to come up for sale—I recently had to sit through ninety minutes of Meissen figurines—as everyone who attends auctions spends a lot of time doing, the pace can seem maddeningly slow.

MYTH #4

"The auction house owns the property it's offering for sale."

REALITY

Usually it doesn't—but sometimes it does.

I could have disputed this myth more unequivocally several years ago. While some auction houses, like William Doyle Galleries in New York, have always owned some of the objects they sold, auction houses, from the country to the city, more commonly had no financial interest in the objects they were selling. Objects were consigned and either they sold or they didn't. One way or another, after the sale they were gone, either to the new owner's home or back to the seller's basement. The auction houses, in other words, were simply the middlemen. In a dwindling number of instances, this is still true.

Here is one of the ways in which the big auction houses work: Property is moved into an auction house several weeks or months before an auction. Each item is cataloged, with the description of the object and an estimated price range in which it is expected to sell. The object is then assigned to a particular sale on a particular date, scheduled for exhibition, and finally sold at auction. Auction houses are in the business of providing a service between people who want to sell things and people who want to buy them.

At the big auction houses like Christie's and Sotheby's, however, and at some smaller houses that have followed their lead, this iron-clad rule has changed. Now, occasionally, they do take a financial interest in a work of art or a piece of furniture in order to retain the business of an important client. For example, the auction house may guarantee that the entire collection of an important consignor will fetch a certain minimum price at auction. If Christie's very much wants to sell the estate of a wealthy heiress that's filled with Renoir portraits, Meissen porcelain, fine Federal furniture, and jewelry formerly owned and worn by French aristocrats, the auction house might guarantee that the collection in total will bring at least $25 million at auction, and if for any reason it doesn't, the auction house will make up the difference.

The auction house would own the objects or have a financial interest in them if it had loaned the consignor money using the consigned property as collateral. The auction house would then be more interested than ever in making a successful sale, since the consignor, in theory, has already been paid. The fastest way for the auction house to recover the money it lent the consignor is by selling the object. In this case, the auction house's financial interest will be—or should be, at any rate—indicated in some way in the catalog.

"If I scratch my ear, the auctioneer will think I'm bidding. I could get stuck buying something I can't afford, or I could look foolish trying to back down."

REALITY
The auctioneer needs clear communication, and a false sale is in no one's best interest.

In one of my favorite episodes of the old *Dick Van Dyke Show,* Rob, Laura, Buddy, and Sally attend an auction. Much to Sally's chagrin, Rob shows her different styles of bidding—rubbing his ears, twisting his pen—and the auctioneer (played by the same actor who served as the voice of Fred Flintstone) reads his movements as actual bids. Rob slinks out of the auction as the embarrassed owner of a "Grant Ood." If this had happened in real life, it wouldn't have been so amusing, of course.

A well-known collector or dealer will occasionally arrange to bid with a secret signal to protect her anonymity. (See page 108 for a full description of this phenomenon.) While such requests are rare these days, most auctioneers will accept them from a very good customer. But no auctioneer I know will assume that your nose-wriggle or head-scratch, or the twist of your pen or tap of your foot, is a bid without having first, and very explicitly, arranged such signaled communications with you. I can almost guarantee that you'll never go home with a Grant Ood—unintentionally, at least.

MYTH #6
"The amount of the total bid is the final price I'll pay."

REALITY
You pay the hammer price plus, in many auction houses, a buyer's premium, plus sales taxes where applicable.

Before the price-fixing scandal of February 2000, for about a decade Christie's and Sotheby's had similar commission structures, which made things relatively simple for buyers. Now the two largest auction houses, which through their policies set examples and lead the way for the entire industry, have their own commission fee structures once again.

Since then, Christie's, for instance, has charged a buyer's premium of 17.5 percent on the first $80,000 of a sale, and 10 percent on any amount over $80,000 (it had been 15 percent on the first $50,000 and 10 percent on any amount over $50,000). Sotheby's buyer's premium is now 20 percent on the first $15,000, then 15 percent on the next $85,000 to $100,000, and 10 percent on any amount over $100,000. As of this writing, the live auction house charges a 10 percent buyer's premium on Internet sales no matter the amount.

While this can be confusing, there is a simple (but not foolproof) way to make sure your bid limit includes buyers' premiums. Simply stop your bidding at 80 percent of the total amount you want to pay for an object. While this isn't a perfect science (especially since sales taxes vary by state), it will pretty closely work out that, when all the other expenses are added in, the *total* will be what you originally set as your upper limit.

MYTH #7
"I can always change my mind if I find something wrong with the item."

REALITY
Legally, when the hammer falls at the end of bidding, the ownership of that particular piece of property is transferred to you.

It never fails to amaze me that people bid on the wrong object—and win. They come up to me after the sale, embarrassed, and say, "I didn't mean to bid on that chest!" All I can say in response—and I'm always nice about it because I realize that they may be distraught—is that I'm sorry but that it wouldn't be fair to the consignor for us to ignore the winning bid.

Although you should never make such an assumption, sometimes an auction house can remedy such a mistake. At a country auction, for instance, they may be willing to reauction an object immediately on your behalf. If the crowd knows of the error, which, of course, they most likely would, the price it fetches could well be lower than the amount you paid. The house may also be willing to try to arrange a private sale with the underbidder—that is, the person who bid the second highest amount, with the successful bidder making up the difference between the underbid and the original top bid. This can be a sensitive business, though, and often the underbidder, even if he wants the object, will agree to buy it only for less than his original underbid. He is under no obligation to help you out, of course, and he may drive a hard bargain. And in some ways, I can't blame him.

A dealer I know was bidding at auction in Chicago on behalf of a very wealthy woman from California who had given him upper limits of what she was willing to pay for certain works of art. But he got caught up in the moment, bidding, at one point, $75,000 more than his approved upper limit. Naturally, he was the successful bidder. He begged me to relent on the sale of the objects or not charge him the buyer's premium, but there was no way I could do either. I reminded him that he was a grown-up, after all, and an experienced dealer to boot. I wasn't trying to be churlish, but he should have known better. I don't know what he told his client, but I'm sure *someone* wasn't very happy.

So remember that once the hammer comes down, you own the item. All sales are final.

After all, that's why some auctioneers say "Fair warning!"

MYTH #8

"Auction houses are in cahoots with dealers."

REALITY

If anything, they have far different agendas.

In fact, auction houses and most dealers have opposing points of view. The auction house is trying to sell a work of art for as much as possible, using everything ethically at its disposal, from advertising to encouraging buzz, to sell an object. Dealers, like buyers everywhere, are trying to pay as little as possible, using every means ethically at *their* disposal to do so.

Some consignors may feel that auction houses and dealers work together to keep the market afloat, or that auction houses accept lowball bids from dealers with whom they do a lot of business.

I can tell you from experience that both these accusations are totally false. The most important thing any auction house has going for itself is its integrity. I can spend years and years building the reputation of my business, but one false move can destroy it. (The price-fixing scandal that erupted in early 2000 is a perfect example of the speed with which accusations of wrongdoing can damage the reputation of an auction house and affect the bottom line.) No amount of money, no scam between an auction house and dealer or auction house and consignor is worth the price the auction house would pay if found out. And in this day and age of regulatory interest, investigative reporting, and the widespread availability of information on the Internet, there is no question that such collusion *would* be discovered.

MYTH #9
"Auctioneers and consignors run up the bidding."

REALITY
The reputable ones never do.

Most auction houses state that the consignor is not allowed to bid on her own object. In some instances, the auctioneer may bid on behalf of the consignor against the room or absentee bids, but only up to the point at which the reserve (the price below which the consignor will not sell) is met.

There may be some auction houses that allow consignors to bid on their own objects as a way of setting a reserve. The problem with that, as I see it, is that the reserve then becomes a floating reserve, changing at the whim of the original owner. It seems unfair, and I would never permit the practice as an auctioneer or go to an auction house that allowed that.

At Leslie Hindman Auctioneers I absolutely did not allow consignors to bid on their own property. Once at an auction of twentieth-century art and antiques, a dealer had consigned a beautiful Tiffany lamp. There was a reserve on it, of course, but even though others continued to bid after it had been met, which meant the lamp would definitely sell, the dealer himself started to bid on it, trying to increase the final price.

This was unacceptable.

I paused and told the audience that a colleague would restart the bidding on the lamp. As quietly as I could (which, admittedly, wasn't too quietly since everyone was watching me) I walked over to the dealer and whispered in his ear. It might have looked very polite and amicable to anyone watching, but I assure you that my words were firm. He never again bid on one of his own consignments at our auction house; then again, I'm not sure he ever bid on anything again at our auction house.

But that's okay. The integrity of our overall business was more important than any one man's personal business.

MYTH #10
"Auctioneers make up the first bid out of thin air."

REALITY
Not quite.

An auctioneer has to start somewhere. Most auctioneers traditionally start close to the actual low estimate in some cases and in others at about half that low estimate. If absentee bids (also called order bids) on an object have been left with the auction house, the auctioneer will use as her opening bid a figure that is one bid level above the lowest absentee bid she has.

In other words, say that before the auction, two absentee bids have been left on an object with a low estimate of $1,000, one bid with an upper limit of $1,000, another bid with an upper limit of $3,000. At many auction houses the traditional method would be to start the bidding at about half that low estimate, or $500. In this case, however, because there are these absentee bids, the auctioneer will start the bidding at $1,100, which would be the next bid had the person who left the $1,000 bid actually been in the audience bidding, and on behalf of the person who left the $3,000 bid. There are times, especially for an expensive object, in which an auctioneer might want to build some momentum, so she may start the bidding much lower. If there were two order bids, $5,000 and $8,000, she might bid on behalf of each of the order bidders, going from $2,000 to $2,100 to $2,200 and on and on until she hits $5,500, which would be the first bid after the $5,000 bid (depending on the auction house's increment structure).

At some small or country auctions, the auctioneer will literally invent a first bid. If no one in the audience bites, he will have to try again by lowering it or accepting a random bid blurted out by someone in the audience.

Direct Auctioneers in Chicago is a warehouse-like place that holds marathon auctions, sometimes lasting up to eight hours, every Tuesday. There the auctioneer starts with a bid he thinks might be near what the final bid should ultimately be. He might suggest $200, scanning the audience for a bid. In a moment, though, he *lowers* the first bid to $100, then $50, then $25, then $10. All that within twenty seconds. If there is a bite at $10, a bidding war may erupt, pitting two people on opposite sides of the scruffy skylighted space against each other until the bid inches close to $200. The hammer comes down near where the bidding began. Not once during the many times I have attended auctions there did a bidder ever actually take the opening bid.

In some cases the auctioneer will simply start the bidding by asking the audience for their opening price. If no one comes forward or if someone tenders a ridiculously low bid, the auctioneer will have trouble maneuvering the bidding back into the proper range. This method can be risky for the auctioneer, who has the responsibility to the consignor to secure the best price, so it's not done very often.

ON THE INTERNET

FIVE MORE MYTHS AND MISPERCEPTIONS

MYTH #1
"Once an auction starts, you can't back out of selling."

REALITY
You can, but you shouldn't, except in dire circumstances.

In traditional auctions a client can withdraw a consignment at any time. This change of heart rarely happens, however, and auctioneers frown upon the practice. At Leslie Hindman Auctioneers, for example, we charged the reneging client a withdrawal fee to cover the expenses we had already incurred in storing, insuring, cataloging, and marketing the object.

In online auctions, we are really talking about canceling an auction not before it starts but while it is in progress. Imagine what would have happened if in the middle of a live auction I had said, "Do I have four hundred dollars? Do I have four hundred— Oops! We've decided not to sell this lot."

There are several reasons why an online seller might close an auction early, some better than others. The vase at auction that you never used suddenly seems like the perfect receptacle for the sunflowers you planted last season. Or you have rearranged your living room furniture, and now that rustic cherrywood end table fits perfectly. These are examples of bad reasons to cancel a sale.

Before you sell anything online, consider every reason for *not* selling it. Might you or a family member need the item later on? Does it have sentimental value that would cause guilty feelings once it was in other hands? Are you so unsure of its value that you might do better securing an appraisal before selling it?

Some people cancel sales when their auction has failed to receive bids. Again, I think this is an inappropriate reason to cancel. By putting something up at auction you are taking a risk, and receiving no bids is a part of that risk. Besides, you don't know there won't be bids in the time remaining. If the object goes unsold at the end of the auction, at least your online reputation will not suffer.

Also unethical in my opinion is to start an auction, then sell the object to someone, bidder or otherwise, who calls to offer a lot of money for it if you'll end the auction early. Even if it's *a lot* of money, you agreed to take that risk when you initially decided to auction the object. In this case, the risk is that you won't profit as much as you'd like. I really believe in playing by the rules, and those who bid on your object and have followed the rules should be accorded the chance to become the successful bidder.

The only reason for calling a halt that is truly justifiable is if the object breaks or tears or is damaged in some other way after the auction starts.

If you do cancel an auction, you'll still be required to pay whatever listing fees the auction site charges. If there were bidders, it is common courtesy to e-mail them and announce the auction's early close. Don't be surprised if they're not happy.

If you close an auction in which a bidder has already met the reserve, you will owe that person a detailed explanation. Just as a buyer is required to complete a transaction in which he is the successful bidder, the seller is required to complete it as well. In this instance, you are breaking what should be an ironclad agreement between two people.

Closing auctions early is serious. Those who had already bid on the object will be disappointed. They will most likely leave negative comments if you are on a site that solicits review of seller and buyer behavior. You should expect this and accept your culpability gracefully.

There is a way both to close an online auction early and not close it at all: bid high on the object yourself. In other words, win your own auction (this is forbidden in most traditional auctions). Bear in mind that you'll not only have to pay the listing fee, but in this case you will be required to pay the commission as well (more about fees later).

MYTH #2
"Once you've made a bid, you can't take it back."

REALITY
It's frowned upon, but reneging on a bid is possible in online auctions.

A colleague of mine is an avid fan of Edith Wharton, the author of *Ethan Frome, The Age of Innocence,* and many other early-twentieth-century novels. He was looking for one of her more obscure works in used bookstores, but without luck. Finally it was offered at auction on eBay. It wasn't expensive, and he immediately bid $25 by proxy, which meant that, as competitors bid against him, eBay would bid on his behalf up to that amount.

As luck would have it, about three days later the same book appeared at auction on Yahoo! Well, he couldn't remember if he had bid on the book already on eBay or had just thought about bidding, or whether he had originally seen it on Yahoo! first and not bid. (He's not as addlebrained as he sounds; if every day you look at a lot of different auction sites and bid frequently, you can easily get confused.) Anyhow, he bid again, but this time only $15.

Within a day he learned of his mistake—bidding different amounts on two different auction sites for different copies of the same object.

In this situation he had several choices: He could proceed with both auctions and hope to be the successful bidder on only one of them, preferably the less expensive one. Or he could go through with both auctions, end up being the successful bidder on both, pay for both, and have two copies of the book. Or he could retract one of the bids, keeping in mind that not all auction sites would allow people to retract their bids. Retracting a bid, however, does sound like the easiest choice. It would save him a few bucks and spare him the inconvenience of having duplicate copies of the same book, which, of course, he could immediately reauction, but with no guarantee of getting his money back. Still, retracting a bid, like canceling an auction, should not be a choice easily made.

There is really only one good reason for retracting a bid, and that's if the description of an object changes significantly after you place your bid but before the auction closes. Say, for instance, that a cabinet described as 48 inches high—a perfect size for your den—is later found to be 54 inches high and so described at a later date. Retracting your bid in this instance would be perfectly acceptable.

Some people would say that if you mistakenly bid $100 on an object when you meant to bid $10 that you should feel free to retract it. Although I don't think you should have to spend ten times as much as you intended, I believe it is the bidder's responsibility to avoid this mistake in the first place. Before your online bid is accepted you are always given a chance to review your bid and change your mind. To have bid $100 when you meant $10 means not only that you typed the wrong number but also that you paid no attention when you had the chance to review your bid.

Some invalid reasons include realizing after you have bid on an object that you can't afford it or merely changing your mind. Bidding is serious business, and as a customer you should strive to behave during the auction as professionally as you expect sellers to behave.

If you do retract a bid for any of these poor reasons, contact the seller immediately and explain yourself. Doing so will go a long way toward making amends. That person will know you feel bad (and you *should* feel bad) and that you're sorry for any inconvenience you have caused (you should feel sorry). This good relationship is important because the online auction world is a community. A seller may someday be a buyer, and vice versa, and every bad transaction can become part of your online auction reputation.

I would hope in these situations that the seller would be kind and understanding, but she may be angry and she may express her anger by not allowing you to bid on any of her future auctions. The fact that you've retracted a bid will be on your record, to which anyone can have access. Other sellers may not allow you to bid on their auctions, either.

Keep in mind that if you do retract a bid, all your previous bids in that auction are erased as well. In other words, if you bid $10 and later mistakenly bid and retract $50, your $10 bid is eliminated, too. If you are still interested in that item, you have to rebid $10.

My colleague made a mistake by bidding twice. To me, that is not a good enough reason to retract a bid. It was not sufficient for him, either, and he ended up bidding successfully in both auctions. Now he has two copies of that obscure Edith Wharton novel, both of which he keeps as a reminder of a situation in which he learned a valuable lesson.

MYTH #3
"Sniping is bad."

REALITY
I'm going to play the contrarian here: No, it's not.

To snipe doesn't sound very nice. My dictionary defines it as "shooting at exposed individuals from a concealed point or vantage." Worse, as a noun, it defines a snipe as "a contemptible person." But I'm going to disagree with Mr. Webster on this.

In the online auction world "to snipe" means to bid minutes or even seconds before an auction ends, so that your competition has no time to make another offer.

Many people don't like snipers—and the term doesn't exactly help their reputations—but I think the idea of sniping is misunderstood. After all, in traditional auctions, people can bid as the hammer comes down. That bid is valid as long as the auctioneer hears and accepts it.

This is how sniping works. In the closing moments of an auction the bidder enters an amount he thinks will top the current high bid. To find out where he stands, he hits the refresh button to bring the latest information to his computer screen. Then what? The risk is that the current high bidder's proxy bid might still be higher than the sniper's bid, and he may not have time to bid again. (A proxy bid, remember, is one in which a person bids his maximum and the site bids on his behalf up to that amount.) The risk for the current high bidder is that he might not originally have bid enough.

If you want to avoid snipers, the best method is to bid your true maximum in the first place. That way it won't matter if you get sniped, because any bid higher than yours is more than you wanted to pay anyhow.

Some auction sites discourage snipers by extending auctions past their original deadline if there is a bid within the final three or so minutes. If so, the auction is extended again and again until there are no more bids. In this way, it most approximates a live auction in that it ends when there are no more bids.

MYTH #4
"Amazon, eBay, and Yahoo! are the only games in town."

REALITY
There are hundreds of online auction sites.

The popularity of eBay, I think, stems in part from its being the first online auction site. It attracted the initial publicity and interest with the lure of easily buying and selling art and antiques, and continued to take advantage of its position as the forerunner. For quite a while it had the entire marketplace to itself, until Yahoo!, Amazon, and other Internet businesses started their own auction sites. The newcomers have not made a dent in eBay's powerful position. Traditional auction houses waited even longer to launch their own auction sites. Sotheby's, one of the largest, most powerful traditional auction houses in the world, opened its site for bidding only in January 2000, five years (a lifetime on the Internet) after eBay was established.

Because everyone knows about eBay, it continues to grow. For beginners—in Internet auction lingo, "newbies"—starting at eBay is convenient and fast. It has become almost synonymous with Internet auctions, just as Kleenex is to facial tissues or as Jell-O is to gelatin desserts. And once people become comfortable with a site, they tend to stay. They get used to the rules, the look of the screen, and the click of the mouse. For more than any other reason they stick around because they like it. In fact, because an Internet auction is always there, Internet auction bidding can become an addiction for some people.

Whereas the reputations of brick-and-mortar auctions as stiff and snobbish have been formed over centuries of existence, the relative newness of Internet auctions has allowed them to create their own personalities. When eBay was founded there were no rules— some people compare the Internet to the Wild West, and I think that's an apt characterization. It's "Shoot 'em up, cowboys" all the way! "Let's put on a show! Anything goes!"

Although eBay, Amazon, and Yahoo! auctions are the Big Three, they are by no means the only games in town. Many others are nipping, or attempting to nip, at the heels of the big boys. Internet versions of mom-and-pop shops—small enterprises run by individual antiques dealers or stores—pop up every day.

There are also hundreds of specialty sites—known as vertical sites—such as pottery.com, whose specialty is obvious, and beaniex.com, which specializes in all Beanie Babies all the time. Stampauctions.com, justglass.com, sportingauction.com, and winebid.com are just a few examples of the range of sites available.

MYTH #5
"Only low-end works of art and decorative objects are selling."

REALITY
It seems to be changing.

Certainly the $10 Care Bears on eBay and $50 Bakelite portable radios on the Yahoo! auction site are selling at a faster clip than high-end antiques such as the bronze signed-and-numbered Tiffany lamp that was offered for sale not too long ago in a ten-day auction on eBay with a minimum opening bid of $26,000. Not only did it fail to sell; it did not receive a single bid.

At a traditional auction potential buyers can get to know the works of art and decorative objects in which they are interested by personally viewing and handling them. There is no way an online auction can approximate traditional auctions in this manner. Most sellers post color photographs of their objects online, but there is and always will be a distance, an invisible wall, between buyer and object. This invisible wall is even stronger between buyers and higher-end objects. Taking a chance on something for pennies is one thing, but once the objects are worth real money, the invisible wall becomes a significant barrier.

Still, as the community of traditional auctiongoers becomes more comfortable with online auctions, and as the world of Internet auctions matures, the barriers that keep people from bidding on higher-end objects are starting to break down. Not too long ago when something pricey did sell online, it was actually news. Today, expensive things sell all the time. A miniature Norton stoneware crock, for example, attracted seventy-nine bids on eBay not too long ago, eventually fetching $10,010. A daguerreotype—an early photograph produced on a silver-covered copper plate—of a lazy St. Bernard brought $11,100 on eBay as well, and the auction site sold a blood amber glass pickle bottle, originally purchased for $3 at a tag sale, for $44,100. A three-dollar gold piece, circa 1884, sold on the Hobby Markets auction site for $23,000; the site also sold a bottle of 1870 Lafite-Rothschild wine for $12,650. Someone paid $24,500 on AuctionUniverse for a 1976 print of *Moonrise, Hernandez, New Mexico,* by Ansel Adams.

Andy Warhol's *Marilyn,* a 1967 silk-screen print, sold on ArtNet for $34,650, while Marc Chagall's color lithograph from 1980, *Red Maternity,* sold for $22,500.

Wolf's, a decades-old Cleveland-based auction house that has totally replaced traditional auctions with online auctions, was able to fetch $187,000 for an oil painting by the American artist James E. Buttersworth.

These are just a few of the many, many higher-end objects that have sold recently in online auctions. None of them made much of a stir in the media because their sales are no longer necessarily that newsworthy. That, if nothing else, is proof that the online market is there for higher-end works of art and decorative objects.

4

Five Auction Blunders and How to Avoid Them

Most auction buyers who have done their homework leave the auction house either pleased with their purchases or empty-handed, but in either case content. One of the most interesting aspects of being in the auction business is watching some potential buyers arrive happy and excited and leave with long, dejected faces. These are people who have succumbed to one of the five easiest—and easiest to avoid—auction blunders.

1. Bidding on the Wrong Lot

This is the type of mistake that never ceases to amaze me.

Auctions are by their very nature social events. At auction, you see friends you haven't seen for a while. You meet other collectors with whom you share interests. There are dealers to chat up, auction house experts whose brains you can pick for free. It's fun and lighthearted. There's anticipation in the air. And I believe that's how auctions should be.

Mistakes do happen, though. Auctioneer Charles Hamilton, himself a collector, poked fun at himself in his now out-of-print book *Auction Madness*. He recalled at a sale at Phillips in New York where he had bid "with great zeal" on two old percussion rifles, which he had planned to hang on the walls of his country house. Gleeful at being the successful bidder at what he believed was a fraction of their value, he went to the shipping department to pay for and retrieve the guns only to learn that he had bid on the wrong lot and was now, as it turned out, the not-so-proud owner of a stuffed finch sitting under a high glass dome. His wife, never one to pass up a good laugh, displayed the bird in their dining room, telling guests about her husband's error—proof that even the most experienced auctiongoers can make silly mistakes.

I have a friend who considers herself very clever when it comes to buying at auction. She goes to all the presale exhibits. She studies price guides. She even carries a miniature black light to check porcelain for cracks and hairline fractures. And to her credit, her home is filled with beautiful furniture and works of art mostly bought at auction in Chicago and New York. What is funny is that whenever someone compliments her on something in her house she always says a bit wearily, "Yes, it's nice, but you should have seen the *other* sofa I wanted to buy. But as usual, I was talking and missed it." My friend, at least, knows herself pretty well.

Mistakes are also often made on addendum lots. These are lots that have been added to an auction at the last minute, after the catalog has gone to press and sometimes even after the presale exhibition has started. The confusion comes in because instead of tacking these lots on to the end of the auction, most auction houses insert them into the auction order where like things are being offered. If lot 100, let's say, is a black leather Mies van der Rohe Barcelona chair and a last-minute addition to the auction is a black leather Mies sofa, this sofa might be called lot 100A. If you are getting reacquainted with Sally from Springfield, you might bid on lot 100A thinking it is lot 101, and get quite a surprise when you go to retrieve it. Because addendum lots are added late, however, they are often great bargains because fewer people know about them.

In the end, just keep in mind that you are at the auction with a purpose in mind—to acquire lot 75, that great George III mahogany long-case clock, perhaps, or lot 423, a circa 1960 brown, orange, and green plaid Chanel suit previously owned by Marlene Dietrich—and you don't want to miss your chance of owning them, so here is my strategy, in one word: *focus*. A lot of people will tell you that you can judge when your lot is coming up by the pace of the auction, giving you ample time for bathroom breaks and chatting. If the auctioneer is going at a typical pace of 100 lots an hour, and you are interested in lot 50, you may believe that you have thirty minutes or so to play. Maybe you do, and maybe not, but I don't think the risk is worth it. The auctioneer may pick up the pace over a series of a dozen lots to keep the action moving forward; things may slow down because a few lots have sparked little interest. Lot 30 may be offered after only twenty minutes, while you're still in the lobby looking at your friend's new shoes.

One of my former auction house colleagues, Nate Berkus, is today a well-known Chicago decorator. He attends auctions around the world, from here in Chicago to London to Monaco. And believe me, he's as social a butterfly as they come. But he never misses an object at auction because he long ago came up with a simple method for forcing himself to focus. If he is interested in the Le Corbusier lounge chair, lot 350, for instance, he circles lot 345 in his auction catalog. That's his visual cue that it is time to stop talking, collect his thoughts, refer to his notes, recall his upper limit, and, most important, to *pay attention*. This method of circling whatever lot is five lots before the one in which he's interested "hasn't failed me yet," he says.

Richard "Buzz" Norton, a well-known dealer in French and English furniture and decorative objects, has a slightly different—and more ascetic—way of making sure he doesn't miss the chance to bid on something he wants. "I sit alone," he says. "Just me and my thoughts." It is easiest to miss out, he says, when the lots you are most interested in are close together. You have to remember how much you're willing to bid on each, and quickly recalculate your upper limits should you be unsuccessful on one lot and wish to bid more on subsequent lots, which may follow within seconds. "I assure you," says Norton, "sitting alone greatly helps."

2. Succumbing to Auction Fever

Who gets struck by the dreaded disease known as auction fever? The same people who as kids raised their hands the very second the teacher asked a question. "Ooh, ooh," they'd shout, "me, me!"

I'm no doctor, but when I'm standing at the lectern in front of a roomful of people, I can spot a victim of auction fever as far back as row 50. It is the person who has to be the first bidder on every lot he wants. He's the guy who thrusts his paddle into the air and waves it back and forth as if he's greeting a returning armada. He's the guy nervously pacing back and forth along the sidelines. He's the guy who avidly looks for every person who dares bid against him. He's the guy who buys everything at top dollar. And he's the guy most likely to approach me later begging me to cut him a deal because he has overpaid for everything and his wife is going to kill him when she finds out.

Some people, of course, absolutely revel in their auction fever. These people are susceptible to the belief that they will never see another whatever-it-is like this one again. My favorite response to the belief that you'll never find another pair of Chinese cloisonné vases this beautiful, another Superman comic book in such good condition, or another George III mahogany chest so unusual comes from a Chicago dealer known for his extravagance and extravagantly good taste. "It's true," he says, "you won't. You'll never see that exact piece again."

Then again, another dealer I know has just the opposite opinion. "If it was made once by man, it can be made by man again," he says.

Some people get attacks of auction fever because a particular object is so rare. My favorite comment regarding this type of auction fever sufferer comes again from Charles Hamilton, who says, for example, that if a bibliophile who pays more than $100,000 for Edgar Allan Poe's rare first book, *Tamerlane and Other Poems*, was actually forced to read it before buying it, the book wouldn't fetch more than a dollar. In other words, it is not the book itself that is so important; it is instead the book's rarity. That may be a cynical view, but perhaps true nonetheless!

People can succumb to auction fever at a country auction, where the selection varies from pine chests of drawers to wrought-metal doorstops, as easily as they can at an invitation-only evening at Sotheby's where record prices are set for paintings by Amedeo Modigliani and sculptures by Henry Moore. But the worst cases always occur at celebrity auctions where the desire to own any shred of a favorite star's belongings is out of proportion to the fair market value for those objects. Can there be any other excuse for the $10,000 someone paid for the gabardine tuxedo Diane Keaton wore to the Oscars in 1992, when she wasn't even nominated?

I wouldn't be surprised if those bidders, though happy and proud as the auctioneer pointed to them and declared them the successful bidder, woke up the following morning feeling the pangs of buyer's remorse, or what in the auction business is known as "the winner's curse."

A person who goes to auctions regularly is unlikely to come down with auction fever. But if you are susceptible, there are certain preventative measures you can take. Here are some cures for what ails you: The easiest thing to do—what I call the spoonful-of-sugar cure—is simply to take a friend along with you. As I see it, auction fever is all about the drive to win at all costs. It's about the adrenaline rush you get when making a purchase. Most of all, it's similar to buying something while you're on vacation. The atmosphere is charged. It's easy to rationalize buying something, at any cost, to make the effort of attending the auction seem worthwhile. And knowingly overpaying has a certain appeal. That's why there are gourmet food shops on cruise ships and Bulgaris in Aspen.

Having a friend with you will help put things in perspective by serving as a tangible reminder that you have telephone bills waiting for you, the kids' braces coming up, and a mortgage, all of which you could pay for if you just held your hands—or had someone else hold your hands—and didn't place those ten crazy bids for Marilyn Monroe's copy of *The Joy of Cooking*.

"There's only one way I can escape the terrible tension of any auction," wrote the nineteenth-century French novelist and art critic Edmond de Goncourt. "I read my copy of Plato until the critical moment of bidding."

For those who are simply never going to learn not to lose control at an auction, there is a more serious measure you can take: Leave absentee bids and stay home. Or leave absentee bids and attend the auction. That way, what will be will be, *que sera sera.*

My friend Dan does that every time he sees something he wants at auction. In fact, he'll proudly tell you that he never actually bids at auction. "I've been burned once," he says sheepishly, "and I did it to myself, too, which hurt the most." As a novice auctiongoer he once lost all control, bidding so much for a pair of old wicker garden tables that he was unable to pay his rent. "I didn't even want them that much," he told me, "but I'm competitive by nature and there was no way I wasn't going to win." Following an embarrassing phone call to his mother asking to borrow rent money, he vowed never to bid live at an auction again. Now he places absentee bids only. The cure might seem drastic, but the way he sees it, certainly no more drastic than having to ask his mother for money again!

3. The Opposite of Auction Fever: Cold Feet

This is one of those blunders about which lots of people would ask, "Well, isn't it better to miss out than spend too much?" And I would say, "Yes, of course it is." But spending more than you can afford, or more than you feel the object is worth, and not buying at all aren't the only alternatives. In my experience, it is as easy to be timid and overly cautious as it is to get carried away by auction fever.

Countless times regretful bidders have told me, "I should have bid more. That whatchamacallit was beautiful, and for a little more money I could have gotten it, but I chickened out."

Remember, too, that at most auction houses the published estimates are on the conservative side. They do this to engender interest from buyers, of course, but for other reasons as well. A conservative estimate means that the lot will probably sell at least within that range, and possibly for more. Either way, the consignor goes home happy. A former auction house furniture expert I know who is now a dealer insists that people shouldn't feel guilty if they pay more than the high estimate for an object. "The estimate is really just an indication of the wholesale range," he says.

My friend John collects watches. A few years ago he had been eyeing a great 1920s platinum Cartier watch at auction. He was willing to spend $3,500, which was the high estimate. When it reached that amount, he stopped bidding, proud of his self-discipline. The watch eventually sold for $3,800. To this day he still kicks himself for having missed out. "Even then the watch was worth at least $10,000 on the retail market," he says. And today, he muses, who knows what it would be worth? "I was being 'responsible,'" he told me, using his fingers to illustrate the quotation marks. "Sometimes that's an auction blunder."

The way to avoid overcaution is to set a top price you're willing to bid. This will free you from fear of spending too much—if, that is, you stick to your resolution.

Let me tell you a story about a friend of mine. She fell in love with a set of twelve porcelain bowls designed for turtle soup. Turtle soup bowls are slightly smaller than regular soup bowls because turtle soup is so rich. The bowls she wanted were absolutely charming, with gold leaf turtles at the bottom of each bowl so that when you finished your soup you saw a darling hand-painted turtle. They were glittering, fabulous, absolutely unique bowls, and my friend really wanted them.

Still, she was cool and collected enough to set herself a top limit of $500 by asking herself these questions: If they sell for $550, will I be sorry I didn't get them? If they sell for one more bid will I hate myself in the morning? Her answer to both questions was no, so when the bowls sold for $600 she was able to take the $500 she didn't spend, invest it in the stock market, or just put it away until the next set of turtle soup bowls came onto the market.

Only you can set an upper limit of what you are willing to spend on an object or work of art. After all, only you know what it's worth to you. But you can do several things to help you make the right decision.

As I have said before, the buyer's best protection is to study up: Go to the pre-sale exhibit and look carefully at any lot under serious consideration. Troll the marketplace comparing similar objects. Consult price guides like *Warman's English & Continental Pottery & Porcelain* by Susan and Al Bagdade. Talk to the auction house experts. And develop over time what some in the antique business call "art eyes," the ability to sense good-quality work and know its value.

Take into account, as well, what position in your collection a particular piece would hold. Let's say that a poster from a 1968 Jefferson Airplane concert at Fillmore East in New York comes up at auction. If you collect pop music memorabilia, and if this poster would be the gem of your collection, you might be willing to pay way more than the fair market value. If you would pass it every day hanging in your hall and get pleasure each time, well, that's a feeling money can't buy. However, if this acquisition would simply be yet another poster from a 1968 Jefferson Airplane concert at Fillmore East in your collection, you would probably be wise to moderate your upper bid limit.

Once you decide on an upper limit, write it down in your catalog right next to the listing. That way you won't forget it in the heat of battle.

If you remember all of this advice, you'll rarely miss out. You won't feel that dreadful twinge of guilt for holding back one more bid and losing out on something you would have cherished.

4. Not Investigating Objects That Failed to Sell

You hate to be, as they say in this business, a bottom feeder, but sometimes that's the best way to get the best deals. When a piece of furniture or a work of art fails to sell, something has to happen to it. The consignor might load it into his station wagon and take it home, or he might try to reconsign it to a future auction. But just as often, he is willing to sell it at below the reserve.

Dealers, who are comfortable with haggling and ambitious in their search for bargains, keep close track of objects that fail to sell. Even when they dislike the piece or it is not the best example of its kind, if they can snatch it up for a good price and sell it out of their shop for a healthy profit, they move swiftly. They seek out the department expert asking if the consignor is interested in selling. They might offer a dollar amount right then and there, tempting an otherwise reluctant consignor with the joy of instant financial gratification.

"Privates," on the other hand, don't always know they can do this. They are embarrassed, or they don't want to seem pushy. They leave the auction empty-handed, wrongly assuming that the object they pined for is out of their reach. You might not be as comfortable as a dealer with the ins or outs of how auctions work (though this book should fix that!), but there are no laws, no rules, that say an auction house cannot try to arrange a private sale between you and a consignor as they would between a dealer and a consignor.

But time is of the essence here. Immediately after an object fails to sell, write a note saying you would be interested in buying lot such-and-such. Give the note to one of the auction house employees, preferably the expert who cataloged the sale and knows the merchandise and consignors best and who will take it from there. There may be a bit of haggling, but keep in mind that in this case you pretty much have the upper hand. After all, if you don't buy it, the consignor may lose money and time, so he is likely to be quite willing to part with it for less than he originally hoped for.

5. Keeping Up with the Joneses

Novices frequently assume that the other bidders know more than they do, so they try to keep up. But think again. In reality, it all depends on exactly who is bidding. A couple of years ago we handled a single-owner sale of the property of a prominent midwestern couple who had owned a Canadian hunting lodge. They had all kinds of cuckoo clocks, heavily carved tables and chairs, antler chandeliers, and wildlife trophy heads, all of which made for an unusual and exciting auction.

A man who was attending his first auction had flown in his family on his private plane. He was an extremely competitive businessman who had not examined any of the objects in the presale exhibition. And every time he started bidding he couldn't stop. He would close his eyes and raise his paddle until he heard me say, "Fair warning!" and "Sold!" Even his wife couldn't restrain him. Collectors who had come to the auction were astonished by the prices he paid. He ended up buying over $200,000 worth of objects in a single Sunday afternoon.

Every auctioneer knows that it takes only two bidders to make an auction, or one bidder and a reserve. Occasionally, this competitive businessman would come up against a collector who also wanted the object and was almost as stubborn as he was. They would bid against each other until the collector finally cried uncle. As in cases of auction fever, the final amount bore almost no relation to the value of the objects.

This happens all the time. Recently, for instance, a well-known public official and partner at a major international law firm walked into an auction house in Chicago, took a seat, saw something he liked, and started bidding. What had caught his eye was a group of six black-and-white prints with railroad themes. Their estimated auction price for the entire lot was listed in the catalog as $125 to $150. The bidding was fast and furious, ending in a bidding war between two bidders, both of whom wanted the prints very badly. The lawyer, a naturally fierce competitor, eventually wore down his foe. He paid $450 for the prints.

What's wrong with this picture? Well, the lawyer was bidding against a railroad buff to whom the prints' value was far greater than their price would have been in the general market. He bid up the lawyer not out of spite but out of desire. The lawyer, not knowing who the collector was or why he was bidding so furiously, let his own desires get the better of him. Did he pay too much? Absolutely.

A friend of mine who works at an auction house in California told me it's been her experience that as more and more private bidders attend auctions, this blunder is getting worse, not better. True or not, it's understandable that average auction-goers and collectors might be intimidated into thinking that dealers know a great deal more than they do about an object. You could at least make a case for following their lead in bidding. It is counterintuitive, however, to think that average auctiongoers and collectors know more. For some reason, though, most of us assume we know less than our neighbor.

My friend in California also thinks that as more "privates" attend auctions, the bidding is becoming fiercer and more competitive, because making a profit isn't the main purpose of private bidders, as it is for most dealers. Bidders who project confidence can be intimidating to auctiongoers who are less sure of themselves.

Far be it from me to analyze your self-esteem problems, but you have just got to tell yourself over and over that you know what you're doing—assuming you *do* know what you're doing. Remember that when you think another bidder knows more than you, you could just as easily be bidding against a stubborn collector, someone so competitive he must have the object at any price, or someone who simply has not done any homework about an object's value.

It wouldn't be fair, however, for me not to give you a contrarian's view here. A decorator from Houston who used to attend my auctions once told me that he was always aware of other people bidding against him and often took that as a sign that the object, even if he didn't really know anything about it, was worth more than he had originally thought. "A flurry of paddles makes me try harder," he says. After all, the way he sees it, if an object at auction is worth only what someone is willing to pay, then if a lot of people are willing to keep bidding, it must be worth it. I think that's a pretty funny way to look at it, but if it works for him, who am I to argue?

Still, I really think there is no substitute for doing your homework, setting an upper limit, and sticking to your guns. Even if someone at the auction does know more than you do, that person's upper limit should have no bearing on your behavior. It doesn't make sense to pay more than you're comfortable with just because the guy four rows ahead of you looks like a genius.

5

The Ten Criteria for Determining Value

The value of anything at auction—or anywhere else, for that matter—is whatever someone is willing to pay. The marketplace rules! But the only way to truly judge the worth of a work of art or a decorative object is to understand the ten criteria for determining value.

These are the same criteria art professionals—from dealers to museum curators to appraisers—use when assigning valuations to fine art, antiques, and collectibles, regardless of the medium. Because I have been in the auction business for so long, these criteria are second nature to me. They're that way to the more than seven hundred "eppraisers" in my own business, Eppraisals.com, which provides online appraisals, using these criteria, digital images, and information provided to us by our clients.

As you amble around the presale exhibit and investigate the objects at auction, keep these ten thoughts in mind. Ask yourself if the object in which you're interested reflects the positive aspects of these ten criteria. If it does, you'll be able to judge more easily whether the object is worth $10 or $10,000. If it does not, the same question arises—$10 or $10,000? Either way, you'll at least have some basis for your decision.

These ten criteria—authenticity, condition, rarity, historical significance, provenance, size, medium, subject matter, fashion, and quality—will help you decide if what you want is worth the cost.

A Is for Authenticity

Is it real? Is it what the catalog says it is? Without an accurate identification there is no way to value anything properly. The difference between real and fake can be the difference between one dollar and a million.

There are no hard and fast rules for determining the authenticity of an object. A signature can be forged, after all, as can labels and many other things that might seem to be indications of authenticity. No one thing proves that a work of art is authentic; only a group of criteria will allow an expert to deem an object the real McCoy.

This was the case in October 1998, when Alan Wintermute, an impeccably dressed, fastidious Old Masters expert at Christie's in New York who might have walked straight out of Central Casting, received a photo of an oil painting from a woman in New Orleans. "The picture had been in her attic for years," Alan told me, "and she had no idea who painted it or if it had any value beyond the cost of its canvas and frame." She had inherited it from her parents, and believed that her grandmother had bought it at an estate sale in Texas some thirty or forty years earlier. She said she came across Christie's through the Yellow Pages.

The painting measured about 20 inches by 16 inches. From the Polaroid snapshot, Alan says, he could see that the painting was oil on unlined canvas, and he believed it was from the hand of Gaetano Gandolfi, one of the most talented members of a dynasty of artists who dominated painting in Bologna, Italy, throughout the eighteenth and early nineteenth centuries.

"Although the reputation of Gandolfi had declined until he was a figure of near obscurity by the twentieth century," Alan says, "he had begun to be rediscovered and collected again quite avidly by the 1970s." In the 1980s and 1990s several books had been written about him, and one major international loan exhibition of his works had been organized. "If this painting had arrived in America in the nineteenth century, its origin would soon have been completely forgotten, and it probably would have sold for pennies in a garage sale in the 1950s without anyone having a clue to its true identity or potential worth."

Alan telephoned the owner and explained that, judging from a photograph, he thought it might be worth $40,000 to $60,000 at auction, considerably more than your typical garage sale find. And, of course, he told her he would be happy to sell it on her behalf in Christie's January auction of important Old Masters. The owner agreed to send him the painting.

When it arrived in New York, Alan was relieved to see just how beautiful it was—small, elegant, and in perfect condition. In fact, he says, it had almost certainly never even been cleaned—something the market places a premium on. As the canvas was in its original unlined state, Alan flipped it over and read, painted on the reverse in the artist's own hand, the painter's monogram and the date of the painting: "G.G. 1791."

This was about as authentic as authentic could be.

Although the sale contained many important paintings, including a Velázquez, during the weeklong viewing before the sale no painting elicited such admiration and widespread attention as the Gandolfi. Alan's original estimate of $40,000 to $60,000 remained, which, he says, raised the level of excitement about it.

The owner, who had never been to New York before, flew up for the sale with her sister. "I didn't want to raise her hopes too much—just in case they might be dashed—but I did want to prepare her for her good fortune," Alan says, so he told her several times that he was quite convinced that the picture was going to make much more than the estimate. "I could see that she thought I meant $5,000 or $10,000 more.

"The night before the sale she asked for a restaurant recommendation for somewhere 'nice, but not too expensive,' and I suggested three of the best and most costly places in town and told her to really treat her sister and herself," he says. "By the time her credit card bill arrived, she would have no difficulty in paying it."

On the day of the sale, bidding started slowly on the Gandolfi, but grew and grew as ever more bidders jumped in. At around $350,000 bidding stalled and, Alan says, he noticed that sitting in the audience, the owner was sweating and looking slightly queasy. Bidding resumed, and when the hammer came down at $660,000, "the owner was barely conscious while her sister was laughing uncontrollably."

Reporters swarmed around them, and the sale of their painting became one of the stories of the week. It made the world-record price for the artist. Had it not been an authentic Gandolfi, the picture never would have been coveted as it was. It never would have realized such a high price. And those two sisters from Texas might never have had a chance to visit New York.

C Is for Condition

Condition is one of the most important of these ten criteria of value. Basically, it defines what kind of shape the object is in, how far off it is from the day it was created, when the artist or artisan shouted *voilà!* Once you see and understand its condition, then only you can decide if it's something you can live with. But I think you should always buy the best you can afford—in fact, it's better to buy something of lesser overall quality in great condition than the opposite. Just remember, an object that's scratched or dinged or ripped or cracked today is going to be just as scratched or dinged or ripped or cracked tomorrow, and the day after that. Bad condition is bad condition. It's just not worth investing your money in an object that isn't the best.

What constitutes good condition, of course, depends on the type of object under consideration. A painting whose canvas seems to be in perfect condition, that is unchipped and clean, may be considered in poor condition if over the years it has been varnished too often, lending it an unpleasant sheen. Rips, of course, even when undetectable to the naked eye, can also lower a picture's value. In the late 1990s, a painting in perfect condition by Alfred Sisley, the nineteenth-century Impressionist painter, would have been valued at auction at about $4 million. When one that appeared perfect in every aspect came up for auction in 1997, the auction house, as well as collectors who knew of the picture, became very excited. But under a black light it became apparent that the picture had at some point in the past been ripped horizontally from side to side. Though the repair could not be seen by anyone not carrying a black light (in other words, almost no one), the picture fetched only $2.3 million.

Condition affects some categories of objects more than others. In the past several decades toy collecting has become particularly trendy. People collect not only Lionel trains, Barbie dolls, and old Corgi cars, but baby boomers have honed in on toys from their childhood—Mr. Potato Head, board games like Clue, Lego sets, and Easy-Bake Ovens, among many others. Collectors prize condition above virtually all else in this area because toys generally were not made from the sturdiest materials and were meant to be used. If you find a Barbie in perfect condition, in its original box, you'll have a real prize.

R Is for Rarity

All ten of these criteria are subject to one overriding law—that of supply and demand—none more so than the rareness of the work of art or object. Rarity, of course, means that there are few of whatever it is, but that is too simplistic. After all, a rare object is valuable only if people exist who covet it. In other words, there has to be a demand for the supply even to matter.

Additionally, an object is rare only if few of them were made in the first place. For Easter 1884, Czar Alexander III gave his wife an egg fashioned from jewels and cloisonné by the house of Fabergé. He followed the next year with another Fabergé egg, and every Easter thereafter. His son, Czar Nicholas II, carried on the tradition by giving his own wife, as well as his mother, a Fabergé egg each Easter. In all, Fabergé produced sixty Imperial eggs. The best-known of them is perhaps the one with the grille on top from which emerges a rooster flapping its wings. Malcolm Forbes paid $1.7 million for it (and you can see it at the Forbes Magazine Building in New York).

Let's see, sixty eggs. That's only five dozen—barely enough for a few Easter omelettes. Now, that's rare.

Pablo Picasso, on the other hand, is regarded by many as a great artist, but, unlike Fabergé, he was extremely prolific. Picasso's best work may be rare, but his work in general seems to be *everywhere*.

So not only does rarity require that few copies or examples of an object were made in the first place, but it helps if even fewer of them survive.

Honus Wagner was one of the greatest baseball players ever to have played the game, even though he has been largely forgotten today by all but the most avid baseball memorabilia collectors. A shortstop, star hitter, and great fielder for the Pittsburgh Pirates from 1897 to 1917, Wagner was one of the first five players inducted into the Baseball Hall of Fame in 1936 in Cooperstown, New York. It is said that he was an early pioneer in the antismoking movement, insisting that a card issued in 1909 with his likeness be removed from tobacco packages lest children start smoking. Casting doubt on this legend is the fact that Wagner was well known for always having a wad of chewing tobacco in his cheek and that his picture appeared on cigar boxes and cigar bands. True story or not, very few of the 1909 Honus Wagner cards have come to light.

Some common antiques and collectibles have rare aspects that can increase their value. Fiesta ware is incredibly popular with collectors, but yellow, orange, and other colors are too common to be valuable. However, find a medium green piece—similar to the color of a spearmint-green Tic-Tac—and you've got yourself a highly desirable piece that will command top dollar.

Other characteristics that contribute to an object's rarity include a common object in an uncommon size. An unusually big Meissen porcelain platter or a teeny-tiny handwoven American basket, for instance, can bring a high price at auction.

Keep in mind, however, that something can be so rare as to be uncollectible. If there is no market for an object because there just are not enough of them to create a demand, then the object is worthless.

P Is for Provenance

Provenance is the history of an object's ownership. (Following periods of upheaval, such as World War II, the record of provenance also establishes whether the work has passed legally from one owner to the next. The recent disclosure by several major museums of gaps in provenance in works in their collections may help to restore to their rightful owners some of the works looted by the Nazis.) To some people, the former owners of the work are unimportant, but to others, especially dealers and serious collectors, knowing the provenance of a work of art is one more way to authenticate it. "There are just too many fakes out there," says Chicago dealer Richard Norton. "Today they take ancient Chinese pots, literally cut off the bottoms, rebuild the top and refire it so there's virtually no way to know it's not real. Under these circumstances, provenance becomes even more important."

Knowing where something has been—whether it was in Mrs. Potter Palmer's attic for sixty years or passed down in one family over six generations—can make a huge difference in an object's value.

Provenance, of course, is what celebrity auctions are all about, as well: Barbra Streisand owned that Stickley sideboard; George Burns owned that humidor; the Duchess of Windsor owned that jewelry.

The sale of the duchess's jewelry is a good illustration of the power of a good provenance. In spring 1987, the duchess's estate chose Sotheby's to sell her jewelry. The sale took place in Geneva, Switzerland, under a tent at the Beau-Rivage Hotel, with an international collection of jet-setters, celebrities, social dinosaurs, important collectors, onlookers, hangers-on, and just about anyone else with enough money and ambition to attend.

In approaching the collection, Sotheby's knew the value of the owner's name. The duchess was the first to wear wonderful animal brooches that Cartier had made for her, and the collection overall reflected her passion. It was composed mostly of wonderful Cartier-designed gems from the 1930s and 1940s. But exactly how much should the provenance add to the price? How do you take into account what was increasingly becoming known as the Windsor factor?

Ultimately, Sotheby's placed estimates on the jewelry based on its intrinsic value. Anything above that would have to be determined by the auctiongoers. And determine it they did, bidding about eight times the estimate, for a total of $50 million.

A little more than a decade later the power of the Windsor factor was at work once again. Sotheby's sold the contents of the Windsor estate in the Bois de Boulogne in Paris. It was consigned by Mohamed al Fayed, who had bought their home from the Pasteur Institute completely intact.

The sale was—well, it was just astounding. For example, a box containing a piece of the Duke and Duchess's wedding cake, estimated to sell for $500 to $1,000, sold for $29,000. A George III silver basket, a wedding gift to them from Winston Churchill and his wife, Clementine, was estimated to bring $15,000 to $20,000. It fetched $79,500.

Provenance, in a sense, can be a security blanket: if a work of art is consigned by a connoisseur, it ensures that someone else important, someone whose choices were less limited than those of the average buyer, thought it was great.

H Is for Historical Significance

This sounds like provenance—but it's actually quite different. The desk upon which President Kennedy signed the Nuclear Test Ban Treaty. The ruby red slippers Judy Garland wore in *The Wizard of Oz*. The Declaration of Independence.

This last example actually came up at auction at Sothebys.com on June 29, 2000, one of the most remarkable sales of a remarkable piece of Americana—online or off—from beginning to end.

It all began in 1989 when a Philadelphia man bought a $4 painting at a flea market, hoping to salvage the frame. Dissembling it, he found a folded copy of the Declaration of Independence, which he assumed was a nineteenth-century copy. Finally, however, a friend persuaded him to get it appraised, which he did at Sotheby's. To his great surprise, the specialists at Sotheby's declared that this Declaration was one of the originals printed on July 4, 1776.

It was first sold in 1991, to Visual Equities in Atlanta for $2.4 million, a record at the time for printed Americana. Visual Equities tried to sell it two years later, but failed due to a downturn in the market.

When the document came up for auction in 2000, however, the economy was roaring and record prices were being set on a regular basis. In addition to great timing, this Declaration of Independence was one of only twenty-five known to remain in existence. All were already in museums or other institutions, or if still in private hands, were already promised to museums.

This meant that this Declaration of Independence would be the only one that could conceivably ever remain in private hands. That's the kind of cachet few objects can claim.

It sold to television producer Norman Lear and a partner for $7.4 million ($8.14 million with the buyer's premium)—23 percent higher than Sotheby's high estimate and a record price, not to mention a piece of history in and of itself.

S Is for Size

It should go without saying that in collecting, size doesn't (necessarily) matter. Bigger isn't absolutely better. A Sam Francis oil on canvas, like the one offered for sale not too long ago at Christie's, measuring 9 by $10^1/_2$ feet won't be as easy to sell as a smaller picture, because even important collectors don't always have that kind of wall space.

A couple of years ago two similar early-1900s Tabriz rugs were included in the same sale. One was 11 by 7 feet, 11 inches, with an estimate of $10,000 to $15,000. It sold easily for just below the high estimate. The next rug was a glorious 27 feet, 8 inches by 16 feet, 10 inches, with an estimate of $80,000 to $120,000. It was an incredibly beautiful rug fit for a pasha, but it was just too big for most rooms, and it failed to reach its reserve.

With jewelry, most people would say that bigger is better. After all, who wouldn't want a big ol' diamond? But once again, it isn't necessarily so. We had two sapphire-and-diamond rings for sale at Sotheby's in Chicago, both exceptionally beautiful. The smaller of the two was an 18-karat white gold ring with a center emerald-cut sapphire weighing 2.3 carats, and six tapering baguette diamonds mounted in white gold. It was estimated to sell for between $2,000 and $3,000. It sold for just under $2,200.

The larger, more fabulous ring had a center emerald-cut sapphire weighing 9.33 carats and two emerald-cut diamonds weighing about 1.10 carats mounted in platinum. It was estimated at $15,000 to $20,000. While it was gorgeous, its size would have made it impossible to ever wear except at the fanciest, not to mention most secure, events. It failed to sell.

M Is for Medium

Is it an oil painting? A print? A drawing?

Three pictures—an etching, a drawing, and an oil painting—by the nineteenth-century French genre painter Jean-François Millet, all rendered in the 1850s, sold in New York during the hot art market years of the late 1990s. Two sold at Sotheby's, one at Christie's. As a group, you'll see how medium can affect price.

One was an etching titled *Les Glaneuses* (The Gleaners), from 1855–1856. Gleaning was an age-old practice in which the poorest members of a community were allowed to gather and keep for themselves any grain left behind by communal harvesters. During this period Millet was becoming increasingly aware of the political and economic significance of these poor laborers. The etching was in a Sotheby's sale in fall 1996. It was a nice image printed in brown ink, estimated to sell for between $5,000 and $7,000. But etchings, which are produced in editions sometimes numbering in the hundreds, aren't as rare as paintings, and the estimate proved too high. It not only didn't sell for much; it didn't sell at all.

A few months earlier a drawing by the artist had come up for sale at auction. It was also called *The Gleaners* and completed in 1853. The drawing was of exceptional quality, and a significant work of art. It had been previously unknown, but once rediscovered it quickly became one of Millet's most memorable compositions. In an emotionally telling gesture, one of the gleaners presses her hand against her straining back as she struggles across a harvested field. The drawing had a presale estimate of $100,000 to $150,000. It fetched $167,500.

A few months before this sale, Millet's unrelated though similarly titled oil painting *L'été, Les Glaneuses* (Summer, The Gleaners), also completed in 1853, was estimated to sell at auction for $800,000 to $1.2 million. It was one of a set of pictures depicting the four seasons that had been commissioned from the artist by a then-famous Parisian architect. The pictures turned out to be significant in Millet's artistic development, a consolidation of his personal painting style. It sold for $3,412,500.

Trios of pictures by the same artist selling for vastly different amounts of money are common. A Matisse print from 1929 sold in 1989 for $150,000, a record at the time for a Matisse print. Within a month of that a Matisse drawing, which had been on the block a year earlier and sold for $250,000, sold again in London for $530,000. In October 1989, a painting by Matisse fetched more than $12 million.

I could go on and on. But I think you get the idea. The medium in which something is created is an issue of supply and demand, of course, like anything else. But paintings are by their very nature rarer than drawings, which are rarer than prints.

S Is for Subject Matter

As people in the auction business often say, "A little girl with rosy cheeks and a bouquet of flowers will sell for more than an old man with a grizzly beard, period." Other perennial best-sellers include pictures of nudes, landscapes, and pets. Religious scenes tend not to do so well, though they're big with museum curators. I guess people just don't want to live with a picture of the Madonna and child sitting on a golden throne or of *Martin Luther and His Friends* hanging in the den.

Again, a trio of pictures proves that subject matter is more than just a matter of taste—for many people, it's a matter of value.

Norman Rockwell, who created covers for the *Saturday Evening Post* for forty years, was the quintessential American artist, a master at showcasing the everyday pastimes of people at work and at play, in moments of quiet repose and thrilling exuberance. His paintings of a family oohing and ahhing at the Thanksgiving turkey as it's brought to the table or of the young girl looking at herself in the mirror contemplating her impending womanhood are American icons.

Three of his magazine-cover illustrations that had been a part of a large Midwestern corporate collection were sold in 1994. The canvases were all about the same size and in equally good condition, and each had a clear and authentic signature. Because of these similarities, they make for an interesting example of how subject matter—which in the case of these three pictures was their main differentiating factor—can affect value.

One of the pictures, though it depicts an adorable cheery cheeked little girl with a flower, was set against a background of war, which isn't considered one of Rockwell's most desirable subjects. It was estimated to sell for between $50,000 and $75,000, and sold for just under the high estimate, at $70,000.

The next picture is a classic Rockwell: an image of small-town America, with a bright new fire engine juxtaposed against its passé predecessor, meant to illustrate Rockwell's—and America's—can-do spirit and optimism. Certainly collectors would find such a quintessential scene more Rockwellian, and desirable, than a war scene, and this was proved true by the $220,000 it brought at auction.

The third picture was an even more ideal Rockwell scene. Called *The Fumble*, it was painted in 1925 and illustrated two themes that Rockwell returned to often: youth and sports—in this case, football. Estimated to sell for between $100,000 and $150,000, it sold for more than twice its high estimate, fetching $400,000.

F Is for Fashion

Just as hemlines and heels go up and down over the years, so too do trends in collecting. Tiffany lamps and Frank Lloyd Wright furniture were for many decades so out of fashion among collectors that you could barely sell them at flea markets. Now the very wealthy can barely afford them at auction.

Taste changes. Federal-style furniture was popular in the 1920s, out of favor by the 1950s, and back in the collecting limelight in the 1980s. In 1888, a picture of a sheep grazing in a meadow by the nineteenth-century Dutch painter Anton

Mauve, who was known for his renderings of rural life in the Netherlands, sold for about $8,000, a fair amount of money back then. By 1904 the craze for sheep-grazing-in-a-meadow pictures had really taken off and the picture sold for $40,000, which was a huge amount of money for the time. In the decades that followed, however, Mauve's pictures lessened considerably in popularity—until the early 1990s, when in a rather small way Mauve sparked some interest. One of his typical rural scenes sold for $42,000, which wasn't such a bad price, and there was some buzz in the art world that Mauve was back.

I don't think so. After all, $42,000 was less than a one-half of one percent increase in about ninety years, not exactly an amount on which to base a trend.

Even fashion goes in and out of fashion. Collecting purses, for instance, is hot right now. Kelly bags, which were made by Hermès originally in the 1950s and named for Grace Kelly, are the fashion-collecting trend *du jour*. A brown alligator Kelly bag, stamped "Hermès, Paris" and estimated to fetch $1,000 to $1,500, recently sold for $6,900; a green leather Kelly bag, stamped "Bonwit Teller, Hermès, Paris" and estimated to sell for $800 to $1,200, fetched $4,025. At a charity auction not too long ago a brocade handbag from the 1920s with a lapis clasp shaped like a pug dog fetched $4,025, almost ten times its estimate.

Trying to determine trends in the art and collectibles markets is like trying to track the stock market. There is no one sure method—though one way may be to watch the covers of home decorating magazines. A former colleague of mine at Sotheby's told me that the high seller in its next rug sale was expected to be very similar to one on the cover of that month's *Architectural Digest*.

If you are careful, in both the stock market and the art market, you won't jump on something at the top of the curve. After all, that's when it may begin its descent. Up to a few years ago, for instance, chintzware—china produced between the 1900s and the 1960s with an overall floral pattern that resembles chintz fabric— was fairly unknown. It was inexpensive, easy to find, and didn't really even make a blip on the radar screens of most collectors. But then, for reasons that are inexplicable, chintzware took off. Now it's expensive, harder to find, and according to some dealers I know, on top—in other words, this is not a great time to start collecting chintzware. From its current pinnacle it can go in only one direction. Unless, of course, you're a contrarian and believe that what goes down must eventually rise, phoenix-like, once again.

Q Is for Quality

This is really a catchall for the entire group of ten criteria, a reminder that value is a combination of all of these things. In other words, is it the best there is of its kind?

There aren't many examples of "the best of its kind," but one is Vincent van Gogh's painting *The Portrait of Doctor Gachet*. Everything about it is perfect, from subject matter—Dr. Gachet was van Gogh's physician—to condition to provenance to significance in the history of art. And its quality was reflected at Christie's in May 1990 in its $82.5 million price, which broke all records for a painting. It was bought by Japanese industrialist Ryoei Saito. The sale, from start to finish, lasted three minutes.

Quality is not just a consensus of snobs or co-conspirators, but judging quality is not something you can teach. Part of it has to do with a comparison to similar objects—how the piece stands up to the artist's or craftsman's previous work, how pleasing and carefully executed the composition is, how good the materials are, and so forth. For the expert, judging quality is no more mysterious than deciding, through the senses in combination with experience, whether one peach on the produce stand is of higher quality than another. Knowing quality when you see it is something that, over time and with an educated eye, just develops. After a while, good things, high-quality things, just look good. They look right. And they *are* right.

Notably missing from these ten criteria is age. Although it is important to several other criteria—authenticity and fashion, for example—just the age alone does not significantly affect the value of a piece brought to auction.

2

Getting Ready

6

Why People Buy at Auction

People buy at auction for lots of reasons. *Lots*. They can get great bargains and unique high-quality works of art and antiques, not to mention a myriad of other things, like well-built though not necessarily antique sofas, contemporary paintings, leather-bound gilded books to line their shelves, Beanie Babies and Barbie dolls, kitchen collectibles—and virtually anything else you can think of.

You might buy something that belonged to a famous celebrity—one of Johnny Cash's hunting guns, maybe, or Ethel Merman's dressing table, which Christie's in New York sold. You might buy a one-of-a-kind sculpture or an Art Deco soup tureen that only you recognized was made by the master silversmith Jean Puirforcat. You might purposely overpay for a painting by Jasper Johns just to read about yourself in the papers the next morning. I'll talk a bit more later on about each of these reasons why people buy at auction.

But I think there's something more, something often left unspoken, something that can include each of these reasons: the thrill of the chase.

Coming Down with Auction Fever

You visit the presale exhibition, say, and out of the corner of your eye, beyond a pair of Georgian candlesticks, on the other side of a Régence-style clock-case, in the distance past an original Art Deco seat from Radio City Music Hall, there *it* is: a gorgeous, pristine eighteenth-century Philadelphia highboy that would look perfect at the far end of your living room. Your prey is in your sights. You amble over nonchalantly and circle it. You open its drawers, even upend its drawers to inspect the joinery. You peek into its nooks and crannies, all the while thinking to yourself, *I have to have this.*

Then you go home and measure and try to envision how the highboy might actually fit into your living room. Of course, the sofa will have to migrate to the other side of the room, the media center will find a new home in the spare bedroom, and the grouping of six silhouettes on the wall will have to come down—all to make room for the highboy.

You spend a day shopping in local antiques stores to see what similar highboys are selling for at retail, and finally you establish your price.

And then it's auction day. You arrive early, register, get paddle number 412, and wait until the highboy comes up. The bidding starts slowly. A man in a charcoal-gray pinstripe suit and pinkie ring lifts his paddle. A woman wearing a trench coat and dark sunglasses sitting two seats down from you bids next. Then the man, then the woman again. You sit tight, waiting. Another man, standing in the back of the room wearing jeans and a Yankee baseball cap backwards, enters the fray, upping the ante by starting a bidding war with the pinstripe-suited man. Finally baseball cap drops out, looking frustrated.

The auctioneer scans the room, and now you jump into the action. The pinstripe-suited man seems startled and slightly annoyed to have a new competitor. He bids, you bid, he bids. You bid once more. This time, clearly in your mind but unbeknownst to him, this is your last bid, your upper limit. Self-discipline becomes you.

The auctioneer, looking at the man, coos in a slightly cheeky way, "You, sir?" A pause, the man shakes his head silently from side to side, and the auctioneer scans the room once more. Finally, with no one else offering a bid, he says, "Fair warning!" Another pause, only an instant really, but to you, it seems endless. Your heart is beating rapidly. You realize you're gripping the paddle as if you're holding on for dear life. And then—*boom*—the gavel hits the lectern. "Sold!" says the auctioneer merrily, "to paddle number 412."

An indescribable wave of joy sweeps over you. Sure, your victory came at a price—the highest dollar amount you were willing to spend—but it was a price you established yourself. Not only are victory *and* the highboy both yours, but they are yours on your terms and not a penny more.

The Best Price

A major reason to buy at auction is price, of course. Here, though, is where there's been an evolution over the past two decades. About 70 percent of those buying at auction used to be dealers. They wouldn't pay more than around 50 percent of what they thought an object would sell for at retail. That meant the 30 percent of private buyers like you could get a great deal by bidding just a little bit more, forcing the dealers to drop out.

That, alas, is no longer necessarily true. In fact, today the numbers have pretty much flip-flopped. That, at least, is what Diana Brooks, former president and CEO of Sotheby's told *Art & Auction*. Now, because of ways in which the art market—auction houses, dealers, galleries, and museums—has changed, fewer dealers are buying at auction. Today, the 70 percent instead corresponds to the number of private collectors and individuals buying for themselves. That means that most bidders no longer drop out after the bid reaches roughly half of the object's retail value.

No one knows the exact number of dealers versus privates, but Lita Solis-Cohen, a prominent writer in our industry and a reporter for *Maine Antiques Digest*, says that dealers are now going to auctions all over the country, and even the world. "They're always returning my calls from their cell phones," she says. "'Lita, I'm on the road,' they tell me, on their way to God-knows-where."

It's a dealer's business to know where the auctions are and what's selling at them that might be valuable to their business. It used to be hard to keep track of everything, but today newspapers and magazines publish auction listings and auction house Web sites keep their clientele informed.

No matter if the number of dealers at auction is on the increase or decrease, their importance continues. Wealthy collectors—both old hands and novices—rely on dealers to sort through the morass of stuff out there and, in effect, by their recommendation, vet works of art and objects.

The dealer does the research, the dealer authenticates the objects, and the dealer often does the bidding, either for a fee or as a favor, on the collector's behalf. Many collectors like to remain anonymous at auction, so the dealer who bids for a client preserves that client's anonymity and prevents other collectors from bidding up the price just to be annoying or spiteful. And don't forget, when a dealer bids on behalf of someone else, it lessens the competition for everyone.

In addition to the dealers and privates who make up most of the buyers at auction, there's another group—museum representatives—that while not significantly represented in number are nonetheless significant. These are the people who supply scholarly approval and whose research adds to our understanding of many works. They have the tools and the know-how to authenticate old and complex things, to write books and journal articles. The items they buy tend to be the best, and what they buy for their museums will probably never be on the market again. They buy the best and, at the same time, diminish the quality of what's available commercially.

Despite the number of knowledgeable dealers, educated privates, and museum curators at auction, though, smart auctiongoers, those attuned to art market trends and those who understand how auctions and auction houses work, can still find great values—and sometimes unearth terrific bargains.

One of the specialists who used to work with me tells a great story about a trip his mother took to New York. She and a friend were doing a bit of shopping when they happened to notice a well-dressed woman of incredible, dazzling beauty. That same night, coincidentally, at a formal charity ball they were attending, they saw the same woman, in an incredible, dazzling gown equaled only by her own good looks. His mother couldn't resist, and approached her to ask where she had gotten the dress. "You like it?" the woman asked. "Dead people's clothes. At auction."

Chris Coy, who used to work with me in the auction business and now conducts house sales in the Chicago area, has a keen eye. He knows his malachite from his majolica, his settee from his sofa from his settle (they're all different). But part of being a savvy auctiongoer is more than academic—and I mean that literally as well as figuratively. When Chris goes to presale exhibits he really, really looks at everything.

At an auction not too long ago, he told me, he was a bit disappointed. There was nothing in particular that he was interested in buying. As he was about to leave, though, he noticed a redware hound dog on a shelf behind the grillwork doors of a cabinet that was for sale in the auction. He walked over, opened the cabinet, and saw that the dog was in the sale, too. The auction house had put it there for display—not a very good idea. Chris left an absentee bid of $250, and was the successful bidder for just about $100. Once he got it home, though, he began to suspect that maybe it wasn't just any old clay dog, but a special clay dog. He sent it to Sotheby's for an appraisal and learned that it was in fact from the Shenandoah valley, circa 1890, and was worth about $1,000. "You don't find sleepers like that at auction very often anymore," he told me, "so when you do, it's that much sweeter."

Like Chris, a friend of mine, a chic young interior designer in Chicago, is an inveterate shopper at auction. In fact, he furnished his entire home with auction finds. Let's take a virtual tour of his house, starting in the library, which he designed around an armoire he bought for $900 and fitted with shelves for another $200 to hold his stereo and television equipment for a grand total of $1,100. He later found a similar armoire at an antiques store he frequents when shopping for his tony clients. This one, not yet fitted-out for modern equipment, cost about $1,800, so he came out ahead, though not by 50 percent, as he would have twenty years ago. Still, the money he saved is money he had to spend when, several weeks after buying the armoire, he attended another auction and bought three contemporary nesting tables in the style of the twentieth-century designer Billy Baldwin for only $100; two side chairs somewhat sculptural in shape for $150 each; and for his bathroom, an unusual Asian table he planned to use as a counter. Not only is it now a conversation piece, but it was a bargain at $300.

He's not afraid of reupholstering either, and though he paid more to re-cover his $400 auction-find sofa and the two side chairs than he paid for the furniture itself, the overall price for his unusual, high-quality furnishings, including the reupholstering, was far less than it would have been at retail. The down-filled sofa is now covered in a bright Scalamandré striped silk, the armoire has interesting hardware and lovely old wood, and there is unusually good carving on the Asian table.

His reason for shopping at auctions is simple: a good eye—that is, an ability to spot a bargain—has helped him own finer things than he could otherwise afford.

The Find

Another attraction for buyers is that auction houses are selling mostly one- or two-of-a-kind pieces. In a world where there's a Pottery Barn or an Ethan Allen on every corner and a Spiegel catalog in every mailbox, it's not easy to be original anymore. You really have to work at it. At auctions you can often find unique pieces that have aged well and that have a story to tell. They weren't necessarily manufactured for the mass market, either, which makes them that much more special.

At one recent auction, for example an elaborately carved 1920s Chinese "opium bed" was an extraordinary work of art. It was red-and-black lacquer with wonderful hand-carved Chinese scenes covered with gold leaf, and it sold for $1,100. The frame was close to 8 feet tall, 3 feet wide, and 6 feet long. It was, needless to say, the kind of incredible, exotic piece you can build a room around.

At another auction a 5-foot-long carved carousel figure of a pig (that's right, a pig) wearing a brown saddle and a periwinkle blue ribbon-tied harness, fetched $3,910. Imagine what a showstopper she would be in a grand entrance hall or a child's nursery.

A friend of mine was the successful bidder on a set of thirty-six framed photographs of celebrity diners such as Phyllis Diller, Tony Bennett, Jack Benny, and even Bozo the Clown that had originally hung on the walls of a now-defunct famous Chicago restaurant. My friend paid less than $200 for the collection, which is now the focal point of an entire wall in his funky lakeside apartment.

In another auction a box lot of wastepaper baskets was for sale. They were all interesting-looking, some old, some not too old. One was decoupage, a few were metal, a few were basketry. The entire lot went for a pittance, and whoever owns them now has an interesting (and useful) collection strewn throughout her house.

Auctions are full of good-looking but utilitarian pieces of furniture, from sofas to end tables to dining room buffets to bakers' racks. It's not all *art* and *antiques*, and not all auctiongoers consider themselves collectors.

The Selection and the Research

For many people, though, and especially for collectors—as opposed to dealers or decorators, for instance—the enormous selection offered by auction houses has great appeal. It's one thing to nose around a series of antiques stores looking for American furniture and decorative objects, for instance, but quite another to go to an auction house like Garth's in Delaware, Ohio, or Northeast Auctions in Portsmouth, New Hampshire, both of which specialize in American furniture and objects.

Better yet, at least at the better-known and respected auction houses, the objects for sale have been vetted by professional experts. That's not to say you can't get burned or that you shouldn't inspect each object as closely as you would in a retail establishment, but at least one level of expertise has already conferred on the lots being offered.

Just for Fun

In big and small cities alike, from country auctions where home-baked blueberry pies and mulled apple cider are sold only yards from hope chests and weather vanes and hand-stitched quilts, to glittering nighttime auctions at Christie's where tuxedo-clad collectors arrive in sleek limousines and munch on blini and caviar as they stroll into the salesroom, auctions are social occasions, places to meet and greet, network, and party. At Leslie Hindman Auctioneers, for instance, we hosted parties all the time to commemorate an important or unusual sale. They attracted attention in the collecting community and in the press, they often influenced a lot of new people to come through our doors, and of course they were always a lot of fun.

The Lyric Opera of Chicago, located in a grand building erected in 1929 on the banks of the Chicago River, has always played a major role in the city's cultural life. Known throughout the world as the home to spectacular presentations, extravagant sets and scenery, and costumes designed with wild flights of fancy in mind, the company decided a few years ago that its storage warehouse, on the south side of the city, was overflowing to the breaking point. In other words, the opera company needed to clean out its closets.

We were approached to hold a sale of many of the holdings, which included decades' worth of props and sets. The individual objects were utterly fascinating, and even the most mundane things, like wooden crates stamped with "Madame Butterfly, 1942," were thrilling to see. We filled seventeen semis with objects to be sold. In celebration, we hosted a festive party. Hundreds of Friends of the Opera came, many of whom had never been to our establishment before. Opera music wafted through the air, guests sipped wine and spent several pleasurable hours oohing and ahhing at the objects displayed in our exhibition area. Better yet, many of our guests that evening left absentee bids and many more showed up days later at the auction itself. It was a bigger success than we or the Lyric Opera had ever expected.

We hosted another wonderful event in conjunction with my auction house's tenth anniversary in 1992. The Dewar's Scotch people were running a series of magazine advertisements called "Dewar's Profiles." I was lucky enough to be chosen for one of its profiles, and I posed swathed in a lush royal purple gown, my upswept hair bedecked with flowers. It was a great coup for the auction house, and I was proud to be a part of it. To celebrate the unveiling of the ad and our anniversary, *Town & Country* magazine and Dewar's sponsored a party. Not surprisingly, we had an auction of furniture and other decorative arts at the same time, and the party was once again held in the exhibition space. My staff and I had really thought of the event as a time to let down our hair and celebrate. Our guests, however, shopped! That auction turned out to be one of our most successful, a great way to celebrate our first decade in business.

In 1998 Sotheby's was selling more items from the estate of the Duke and Duchess of Windsor. You might recall that the duke and duchess were besotted by pugs. Aside from their own, which slept on monogrammed linen sheets, drank from silver bowls, and had pillows made in their likenesses, the duke and duchess had pug figurines, pillows embroidered with pugs, and pug pictures. So when Sotheby's was set to sell much of this pug paraphernalia it seemed only appropriate to have a pug party. The auction house invited human guests to bring their pugs to tea. The party was standing room only—even if half the guests were standing on four legs— and the press, not surprisingly, loved it!

Celebrity Appeal

People also attend auctions to buy items that once belonged to famous people. The navy blue velvet ball gown worn by Princess Diana at the 1985 White House state dinner where she took the now famous dance with John Travolta eventually fetched $222,500 at a Christie's auction. Not surprisingly, Elton John's handwritten copy of the revised lyrics of "Candle in the Wind," updated for the funeral of Princess Diana, was auctioned off in 1998 at a Beverly Hills fund-raiser. It sold for $400,000. At another sale, Elvis Presley's American Express card fetched $63,000. And I sold the one millionth Schwinn Stingray bicycle, made in 1968 when it was *the* hot bike, for $14,000.

At some celebrity auctions, there truly is something for everyone. For a buyer with a taste for blue-blooded linens, $1,600 might seem like a bargain price for the sheets from the estate of the Duke and Duchess of Windsor. At the same auction, the desk at which the Duke of Windsor, then King Edward VIII, signed the articles of abdication, sold for $375,000.

Fifteen Minutes of Fame

Finally, some people buy at auction for one more reason, although they might not readily admit it: personal aggrandizement and publicity. For days after the auction, the press followed businessman Jim Pattison, who in 1985 bought John Lennon's psychedelic 1965 Rolls-Royce Phantom V for $2,299,000 at Sotheby's. After the Jacqueline Kennedy Onassis auction, newspapers and television shows mentioned such celebrity bidders as Arnold Schwarzenegger and Joan Rivers. The owners of the Franklin Mint bought Mrs. Onassis's double strand of costume pearls for $211,500 so they could be displayed in the company's museum for the tour groups that flock there. And the pearls were reproduced, as well, to sell for a couple hundred dollars each. The two businessmen who paid $1,150,000 at Christie's in 1999 for the tight, rhinestone-studded dress Marilyn Monroe wore in 1962 at Madison Square Garden when she breathily sang "Happy Birthday" to President Kennedy were interviewed by Katie Couric on *Today* barely twelve hours later. When they mentioned not only the name of their collectibles store in New York but the street on which it was located, I swear I saw Katie Couric wince.

In the end, of course, it doesn't matter why anyone buys at auction. The fact is, they just do. Your neighbors. The guy around the corner. Me. And, most important, you.

ON THE INTERNET

WHY DO PEOPLE BUY ONLINE?

People participate in—and in some cases, become addicted to—Internet auctions for many of the same reasons they have been attracted to traditional brick-and-mortar auctions: there are bargains to be found, objects owned or used by celebrities are offered for sale, publicity seekers can attract attention, and of course, there's the thrill of the chase.

But the Internet is unique, and it differs from traditional auctions in several ways.

VOLUME AND VARIETY

No matter how big Christie's and Sotheby's grow, their salesrooms will never be able to handle as much volume as eBay. Christie's may sell tens of thousands of objects in any given year, but eBay may sell tens of *millions*. That means, of course, that the variety offered by eBay (although not the quality) is necessarily greater.

A lot of collectors have realized that it is fun to limit their collecting to a very narrow specialty. Not only does this accentuate the thrill of the chase, but as the decorating magazines keep reminding us, a whole lot of similar inexpensive objects have more impact than one or two treasures. A colleague of mine, for instance, collects gravy boats. He has them lined up on his shelves like toy soldiers. Some of them are simple in design, but others are elaborately shaped and decorated. Before the advent of Internet auctions, he would occasionally come across a gravy boat in a box lot at a traditional auction or as part of a larger china service. Finding one on its own, let alone several from which to choose, was highly unusual at conventional auctions. However, on any typical day eBay has almost a thousand gravy boats at auction. In the few years since he discovered eBay and other Internet auction sites, my colleague's collection of gravy boats has multiplied in number several times. Without the Internet, he could never have added to his collection so quickly. Traditional auction houses simply cannot compete in volume.

PRIVATE LIVES

Another lure of online auctions for buyers is the relative anonymity of bidding. While traditional auctions allow for anonymity through absentee, telephone, and Internet bidding, most people feel more comfortable and in control if they attend the auction themselves. For those who either can't get to an auction or are awkward about the public aspects of participating in one, Internet auctions provide the perfect solution. (In reality, of course, it's important to remember that every bid you make, and every auction in which you're the successful bidder, is available for anyone online to see.)

TIME AND CONVENIENCE

For our busy lives, the convenience of the computer is also important. You can sneak in a peek at an online auction while you're at your office, during commercials in your favorite television show, or for hours at a time on a Saturday morning. You can think as long as you like before the auction closes, and bid in the privacy of your own surroundings. Bidding online provides no potentially embarrassing gaffes to worry about, no in-your-face competition, no leers from collectors trying to psych you out.

This brings me to a related reason people are attracted to Internet auctions: the ease of these auctions makes them absolutely addictive. Collecting in and of itself can be addictive, as can the Internet. For some people it's a lethal combination. I'm not sure I'm addicted, but I've found myself lost for hours at a time on eBay, looking at dozens and dozens and *dozens* of auctions. I curl up on my sofa with my laptop and a cup of coffee on a Sunday morning, and the next thing I know it's Sunday afternoon. The hours just magically fly by, though usually I feel richer for having learned something during the time spent online—and poorer too, depending on how much I have bid.

Whether or not I can be diagnosed as an online auctions addict, I do know that online auctions are a lot of fun. They're entertaining, sometimes educational, and they feed my competitive spirit. I like to win, and all auctions allow me to do that. Internet auctions merely allow me to do it more often and at any time of the day or night. The fact that I can directly ask the seller a question—any question—about the object gives me a sense of control I don't always feel I have at traditional auctions. I like the sense of interactivity I feel when participating in an online auction.

NO-FEE AUCTIONS

On more practical matters, the vast majority of Internet auctions don't charge buyers' premiums. At brick-and-mortar auction houses buyers pay an additional percentage on top of their successful bids as we discussed earlier; online extras are usually only tax and shipping. In addition, for those with a little savvy and knowledge, Internet auctions, partly because of their huge volume, create extremely efficient markets. A popular collectible, such as a Barbie doll, may sell for more than its actual market value at a traditional auction because it's the only one available there at the moment. Online, however, there may be scores of them for sale simultaneously, providing a clearer choice and truer prices.

Most Internet auction sites have chat rooms or forums in which people can discuss everything from whether sniping is ethical to how to tell American Belleek porcelain from Irish Belleek porcelain. But what these chats are truly about, I believe, is community. They allow buyers, sellers, and others who share similar interests to meet, exchange ideas and advice, and feel a real sense of togetherness. This is unique to the Internet, something that an auction house like Sotheby's or Butterfields can't duplicate.

7

The Presale Exhibition

If you ask me, the presale exhibit—the public display of the works of art, decorative objects, and collectibles for a few hours or a few days before the sale—are more important than the auction itself. It's there that the sales are really made, where potential buyers inspect the goods, decide what to buy and for how much. The auction in some ways is merely where those sales are consummated. How you approach the presale exhibit, therefore, is incredibly important.

Do it poorly and you'll find yourself bidding in a vacuum, making rash decisions, and not only living to regret it, but maybe regretting it while sitting in an eighteenth-century three-legged chair covered in chartreuse Naugahyde for which you paid $42,000.

Do it well, though—thoughtfully, cleverly, and patiently—and you'll bid only on objects you will be thrilled to own and which cost no more than you wanted to pay. After all, as Louis Pasteur said, "Chance favors the prepared mind."

At the presale exhibit you can buy a catalog, which I would recommend. Yes, they are usually expensive ($10 to $40), and yes, the auction house will usually scatter a few around the exhibit, tied with a ribbon or string to a finial or chair arm so you don't walk off with them. But they are irreplaceable for keeping a record of what was for sale and what prices objects fetched, and perfect places in which to take notes.

When I started my auction house in Chicago, I tried hard to outdo my local competition. I wanted to run a different kind of auction house than was currently available in Chicago, where auctions were held in mundane buildings with few amenities. One way, among many, in which I distinguished our auction house was by providing auction catalogs that compared with the best of the big international players like Christie's and Sotheby's.

Catalogs can be beautiful works of art in themselves. Richly illustrated and beautifully produced on heavy stock, even between hard covers, color photography, and historical references throughout, catalogs today can rival the works of art they are meant to describe. Admittedly, it is unusual for the catalog to become a collectors' object, but that's just what happened a few years ago when Sotheby's sold the estate of Jacqueline Kennedy Onassis. The auction house correctly anticipated such a high demand for catalogs not just from potential buyers but people in general who wanted a keepsake of Mrs. Onassis's life, that it set up a toll-free request line. And even at $90 for the hardcover catalog, which by the way, weighed 28 pounds, and $45 for the paperback, Sotheby's sold 105,000 copies. Today you can often find the catalog for sale on eBay and other Internet auction sites.

Catalogs are usually available several weeks before an auction, for anywhere from a few dollars to as much as $40 to, in some unusual cases, much more. Of course, regular collectors, important dealers, gallery owners, and some socialites and other celebrities who attract a lot of attention, may get free catalogs. Some auction houses allow you to subscribe to the catalogs of individual departments as well. So, if you collect furniture and decorative arts, Phillips New York, for instance, will send you catalogs for those sales as if they were magazines. Christie's not only allows you to subscribe, but will send its catalog subscribers price lists after each sale. These are handy references in themselves, especially if you were unable to attend the auction. For sales of American furniture and decorative arts, at Christie's main salesroom in New York at Rockefeller Center, a subscription of four catalogs costs $170. Not inexpensive, certainly, but thinking of them as reference books and not just as sales catalogs might soften the blow to your pocketbook.

Catalogs, as you will quickly learn when you start attending auctions, are a great source of information about the individual objects for sale and the rules and regulations of that particular auction house. It pays, by the way, to read the fine print in the rules. I always tell collectors—from novices to those who have been buying for decades—to read the catalog carefully if the auction house is unfamiliar to them. Even the slightest difference in rules can cost money, not to mention time and worry.

As an auction progresses, mark in your catalog the final price of each object offered. Later on, the catalog will be a valuable reference for future auctions. Over time, your catalog collection will help you follow the ups and downs, not to mention the booms and busts, of the market as well as buying trends.

Most catalogs also provide two kinds of information: the conditions of sale and other rules of that particular auction house, and information about the individual works included in the sale.

The Rules

It may seem like dull reading, but knowing the conditions of sale is essential for any buyer new to the house. Here are the buyers' premium and sales tax, availability of condition reports on works being offered, and the terms of the house's limited warranty, if any—"if any" being the operative phrase. The nitty-gritty details of the auction process—registration, bidding increments, absentee bidding, payment, and shipping, among other things—are usually explained as well.

The actual conditions of sale aren't complicated, but they are comprehensive, including the auction house's right to withdraw objects from the auction, the auctioneer's right to decide the final outcome of a dispute between bidders, title possession, and so on. Virtually every auction house states as one of its conditions that it is not responsible for any mistakes that may or may not appear in the catalog.

I say "or may not" because a few years ago at Leslie Hindman Auctioneers we were consigned a lovely oil painting of a young girl making lace. It looked French, circa 1870, and had a very clear signature in the lower right corner: Giradot. We did the usual research trying to formulate a reasonable estimate but none of the standard references listed the artist. Finally, we consulted a funny little general price guide that had been lying around the office. Sure enough, there was Giradot. The dates corresponded to what we had thought, and we based our estimate of $2,000 to $3,000 on it. The picture sold to an absentee bidder who had never seen the picture in person, only in the catalog. The sale seemed unremarkable.

Soon thereafter, however, we got an irate phone call from him. This isn't a Girardot, he said. Right, we told him, it's a Giradot. There is a Girardot—Louis-Auguste Girardot, an excellent Orientalist painter who lived from 1856 to 1933—whose paintings sometimes sell for more than $35,000 at auction, and he is the artist by whom the buyer thought he was getting a picture. He was betting that *we* had made a mistake in our catalog and that he was going to get a bargain on a Girardot. Though there was no mistake on our part, the buyer wanted his money back! Of course we refused, and to this day I have no idea what happened to his Giradot. It was a pretty picture; I hope it's above his mantel and he is enjoying it.

Some catalogs go out of their way to inform potential buyers of the auction house's way of doing business. For instance, Sotheby's might have a section devoted to export permits and to the United Nations embargo on trade with Iraq, which prohibits it from accepting bids from a person in that country or even from anyone anywhere else if the house suspects the person is bidding on behalf of someone in Iraq. Finally, this section may include information on other services the auction house provides, such as appraisal, adult education, and storage facilities.

The Details

The quality of catalogs and their scholarship varies widely. Country auctions may not have catalogs at all, just a haphazard list of the objects offered that day. Catalogs from other auction houses, like Garth's, outside Columbus, Ohio, are illustrated with good-quality black-and-white photographs on glossy stock. Christie's and Sotheby's, of course, publish well-researched and colorful catalogs as nice as most coffee-table books.

But no matter how fancy or plain, every catalog provides important information, including lot-by-lot listings, and should be read very carefully.

The first words you may encounter in a listing will be something like "Property from the Collection of Mr. and Mrs. Ann and Gordon Getty." Don't attach too much importance to this. You could assume that if important, cosmopolitan collectors like the Gettys owned it, it must be good. Then again, you might just as easily ask yourself why the Gettys are selling it. If a prominent person is the seller you might use that as an indication that the price it eventually sells at will be inflated compared to its intrinsic value. Something like "Property from a Lady," which you see regularly, is pretty meaningless, used mostly to flatter the consigner. "From the Estate of Mary Ball" tells you not just that the owner is deceased but that the objects come from a known collector whose taste you may or may not admire.

More often, though, a listing starts with the title that basically identifies the object, which may be fairly straightforward: "Victorian Brass Inlaid Rosewood Box," or "Joe DiMaggio Rawlings Big Stick Autographed Bat," or "Pair of Aquamarine, Diamond, 14K White Gold Earrings."

Sometimes, however, these labels are anything but obvious. An object can be what the auction house says it is, like the box, bat, and earrings I just mentioned, but often the auction house wants to hedge its bet, adding a few qualifying words that allow the description to be a bit vague. Sometimes the house just doesn't know what it has and is fishing for a way to describe the object without admitting ignorance. You should assume that every statement is subliminally preceded by "In our opinion."

Let's take an example of a picture by Bartolomé Esteban Murillo, a seventeenth-century Spanish painter. If the title is merely his name, the auction house believes the picture is in fact by him. If the listing starts with "Attributed to," however, the auction house thinks that the picture is from the period of the artist and is wholly or in part by him, though it's not making any promises. "Circle of Bartolomé Esteban Murillo" implies that the painting is from the period when Murillo lived and painted and is very much like his work. One catalog defines such a work as a picture by an "as yet unidentified but distinct hand" closely associated with the artist but not necessarily his student.

"From the Workshop (or Studio) of Bartolomé Estebán Murillo" means the auction house thinks maybe the picture was done under the artist's supervision, or by an "unknown hand in the studio of the artist, which may or may not have been done under the supervision of the artist." "School of . . ." refers to a picture by a follower or student of the artist, while "In the manner of . . ." means the picture is in the style of the artist, but possibly from a later date. If it starts with "After," as in "After Bartolomé Estebán Murillo," the picture is most likely a copy of a known work by the artist. Finally, "In the Style of" or "By a Follower of Bartolomé Estebán Murillo" implies that the picture is by a painter working in the style of the artist, but not necessarily his student and certainly not the artist himself. These are important nuances. A picture "in the style of Pablo Picasso" might be lovely to own, but it will not have the same value as an authentic work by Picasso.

Descriptions of the decorative arts follow the same guidelines. There's a big difference between Chippendale and Chippendale-style, between Eames and Eames-like. The title will often be followed by an actual date, like "1865" or "Circa 1900," which means the object was made around that year, or if even that is too specific, something like "Late Nineteenth Century."

Then the description follows. This ranges from the terse—"In white Carrara marble depicting a woman with a lyre"—to the elaborate: "Highly important and rare Louis XIV ormolu-mounted Boulle marquetry small *bureau plat*" (from a recent Sotheby's sale). The information provided about the *bureau plat*, or desk, which was made by the French master craftsman André-Charles Boulle around 1710, explains, in part, how Sotheby's went about determining the desk's origin through comparisons with desks of similar age and style in collections around the world, from the J. Paul Getty Museum in Los Angeles to Musée Condé at Chantilly in France. Boulle's place in the history of design is discussed as well, and this particular desk is cited by the catalog as "a harbinger of the Régence period to come."

In some cases, there will be information on an object's provenance. For instance, in the case of *Self-Portrait as a Heel*, a contemporary painting by the late Jean-Michel Basquiat, which Sotheby's sold in 1999, the provenance read like this: "Estate of the artist, Robert Miller Gallery, New York, acquired by the present owner from the above."

A "William and Mary turned maple easy chair" made in 1700 sold at Christie's in 1998 and had a far more detailed provenance: "The Doggit family, Boston, possible line of descent: Samuel Doggit (1652–1725) or his son Samuel (1685–1745),

Boston and Marshfield, Massachusetts; Noah Doggit (1725–1805), Boston, son; Noah Doggit (1770–1842), Boston, son; Nathaniel Bradlee Doggit (1818–after 1902), Boston, son; Samuel Bradlee Doggit (b. 1858), Boston, son; thence by descent to Brewster Doggit, Wiscasset, Maine; Harry Arons, Ansonia, Connecticut." A provenance like this helps to authenticate the object, increasing its value.

There may also be listings for museum or gallery exhibitions in which the work might have been included, as well as any literature in which it was cited.

Secrets of the Estimate

Finally there's the estimate. Virtually every catalog provides an estimate of the price that the auction house believes the object will fetch. It's usually a range, say, $2,000 to $3,000. I would advise regarding the estimate as what it is: an estimate. Auction houses base their estimates on all sorts of criteria, one of the main ones being what comparable works of art and objects have sold for in recent auctions. See Chapter 5 for the ten criteria I think are most important.

Many works of art, furniture, and decorative objects at auction are sold with a reserve, or sometimes a secret reserve. This is a minimum price below which the consigner does not want to sell. Let's say I consign a mahogany card table that I had inherited from a great-aunt. The auction house places an estimate of $3,000 to $4,000 on it. Fine, I think, but unless I can get $2,400 for it, or what amounts to 80 percent of the low estimate, I don't want to sell it.

Officially, the reserve is kept secret from buyers, but ethically I think it should be less than or at the low estimate. So the reserve on my card table must be $3,000 or less. A river scene from the Hudson River School with an estimate of $1,000 to $1,500 might have a reserve of $800, a Jasper Johns flag painting with an estimate of $800,000 to $1.2 million might have a reserve of $640,000, and so on.

None of this will pinpoint exactly what the reserve is, but the estimate will at least give you an idea of what it *might* be. Then you can judge for yourself whether the object or work of art is something you think would be worth bidding on.

Often the catalog listing will be accompanied by a photograph of the work of art. It may be a postage stamp–size black-and-white or a full-page glossy color photograph. For highly important objects there may be more than one photograph.

Despite this information, however, no catalog can take the place of going to the presale exhibit and studying each object that interests you. Remember, a picture may be worth a thousand words, but it may *not* be worth a thousand dollars!

ON THE INTERNET

REGISTRATION

Naturally, the one feature that does not cross over from the live to the online auction is the presale exhibit. Auction listings are the Internet version of the presale exhibit. I believe they should be taken seriously, written professionally, and judged accordingly.

To make sure you can participate as a seller or buyer, and to find out the site's rules and overall conditions, you will need to register. In most cases, however, browsers need not register until they are ready to become buyers or sellers.

For the most part online sites make registration as effortless as possible, although different sites may require different information. To bid on eBay, for instance, you must give all the usual information—e-mail address, name, street address, and phone number—and you must also choose an ID and a password. On some other sites, such as Amazon, you must also supply your credit card information.

You are required to provide credit card information if you want to sell online, too. That makes sense. After all, sellers are required to pay fees, or commissions, to the auction site, just as they do at traditional auctions, and with a credit card on file the site can automatically charge the seller's account.

Some Internet sites, like most brick-and-mortar houses, require that you have a regular mailing address rather than a post office box, so that you can be tracked down if a problem arises.

Finally, after wading through a series of questions you are not required to answer—such as "How did you first hear about this site?"—you must accept the site's terms of service. Most of us just automatically accept them—reading them seems like a dreary prospect—but there are all sorts of fine print rules and regulations that could be important later on. For instance, some sites allow registrants to have more than one account on the site. This can be problematical because a seller can then act as his own shill, which means he can bid anonymously on his own auctions to jack up the price. Shilling is far less likely on sites that permit just one account per person.

Some sites offer limited guarantees or warranties; others don't. Some sites will mediate disputes between buyer and seller; others will not. Some sites will process credit card payments between buyer and seller; others won't.

These are only a few of a host of subtle and not-too-subtle differences that you'll learn about—and that will ultimately save you time, money, and aggravation—by reading the (admittedly dull) terms of service.

SEARCHING FOR AN OBJECT

Since there is no traditional presale exhibit for online auctions—no viewing hours or evening soirees celebrating art and decorative objects from a great collector's estate—finding objects is the easy part, but deciding if they are interesting is hard. Finding exactly what you're looking for can be a challenge—a challenge that I don't even think should exist.

Some people find the "anything goes" nature of online auctions charming, but that very attitude is also one of the things many people, including myself, find maddening. A prime manifestation of the frustration many people feel is the way in which auction listings are written. The lack of standards and conventions makes searching the listings, as well as writing them, just the sort of challenge that can easily discourage many people. (For specifics on writing online auction listings, see Chapter 13.) Obviously, I have a self-interest in this, as I love and am involved in the auction world and want more people to become involved and comfortable in it.

In the online version of that world, as it currently exists, buyers and sellers alike must work without the convenience and reassurance of universally accepted standards and criteria.

As you input key words in your search for objects, put yourself in the shoes of the seller. How would you describe a nineteenth-century walking stick? Would you call it a cane instead of a walking stick? Is a porcelain disk from which you eat a dish or plate? Are pictures pictures or photographs? To some people pictures are "pics" or "pix." This guessing game is part of the fun of searching online. As you search, you will stumble across new things and come to admire objects you had no idea even existed.

My friend Henry is obsessed with anything and everything having to do with cake. That's right—cake. He bakes incredible double- and triple-layer cakes, and he collects all sorts of cake paraphernalia. He buys cake stands, which online are often called cake plates, cake servers, or cake pedestals. Some sellers even list them, rather formally, as cake salvers. Henry buys cake salvers, too.

And thanks to the vagaries of search engines, Henry also buys cake carriers, cake transporters, cake tins, cake savers, and cake safes. No matter what you call these contraptions, they are used for taking a cake from your kitchen to your neighbors' house. They're kitschy holdovers from the days of Ozzie and Harriet and the neighborhood Welcome Wagon. Henry didn't even know they existed until his cake stand search went in the wrong direction.

You can see how hard it is, though, for Henry to find the item he wants to buy. On some auction sites he has to do a search using all ten of these key words. (Here's an interesting side note, however: because people do occasionally mistakenly list a cake stand as a cake plate, for example—stands have pedestals, plates do not—he is often the only one bidding on it because he's the only one who found it. He's gotten a couple of great bargains that way.)

Another secret method of bargain-hunting is to purposely misspell something during your search, since so many sellers misspell. I know a woman who collects purple slag glass—colored glass with slag, a lava-like substance, in it. She told me she always searches for "slage" glass as well, because so many sellers misspell it that way in the listing. Henry also says that people often write "cake carrer" instead of cake carrier.

Such inconvenience means that you have to be creative—and patient—in your search. Henry searched for cake stands for months before he realized that they were listed in so many different ways.

When you explore the auction site and the offerings that interest you, first fool around a bit. Every auction site has a search engine that will allow you to search an entire site, or you can narrow your search by looking only within certain categories. Some sites let you narrow your search further and still further, until you're looking in a narrow field. This may have some appeal, but if you narrow your search too much you might miss out on a lot of very attractive objects—and more than a few bargains.

That said, however, you can search too widely as well. Try to narrow your search just enough to find what you're looking for in a reasonable amount of time while still searching widely enough to chance upon new ideas and objects.

There are some basic ways and some more advanced ways to narrow your search. The basic ways include understanding how the particular auction site's search engine works (though they're all fairly similar, each has its own idiosyncrasies) and how its categories work. By all means use the auction sites' tutorials and refer to them whenever your search is unsuccessful.

Narrow your search by searching the appropriate categories only. I know an avid collector of books by and about Eleanor Roosevelt. He even owns a first edition of an etiquette book she wrote. He checks eBay and other sites every day for new books. At first he just called up the site's home page and, using the key words "Eleanor Roosevelt," found hundreds of listings. Sure, he told me, there were always lots of books, but there were also Eleanor Roosevelt dolls, Eleanor Roosevelt crystal paperweights, Eleanor Roosevelt paper dolls wearing inaugural ball dresses, and many other Eleanor Roosevelt–related objects. Once he learned to search only in "books," however, his search was narrowed considerably. He found all sorts of books and related printed material as well, including signed invitations to state dinners at the White House, handwritten letters, and photographs.

Choosing the right category is even more important when you're searching for, say, Quimper plates. Quimper is a pottery that's been manufactured since the seventeenth century in northwestern France. I recently did a search on eBay using only the word "plate." I got 36,188 auctions in progress at that very minute. On Yahoo! Auctions I used "plate" and got 10,021 auctions in progress. Well, even on my laziest days I don't have the time to look at 10,021 auctions, let alone 36,188 auctions! Knowing that Quimper is pottery, however, and not metalware or wood, I got a more workable search result by looking only in the pottery category (69 on eBay; 2 on Yahoo!).

Once you've decided on the category in which to search, as Henry learned, using the right key words within the category is important. Keep your key words as simple as possible. Try to stay away from words so common that they'll only broaden your search too much or be ignored altogether by the search engine. Words like "and," "or, "the," and "but" won't do you much good in most circumstances. If you're searching for toys and stuffed animals related to Smokey the Bear, for instance, the word "the" would be helpful. On most sites you would search for "Smokey the Bear," using the quotation marks to gather the words together, just as I've done here. If you search Smokey the Bear without the quotation marks or the definite article (the), you'll find auctions not only for Smokey the Bear but for a boxed set of four CDs by the Zombies (including the song "Smokey Day") and a stuffed animal bear sold by a shop in Las Vegas called Smokey's, as well.

Another way to keep your searches simple is to avoid punctuation whenever possible. Remember to picture yourself writing the listing. Say you're looking for T-shirts commemorating the Chicago Bulls' fourth-in-a-row NBA championship. Do you search for t-shirts, T shirts, T-shirts, or tee-shirts? There are all sorts of ways to say it, some better than others. But the only search that will most likely capture them all is using no punctuation.

If you are looking for photographs of Laurel and Hardy, for instance, and are interested in seeing listings for sets of pictures as well as for one picture, use the asterisk as a wild card: "picture*" will find listings for picture and pictures.

Using the word "and" between words, as in "cake and plate" will get you listings with both the words, "cake" and "plate." Using "cake or plate" will capture listings with either the words cake or plate. If you're searching for cake stands but not cake plates you can often put a minus sign before the word "plate," as in "cake stand –plate" to tell the search engine to ignore listings with "plate" in them. Likewise, to find both cake stands and cake plates, you can add a plus sign, as in "cake stand +plate" to capture postings of cake stands and cake plates. Most auction sites will direct you not to use a space between the plus or minus sign and the following word. These sound like minor distinctions, but once you start your search you'll see just how major they really are.

Instead of narrowing your search, in some instances you'll want to widen it. On eBay for instance, Henry can search using "cake stand" in the listing titles alone or in the listing titles *and* body text. Searching for "cake stand" using only the title search captures only listings that use those exact words. But he'll miss titles using "cake plate." A broader search, however, finds objects using the key words "cake stand" in the title but also listings for which the title might be "cake plate" but that use the word "stand" in its description. In other words, using the broader search increases the chances of finding more listings.

READING THE LISTING

At a typical brick-and-mortar auction there may be 200 to 500 lots. Even larger sales, including a thousand or more lots, are sometimes spread out over several days. But on a typical day at eBay, for instance, as I mentioned earlier, there may be *four million* lots for sale at once. A traditional catalog, if one existed, would be about the size of the *Encyclopedia Britannica*.

Of course, no catalog exists, and each lot, so to speak, is a separate auction conducted by separate individuals, each of whom has her own business practices, ethics, and talents. Not only that, but each listing is written by that person, with all the differences in writing abilities, powers of description, and imagination that people have. As I have lamented, there is no standard way to describe decorative objects and, unfortunately, one man's soup tureen is another's covered vegetable dish.

The Internet auction world is a big messy conglomeration of auction listings divided into thousands of categories through which you must search and sift.

The first words you'll see constitute the title of the object—"Beautiful c 1930 Large Linen Pillowcases"—which the seller has composed. Titles are incredibly important in that they identify the object—or misidentify it. A title might identify a serving dish as "hard-paste" porcelain, but there's no telling how much the seller actually knows about porcelain or how she decided to use that term. Is something really linen, or is it actually a contemporary blend? A title might include the word "antique," but since there is no accepted standard of what an antique is, it is hard to know what the seller really means.

When reading a title, I ignore all modifiers, like "gorgeous," "vintage," "retro," and my personal overused favorite, "fabulous," which has no real meaning. I often see "wonderful," "old," "incredible," "nice," "cool," and "neat." I even see the word "jumbo" used. Do you really want a jumbo antique? I don't!

All of these words are aimed at attracting your attention. Sometimes they work; other times they don't. Either way, do not let them distract you from seeking the serious information you need.

A collector I know has a beautiful country home in southern Wisconsin. It's an old white clapboard house with a wraparound porch, wide-plank maple floors, cozy plaid-covered furniture, and simple decorative objects. He calls it shabby chic. The term "shabby chic" has become ubiquitous in Internet auction titles, and even my friend, who is a sophisticated and savvy auctiongoer, was at first seduced by it. "I would see the phrase and immediately go to that auction," he said. "I guess I thought the seller would be a soul mate." Instead, he found everything from moth-eaten linens to chipped porcelain dishes to a myriad of other objects in disrepair. "It was rare that I ever spotted something that fit *my* definition of shabby chic," he said. And that, I think, is the point about all of these words. They don't really mean anything.

No two people will define "fabulous" or any of these words similarly. Let them catch your attention, but don't pay too much attention to them once they do.

There are many bits of key information on the listing, all of which are important to understand before bidding on that object. These include:

ITEM NUMBER

This identifies the object for sale. If you end up bidding on the object, take note of that number and refer to it on all of your communications with the auction site or the seller regarding it. Some people sell many objects at once, and many similar objects, so referring to a hand-painted tole tray won't be of much help if the seller is auctioning five of them simultaneously.

TYPE OF AUCTION

A reserve auction will be identified as such. Some people, based on principle, will not participate in reserve auctions. Most people don't care, but do want to know. If it is a reserve auction, the highest bidder at the close of the auction will not necessarily be the successful bidder. There may be none, in fact. Where an auction is identified as reserve, it will also usually say whether the reserve has been met. If it has, and if you're the high bidder, you'll get the object. Either way, you'll know right away.

CURRENT HIGH BID

You'll surely want to know what the bid is the moment you log on to the site. If the bid is already $100 and you were looking to spend $20 on a vase, you know that it's time to move on right away. If you're surfing through a series of similar items—say, Gallé vases—and they're all hovering around the same amount, use this information as a learning experience. That's an indication of what the fair market value may be at the time.

TIME LEFT IN AUCTION

Auctions last anywhere from several hours to ten days or more. When Sotheby's first started online auctions with Sothebys.Amazon.com, its auctions sometimes lasted twenty-five days or more. The time remaining in an auction is obviously key to any successful bidder, and will play a role in your bidding strategy (more on this later).

If the end of an auction is several minutes away, you will have to be quick on your feet, or at least with your typing fingers. If the end is a week away, you can think about it longer. That said, however, it is easy to forget to return to the site, thereby missing an opportunity to bid on an object that would have been a cherished addition to your collection. Again, if you are interested initially in an object, maintain good notes. Or take advantage of what eBay, for instance, calls My eBay, which allows you to watch auctions without bidding until you're ready.

START/END

This information is very specific: it is the exact date and time, right down to the minute, of the beginning and end of the auction. If the day you log on is the eighth day of an auction and there have been no bids, the lack of interest from others has a different significance than if it is only the second day of the auction.

FIRST BID

If there are no bids on an object, the first bid is the lowest starting bid acceptable to the seller. If it is a reserve auction, this amount will most likely be less than the reserve, just as in a traditional auction. If it is a no-reserve auction, this is the lowest amount the seller will accept.

A high opening bid—and "high," of course, is relative to the object and the marketplace—doesn't mean that the object is worth that amount, only that the seller thinks it is or, more likely, wants you to think it is. Some objects have low starting bids and yet the current bid is many times that amount; this doesn't mean that bidders are overpaying, just that the seller chose a low opening bid to attract some action.

Other bits of information include the number of bids already offered, the seller's location, including the country he's in, the seller's identification number, and the ID of the current high bidder.

The number of bids will tell you if there's been serious interest in the object already. The seller's location is important for two reasons. First, some people like to bid locally. Right or wrong, they feel safer dealing with someone in their community, and they prefer to arrange for the object, especially a large heavy one, to be picked up rather than shipped. Other potential buyers do not like dealing with sellers from other countries because they find exchange rates confusing—20 pounds equals how many dollars? Also, time zone differences may hamper communication.

∽∼⚮∼∾

From the auction listing you can usually, depending on the site, link directly to various pages, such as the seller's feedback profile. Some sites allow you to link directly to the seller's other auctions, the current high bidder's e-mail, and his feedback profile. Finally, you may be able to send the auction listing to a friend who may be interested in it.

The most useful information on any Internet auction listing is, of course, the description of the object by the seller and the accompanying photographs. On a site affiliated with a traditional auction house the descriptions are written in-house and should be as professional and trustworthy as any printed material they would publish for a live auction site.

On most auction sites, however, the seller doubles as the writer, and writing skills may not be among the seller's talents. Fortunately, there are many well-written and carefully researched auction listings online. They include all the right information, they anticipate a buyer's needs, and they are enjoyable to read. You should always walk away from a traditional presale exhibit having learned something, and the same is true of an hour spent on eBay, Amazon, or any other auction site.

But because there is no standard way to write auction listings, they vary in length, detail, style, and in every other way imaginable. They are sometimes rife with misspellings and grammatical mistakes. I am hardly a stickler for good grammar, but as a potential buyer I can't help but take the manner in which the description is written as an indication of the seller's seriousness and professionalism.

People write descriptions that include opinions not based in fact, or facts merely based on their opinions. "I bought this from the estate of an eighty-seven-year-old woman," went one listing, "so it must be very old." Old, that is, unless she bought it at Wal-Mart the day before she died. "It's in such good condition I bet it's never been used," wrote another seller about an alabaster compote. Many sellers start their auction listing by saying, "I have no idea what this is, but . . ." Many sellers actually may know little about the object they are selling. After all, anyone who registers on the site can become a seller, and the object may come from an amateur trying to clean out Grandma's attic. This can be a blessing if you know something that the seller doesn't (that is, a potential bargain), but it can lead to problems if you are basing your bid on the accuracy of the seller's description.

I always keep a written list of information I need. As I acquire it by reading the description, I note that. If there are gaps after I have filled in my list, I e-mail the seller and ask. As you become more familiar with Internet auctions, you will want to make your own checklist, custom-designing your questions to your own needs. At the very least the listing and your own list should yield a very good impression of the object's condition. When reading a listing be sensitive to every word and nuance. A seller who says an object is in good condition may honestly think the object is in good condition. A hairline fracture, a tiny chip, a perfectly restored leg—if the seller isn't an expert, he may think these things don't matter. But you know better.

When a seller is uninformed about his object, he may fail to point out certain characteristics that you might find undesirable. My friend Jan bought a beautiful hand-painted Bavarian relish dish on eBay. The seller's description was thorough and well written. Unfortunately for Jan, the dish had a faint nickel-sized porcelain stain that was undetectable in the photograph attached to the listing. The seller may not have realized that the stain would detract from its beauty and its value, and Jan didn't think to ask about it before she bid.

Your own checklist can address considerations like these. Jan now always asks a seller about stains, as well as other imperfections in porcelain that are either unmentioned in the listing or invisible in the photograph.

Most buyers want to know an object's dimensions, but you would be surprised at how often sellers fail to include them. I think sellers should give the dimensions of everything they sell, even books, and especially of any work of art, decorative object, or piece of furniture.

Another imperative is that the seller provide an explicit sales policy, but again, many do not. Note the type of payment the person accepts, what sort of waiting period there might be between their receiving the funds from you and their mailing the object, how they charge for shipping, if they charge an additional sum for "handling," and if they require insurance. The notion of "handling" is a tricky one. To most sellers, handling means the amount of money they spend on packaging, which may include packing tape, padded envelopes, tissue paper, Styrofoam peanuts, or bubble wrap, among other things. I think these are reasonable costs to pass on to the consumer. What is unreasonable—and what you should be wary of—is an excessive handling fee, which some sellers charge as a way to increase their profit.

Since you are not the one doing the packing, you will have to use your own judgment about what is excessive. If you collect Bakelite bracelets, for instance, you'll soon recognize a reasonable shipping and handling charge. If each of five different bracelets costs in postage about $3 to send, with an additional dollar for handling, and the sixth seller wants to charge you $6 postage and $3 handling, you can be fairly certain that the charges are excessive, and you are perfectly within your rights to point this out to the seller. One good sign is when a seller states that they charge "actual postage and handling only." This lets me know they are thinking along the same lines as I am and, while it's no guarantee, that they are not trying to skim a profit off the top.

After you have finished ticking off information on your list, it's time to e-mail the seller with questions. No question is too dumb! Asking for amplification on a defect or dimension is as reasonable a request as questioning a shipping charge. Since many sellers honestly have no idea how much an object will cost to send, I ask what they *think* the shipping and handling will be. I let them know I live in Chicago, and even provide my zip code so they can give me information as specific as possible. Their answer is still an estimate, but they at least know I am interested, serious, and responsible. The implication, I hope, is that I expect the same of them. So far, my expectations in this area have always been met. If they know the weight of the object and the packaging, there are Internet sites at which they can input the weight and your zip code and provide you with the exact shipping charge.

There are all sorts of questions you might want answered before you bid. In addition to those I've just discussed, you might contact a seller to clarify his negative feedback. Often the seller will have a good explanation and even the most responsible seller is almost sure to elicit a negative comment or two over time. Some people ask the amount of the reserve, and often—utterly unlike brick-and-mortar auctions—sellers will tell you. On occasion I have asked about alternative mailing options. A seller may ship everything by priority mail, but that can be expensive and is often unnecessary. Better to work that out beforehand. If she never diverges from her policy, you may not want to bid in her auction. Similarly, many sellers say they require insurance. I buy a lot of books about art and antiques online, and for such inexpensive purchases, I'm happy to forgo the insurance and take the risk.

Another area ripe for miscommunication and misinterpretation is a seller's return policy. Merely saying "satisfaction guaranteed" isn't a guarantee at all, at least not of getting a refund for any reason. The seller may mean that if you do not receive the object described by them, they will return your money, while you may take the phrase to mean that the seller wants you to be pleased in every way.

Even though I am an avid fan of communication by e-mail, I think it is a good idea to get the person's phone number as well. Sometimes direct conversation can be faster and more informative than e-mail, especially since people do not always check their mail daily—or minute by minute, as I do. If a person hesitates to give you his phone number, he may not be as serious as you would like. He is, after all, a businessman, even if his corporate headquarters is a makeshift desk between two sawhorses in the basement.

While it is fine to accept some of the information in the description at face value, scrutinizing it line for line is important. I often miss certain pieces of information the first time I read a listing because I'm trying to do too many things at once or I'm speeding through a slew of listings. Before you send an e-mail to a seller, reread the listing to make sure your question hasn't been answered. If it and other questions still apply, e-mail all of your questions to the seller at once. It's annoying to receive a series of e-mails when one would have sufficed.

I've found most sellers eager to answer questions, happy to build relationships with potential customers. Most, in fact, answer promptly. But be patient if a seller doesn't respond immediately. She may be loaded down with e-mail, especially if she is in the throes of several auctions at once, or she may not be the type to check e-mail often. If she never answers, take that as a cue to back away.

8

"As Is" Really Means "As Is"

As you view the presale exhibit, bear one thing in mind: at auction, everything is sold as is.

"As is" means "as is."

When I was working on this book I thought I might end this chapter right here, with those five little words. But after thinking about it for a while, I realized that "as is" deserves a fuller explanation. First of all, the phrase itself refers not just to the condition of the piece—its nicks and dings—but to its date, attribution, provenance, and medium. In other words, caveat emptor. Once it's yours, it's yours, beauty marks and all.

Works of art, decorative objects, and collectibles are sold as is for very practical reasons. There are at most four or five department experts who organize 500 or more lots that will be included in a sale. Each object has to be researched and cataloged. Putting together an event like this is an enormous task, and most auction house specialists take it very seriously. They go out of their way to know, understand, and pass along to you all they can.

But even if a hundred specialists were assigned to each department, it would be impossible to prove that every object is what they believe it to be. No time machine can transport them to the eighteenth century to see Madame de Pompadour use the vanity that now sits in their climate-controlled storeroom. The sellers can point to centuries of documentation and an excellent provenance as evidence that it's most *likely* a vanity that Madame de Pompadour used, but they can't actually *prove* it.

In other words, objects are sold "as is" because the auction house simply cannot guarantee beyond all doubt the authenticity of what it sells.

Many auction houses go a step further than the catalog listing by providing condition reports. Christie's and Sotheby's provide them if asked.

Often the condition report is only a line or two long pointing out a dent there, a chip here, a missing bit of inlay, or whatever. This will be followed by a ten-line paragraph basically saying that the house is not responsible for the information in the condition report.

Sometimes, though, no matter how diligent the house tries to be in disclosing the flaws of a given piece, some buyers just do not take advantage of the efforts. Not too long ago Weschler's, a fourth-generation family-owned auction house in Washington, D.C., was selling a small chest of drawers. It was on display in the center of the exhibition so that potential buyers could see it from all sides. One lady inspected the chest, opened its drawers, looked inside, did most of the usual things, and at the auction she was the successful bidder. The next day, though, she phoned Virginia Weschler in the customer service department. "It doesn't have a back!" the lady said, mildly distressed. "I know," said Virginia, "isn't that weird? That's why we put it in the center of the room." The buyer admitted that she hadn't actually looked at all four sides.

Every potential buyer absolutely has to look at the objects under consideration *very* carefully. Inside. Outside. On top. Underneath. Front. Back. The presale exhibit is not a museum; it is a gallery assembled for one purpose—so that auctiongoers can inspect the goods. As you survey the room, repeat over and over to yourself, "This is not a museum." In so doing, you will constantly remind yourself that what you see may within days be something you own, something you will live with. It could become an heirloom for your family, just as it might have been for another family years ago.

Some auction houses have experts who can tell you about a particular piece. Take advantage of these people. The woman meandering around the presale exhibit might well be one of the auction house's experts in that field. That means she probably helped to catalog the sale. Just think of all that Ph.D. power you can take advantage of.

While no auction house experts will recommend you buy or don't buy something—that is a liability they cannot afford to shoulder—they will answer your questions and point out the beautiful aspects of a piece as well as its flaws. That last part might surprise you but I assure you, it's true. Auction houses are there to make a profit, of course, just like any other business, but an auction house and its experts are only as good as their word. A good reputation can take years to build but only seconds to ruin.

Let's say that I am on the floor at the presale exhibit and someone asks me if an intricate nineteenth-century gold-leaf mirror has been restored. If I know it has been but say it hasn't, that's just bad (not to mention fraudulent) business. I will surely lose you as a customer, and others as well, because word travels fast.

Auction house experts are just that: experts in their field, whether it is horology (the art of making timepieces), American folk art, or Russian icons. They catalog each object included in the upcoming sale using all of the available resources, including their own knowledge and background, whatever information has been supplied by the consignor, and other research. They use all of this to describe, as accurately as possible, the object, its history, and its condition. Then, using all of that information, as well as information about final sale prices of like objects in past sales, they establish an estimate and write the catalog description and condition report.

All of the many auction house experts I have known take great pride in their knowledge. They describe an object in the catalog as truthfully as possible. On the floor they will answer your questions so you can make an appropriate purchasing decision, armed with as many facts as possible and with an understanding that what you buy will come exactly as its consignor brought it in, exactly as you first saw it.

That last point is important. Auction houses, with rare exceptions, do not alter or restore objects they sell. They might polish a piece of silver now and then, but rarely will they make a major alteration. The reason for this is that when restoration is necessary, dealers and collectors who buy at auction prefer to use restorers of their own choosing, people with whom they have worked in the past. In addition, restoration can often diminish the value of an object. Old furniture, after all, is old. Centuries' worth of oils and varnishes undoubtedly lend it a unique patina. This is definitely true of American furniture and decorative objects. In the trade this patina is called crustiness, and it's a good thing. Not only is it beautiful, but it lets you know the chair is not a Bloomingdale's reproduction but a real American Chippendale.

Besides, on those occasions when an auction house does undertake a restoration project, it sometimes fails miserably. A few years ago Sotheby's acquired an early-eighteenth-century Newport desk and bookcase to sell in an American furniture sale. While the chest was otherwise in great shape, its feet were missing. To the experts at Sotheby's it seemed too short to be pleasing. After some research—as it turned out, not *enough* research—they had ball feet attached. Despite the effort and expense, the feet turned out to be the wrong style, and after the sale they were promptly removed. The anonymous collector who bought the chest for $8.252 million lent it to the American Wing of the Philadelphia Museum of Art, where it was exhibited, footloose and fancy-free, while research was conducted to learn what kind of feet would be most appropriate.

9

Scoping Out the Exhibition

Most presale exhibits are not arranged like retail antique stores, with great lighting, ample room to stand back and look, a clerk there at your side helping you, answering questions. Objects are seldom grouped by category or medium. Some furniture may be arranged in small, loosely organized tableaux, but most will be crammed in willy-nilly. Sometimes it seems the organizers have been *un*helpful in their display. Of course, this disarray can work to both your advantage and your disadvantage—to your disadvantage because it may be difficult to really inspect that nineteenth-century carved pine American eagle they've so inconsiderately displayed atop a 7-foot-high eighteenth-century George III mahogany bookcase; to your advantage because maybe no one but you will make the effort to climb up there to inspect it.

Recently I visited a presale exhibition with my friend Blair, an inveterate auctiongoer. It was fascinating to see him work the rooms. At this winter sale, the first floor of the display was jammed with works of art and decorative objects. The contents included carved stone garden figures and Victorian mahogany armoires, gilt-bronze and cut-glass chandeliers, Staffordshire figures, lacquered and inlaid netsukes, lithographs by Grant Wood, soapstone vases, nineteenth-century portraits painted on ivory, bronze mantel clocks, and Bidjar carpets from what was once northern Persia and is now Iran. There were also piles—and I literally mean piles—of prints and lithographs in plastic sleeves with pairs of gilt gold wall sconces placed on top of them to serve as paperweights. On the second level we found more of the same, as well as dozens of box lots of books—wonderful old hardback copies of Proust, Shakespeare, Hart Crane, Charles Dickens, and Sinclair Lewis, among others. Oh, and did I mention the spectacular carved celery-green Venetian rococo-style tête-à-tête (a curving sofa designed so two sitters can have a chat)? The auction house that day had the air of a Turkish bazaar—and it was wonderful. Only a fairly aggressive person could have made sense of this jumble. Blair, however, marched through it like a man with a vision. He took pictures off the walls and inspected their backs. He held them up to the light to look for rips and repairs. He moved chairs so he could walk all the way around them. He repositioned them so he could see them not only close up but from 15 feet away (to see what they would look like seen from the back as you walked into his living room). He pulled console tables away from the walls to look at the backs and to crawl underneath. He ran his fingers around the rims of porcelain ginger jars feeling for chips and nicks. He made sure to hold closed the tops of jars and inkwells so they wouldn't fall and shatter. He picked up cups, pitchers, and decanters by their bodies and not their handles, which may have been cracked or fragile.

He measured bookcases. He took all the pillows off a carved wood and rattan bench to study the pillows and the bench they were covering. He sat in all six of the George III mahogany dining chairs only to discover that three were broken and the upholstery on all six was in dreadful shape. He pulled over several of the specialists working the floor and asked questions. Did they think it would be expensive to shore up the legs of a wobbly set of ebonized-wood and parcel-gilt armchairs? How might a few hairline cracks affect the price of six English Rockingham porcelain dessert plates? Was the frame of a painting called *Adoration of the Magi* original to the picture?

We overheard couples asking each other questions they should have been asking the specialists. About a pair of Victorian mother-of-pearl inlaid black papier-mâché chairs, a man asked his wife, "Do you think we can buy only one?" "I don't know," she said, before they moved on, no more informed than they had been thirty seconds before. A few minutes later I heard a woman ask her friend if a slight rip in an oil portrait could be restored easily. "Beats me," her friend said.

For every sideboard Blair pulled away from the wall to look at the back, another ten people who were interested in the same piece would stand in front of it, maybe open one of four drawers, and make a notation in their catalog. Blair sat in every chair, walked around it, fluffed, needled, and crawled underneath it, while the other auctiongoers never even bothered to test the seat. While Blair opened the inlaid box, checked its locking mechanism, and worked the hinges, others merely ran their hands over it, as if by touching it they would pick up some special vibe.

Falling in love with an object is just like falling in love with a person. There is love at first sight (I have to marry him; I must own that Hepplewhite bowfront chest of drawers), followed by closer examination (he snores at night; the drawers stick), followed by acceptance (his strengths outweigh his weaknesses; repairing the drawers will be inexpensive, and the piece is perfect for the guest room). Sometimes, as with love, the flame dies as suddenly as it flared. It might have been better not to have married after love at first sight; it might have been better not to have bought the chest after only admiring its beauty from afar.

Looking at works of art, furniture, decorative objects, and various collectibles means experiencing them with your senses. Look at them, of course, but also touch them, smell them (antiques often have a pleasantly musty aroma), and even listen to them. Shake things gently. Are chair legs creaking? Does a sofa groan and sigh when you plop yourself down? Things will literally tell you that they are loose.

With every type of antique you will want to do a lot of examining and touching. Some people are fearful; they think the objects are inviolable and can't be touched until they own them. Nothing could be further from the truth.

You wouldn't buy a used car without kicking its tires, or a horse without checking its teeth. So don't buy a dining room chair—especially a used dining room chair!—without sitting in it. Sit in *each* of the dining room chairs in a set. Don't assume that because one is in good repair they all are. I have many memories of people trying to return a set of chairs because they hadn't inspected them all earlier and learned only when they picked them up after the auction that the leg of one chair was attached with masking tape. Look at sets of anything carefully; missing two out of eight fish forks may or may not be a problem. Three fewer soup bowls than you need can turn an otherwise beautiful table setting into a disorganized mess. If three teacups and two saucers are missing, you cannot assume the missing pieces are in the back room. (Remember, "as is.")

The pleasure of buying antiques at auction is that they have a history. They have been used and have developed their own personalities and lives. You need to make friends and become intimate with these things. You don't invite people to your home without knowing them well. It's the same with objects. You need to prod and poke and look at them with an analytical mind-set, even if that removes some of the mystery, and people are loath to do that to the things they love. If you can still appreciate things after you do all of this, you'll have a good sense of whether you'll enjoy them for a long time to come.

The presale exhibit, no matter your approach, can be daunting. So much to look at, so little time. Some people go to the exhibit without first giving much thought to what they're interested in buying. I've found that it really helps to think ahead. Look around your house. What do you need or want? A coffee table for the den? An ottoman for a chair in the living room? A picture to hang above your mantel? Are you looking for a few silver serving pieces to round out a collection of flatware? Does your front hall need a chandelier?

A recently married friend of mine who is furnishing her first house told me, "If you go with a plan, at least you have a mission and a context in which to look at things." Otherwise, she admits, "it can be overwhelming."

Richard Norton, who sells his furniture and decorative arts from an eccentric and crowded space overlooking the Chicago River in the city's Merchandise Mart, says that before he looks at any one thing, he walks around the periphery of the entire exhibit. Then he walks up and down each aisle looking only one way. "If you turn your head you're going to miss something," he says. Only after he's familiar in a general way with what's on display does he go back and look at individual pieces.

Chicago decorator Nate Berkus also makes an initial cursory sweep through the presale exhibit, but before going back to look at specific objects, he says, "I go across the street and have a cup of coffee to energize myself." Even after years of auction experience, as employee and customer, he says he still finds them exhausting. Nate looks at everything in great detail, going so far as to take Polaroids of furniture and objects.

Looking at objects with a fresh eye is imperative. Some people, like Nate, leave and walk around the block, then return later to look again when their reaction is less visceral, less emotional. Others create their own methods of seeing things with a clear and refreshed mind.

A well-known New York collector of contemporary paintings used to stand in front of a painting that interested him, close his eyes, take a deep breath, and clap his hands together in front of him once very loud. Finally, he would exhale. For him this ritual rejuvenated his senses. He meditated for a moment, paused, cleared his eyes and ears so he could look at the picture as if he had never looked at the picture before. Just like wine tasters who cleanse their palate by taking a bite of bread between sips, the collector cleansed the exhibition overload from his mind. And he rarely made a purchase he regretted.

All sorts of rituals can be observed at presale exhibits. I know dealers who always move clockwise to sit in chairs around a dining room table. One collector I know likes to feel the hallmark on a piece of silver, as if reading Braille, before looking at it. At some point, though, these rituals give way to practical considerations. To examine that silver hallmark, for example, the collector uses a small magnifying glass, a tool that is also invaluable for deciphering signatures on pictures, discovering infinitesimal cracks in porcelain, identifying old glass by its random scratch marks, spotting new glass from its even scratch marks, seeing knife marks on dinnerware that might be invisible to the naked eye, and studying mintmarks on old coins.

In addition to a magnifying glass, a few other tools can be useful. Because bronze, copper, and brass are not magnetic, for instance, and the fakes of these metals are often iron (which is magnetic), a small magnet will help test for authenticity. A tape measure can assure you that the red, blue, and brown Serapi rug that would look perfect in your front hallway will actually fit. I can't tell you how often an auctiongoer will buy a rug only to resell it at the next auction because it is a foot too long and he measured it with his mind's eye instead of a tape measure. To check for shrinkage, measure a round table two ways: with the grain and against the grain. If the table is very old, its diameter can vary anywhere from a half inch to three-quarters of an inch. Flashlights come in handy to look underneath tables and chairs, to look inside vases and tureens, and behind heavy sideboards and chests. They can help you see if pieces have been inappropriately glued or nailed together.

Some people, as I said earlier, carry portable black lights (which cost from $15 to $250) with them to reveal overpainting in an oil portrait or cracks and repairs in porcelain that might not be visible to the naked eye. A black light can also help you detect the glue that holds together pieces like those old kerosene lamps that originally were fused. Even dating paper, like postcards, is easier with a black light since newer paper, especially that made after 1945 or so, will glow whiter and brighter than older paper. Newer thread used in textiles, doll clothes, and quilts will glow whiter, as well.

Going to extremes, some people bring a flathead screwdriver to help them remove pictures from their frames. If you want to try this, first ask for help from one of the auction house employees. You are allowed to touch and examine things at the presale exhibit, but it is important to treat the objects with respect.

Bring a pencil and paper, of course, for notes, as well as a price guide for reference.

When looking at an object at the exhibit, note, too, the lot numbers, either on stickers or on tags attached with wire or string. If the lot tag says 35, you will know the lot is that object alone. If it says 35/4, that means there are four objects in that lot and that you have to buy them all. When the tag is a sticker, look even closer. Does the sticker conceal a crack or blemish? Look at the edges of the lot sticker and note if a crack is snaking out from beneath it.

As someone who's been in the auction world many years I can tell you that this business of the sticker is no small thing. Stickers range from the not-too-sticky to the very sticky, and the choice the auction house makes is important. Stickers can change the color of silver plate, lift the gilt off painted porcelain, peel the paint from frames or furniture, and leave residue for eternity. At Leslie Hindman Auctioneers our new-employees' manual included a section on what kind of stickers to use and how to place them on various objects.

If you have a question about that square inch of an item that is covered by the lot number, don't remove it yourself; ask for help from one of the auction house employees, even if you just want him to peel off a tiny corner to see that it's not picking up any of the paint or gilt underneath.

The presale exhibition is your one big chance to do a bit of detective work. Don't allow yourself to feel silly looking at objects, and don't feel embarrassed to ask a specialist a question that you may think is ridiculous. Attend presale exhibits and soon you'll become a savvier auctiongoer than you ever imagined you'd be.

3

Buying at Auction

10

Setting the Scene

I have been to thousands of auctions, as consignor and buyer, as auctioneer and audience, and I have learned that no two auctions are the same. No groups of artworks and decorative objects are the same, no audience is the same as any other, and no two auctioneers respond the same way in all situations. Finesse at the outset often gives way to fatigue by lot 600; surprise and stress are constant.

One tip for novices is to arrive early on the day of the sale. Scope out the space, save yourself a seat, and learn in advance the location of the bathrooms and refreshment concessions. Speaking of seats, auctions are often very long. Don't be surprised to see others more experienced than you bring along seat pads. I admit it seems tacky, but by the fourth or fifth hour of an auction, you will be wishing you had brought one. Take advantage of the time you have before the auction starts. If the presale exhibit is still on display, take another look. Read through the catalog again. Reread the conditions of sale. Make sure your notes are in good order.

Registration at most auctions, from Sotheby's on down, is usually quite simple on the day of the event. The form asks for the usual details—name, address, and so forth—as well as your bank information. Some auction houses, particularly the smaller ones, may ask you to put down a deposit of anywhere from one hundred to several hundred dollars. You can do this on your credit card. Should you not be the successful bidder on anything during the sale, the auction house deletes the charge.

While registering, ask about payment. Major auction houses like Phillips in New York take Visa and MasterCard; Butterfields, another big auction house, does not accept credit cards; while Direct Auctioneers, a relatively small operation in Chicago, does. In other words, there's no rhyme or reason when it comes to payment methods.

As the auction begins, take your seat and observe what's going on around you. Unlike an art gallery, which is usually occupied by a receptionist and the owner, an auction house has a whole cast of characters waiting to greet you and work with you to make the process as easy and entertaining as possible. The staff will sometimes include a security guard, too, but he or she will be dressed so as to blend in with the auction house clients.

At the high-end auction houses every staff member's role is very specific. At the smaller houses, employees will have several responsibilities. One person might serve as a client service representative and a salesclerk, or as an auctioneer and a department specialist. At one auction house I know of, the man at the registration desk also sells hot dogs and doughnuts.

But these employees all have one thing in common: they're there for you. Never forget that. Whatever their role, it is first and foremost to make sure that your experience under their roof is a pleasurable one. Knowing who they are and understanding their duties will lessen any of the anxiety you might have about attending an auction.

The Registration Desk

Before you enter the salesroom you need to stop by the registration desk. Here you'll pick up your paddle or bid card and sign in. Registration-desk employees are trained to move the line along. Their attitude—from warm and welcoming to snotty and sneering—can make or break the experience for visitors, especially novices.

At Leslie Hindman Auctioneers, I always stood around the registration desk before the sale as people came in. I liked to greet the auctiongoers myself, mingle, make them feel welcome, and get a good feel for the crowd.

Client Service Representatives

Auction house employees who work directly with the clients get to know the regular clients and their special needs. Some clients like to maintain a very businesslike relationship and don't demand much attention. Others, however, like to be coddled as gently as an egg.

Buyers and sellers alike have to know that they can go to the client service representative for virtually anything, from condition reports to arranging absentee bids to making an appointment for a private viewing of a presale exhibit if for some reason they can't attend at the regularly scheduled times. Client service representatives may be able to make shipping arrangements as well.

We had a very good client, a high-profile businessman, who often attended our sales. He would arrive with his wife and they would take their time looking at everything from furniture to jewelry. Once, before a jewelry sale, though, we got a call from him asking for a private viewing. He wasn't going to be out of town or anything, but he said he didn't want to run into any of his or his wife's friends at the presale exhibit. No problem. We arranged an after-hours appointment. He came by himself, looked closely at various pieces of jewelry, and left three absentee bids.

Ultimately, he was successful on two objects, a gorgeous $40,000 sapphire ring and a pair of diamond earrings. He was excited about it all, but very serious in his request that no invoice be sent to his home or office. He came in person, again after hours, to pay for and pick up the ring and earrings. It turned out that he and his wife were celebrating an important anniversary and he wanted to surprise her. He took every precaution to maintain the surprise, and our client services representatives helped him along the way. He told me that he would give her the ring on their anniversary and the earrings at a later date. Weeks later, when I ran into his wife at a formal dinner at which she was wearing her dazzling new ring, I could only wonder how excited and surprised she must have been to have received it—and how pleased she would be at the surprise that still awaited her!

Bid Spotters

Auctions progress quickly. Objects are moved from place to place, people come and go, the auctioneer talks nonstop. The atmosphere can be hectic. No wonder, then, that the auctioneer sometimes needs a little help. Bid spotters point out bidders, sometimes even bid on a particular person's behalf, and maintain control of the audience. If the auctioneer is concentrating on a bidding war between two people on her right and a person in the back of the room wants to enter the fray, the spotter takes notice and makes sure that at the appropriate time the auctioneer takes notice as well.

Shipping Department Personnel

More than anyone else in the auction house, members of the shipping department are the true insiders—they know who's buying what, for how much, and where it's going. They often work directly with each buyer to ensure that the work of art or object is packed properly, ready to be picked up on time, and sent, if necessary, in a timely manner. One false move on their part—and I mean that literally—can destroy a precious work of art and a long-standing relationship with a client as well.

Department Specialists, or Experts

Such prima donnas! But like the best real-life prima donnas, the experts who work in each department are usually—hopefully—worth it. Auction houses couldn't exist without them. They're most definitely on top of the list of "most important employees."

These are the men and women who procure the most interesting works of art and objects to include in a sale. They research and catalog each object. They work with consignors to establish a reserve price and a presale estimate. They answer questions from buyers during the presale exhibition, and they hold sellers' hands when necessary. No matter how nonchalant they try to be, department experts are usually obsessed with their area of specialty. At auction houses like Christie's and Sotheby's, specialists head departments in dozens of areas, from Impressionist painting to pre-Columbian art to vintage cars to wine.

The experts are rarely astute businesspeople, but at Leslie Hindman Auctioneers they were allowed to be experts, while others were hired to balance the books. During the auction the department experts are usually up front, consulting, letting the auctioneer know when a special announcement has to be made about a particular lot, and keeping track of who is bidding.

11

Bidding

Of all the reasons people fear auctions, perhaps the most common is the fear of finally taking the plunge and actually bidding.

Bidding is, after all, a public act. As much as the furniture or works of art being auctioned, bidders themselves are on display. You have to call attention to yourself, which not everyone is comfortable doing. You have to shout your bid above the fray or shove your paddle into the air. And you often have to do it again and again. You may risk embarrassment in front of your friends if they think you are bidding too high. You may risk embarrassment if they think you are not bidding high enough.

It is up to you to make sure that this potential lose-lose situation turns into a win-win. If you have done your homework, if you have thought long and hard about which objects or works of art to bid on, if you have set firm upper limits, and if you have just a bit of self-discipline, you will be fine. Trust me.

But that said, there are some things you should know.

In Part 1 you learned how to set your limit. Now stick to it! Dig in your heels, sit on your hands, and practice self-discipline, because once you waver, the game is over. Not too long ago a beautiful Renoir nude was auctioned at Christie's. A gentleman opted out of the bidding at $9.5 million, his upper limit. But then Christopher Burge, Christie's auctioneer, looked at him and in his lilting British accent cooed, "One more?" The man shrugged—yes, why not? And then there was another bid and Christopher returned to the man, who bid again. And again. You see, once he broke his upper limit, once he broke the rules, so to speak, the rules ceased to exist. Then he was bidding in no-man's-land where the sky's the limit. In fact, he forgot he ever had a limit in the first place. That man got his Renoir—for $12.9 million. This happens with multimillion-dollar Impressionist paintings and $50 figurines. Don't let it happen to you.

Listening to the Auctioneer

Christopher Burge knew exactly what he was doing when he coaxed an extra $3 million out of the gentleman who bought the Renoir. He's not one of the best auctioneers in the country for nothing. Being an auctioneer is like being an actor, an impresario, and a circus ringmaster all rolled into one. Christopher Burge embodies all of these talents.

When I first started out, I was very unsure of myself. I had founded the auction house, but I had not planned on being the auctioneer. For our very first auction, in October 1982, we flew in a guest auctioneer from New York, a wonderful friend named Joe Keiffer, who at the time worked at William Doyle Galleries. I was nervous, of course, but Joe kept the auction going at a good pace.

Joe was a dear. The audience loved him. But somewhere around lot 300 he looked at the audience and then back at me. "And now we'll turn the bidding over to Leslie Hindman," he said, a slight grin crossing his face. Although I thought I would die right then and there, I could hardly have said no. To this day I don't remember what I sold or for how much, I was in such a daze. But it was my initiation into auctioneering, and as it turned out, I liked it.

Hugh Hildesley had a similar start at the lectern. He started his career at Sotheby's in London as an apprentice porter in the Old Masters painting department. Today he sits on the company's board of directors and has for many years been an auctioneer there as well. "Ladies and gentlemen," said an auctioneer just before Hugh took to the podium for the very first time, "there will now be a slight pause while I hand over the gavel to Mr. Hildesley." Many years later Hugh wrote of that moment, "It's then that one's life passes before one's eyes. My throat felt dry. I was convinced that I would not remember any of my instructions, and that no one would bid when I offered my first lot. . . . [T]he first four or five lots felt as if they took an hour to sell. Would this torment ever end?"

Like many auctioneers, I never went to school to learn how to do it. I developed my style simply by watching auctioneers in New York, Chicago, and London and reacting to what I liked and disliked. For instance, I liked how polite they usually were, I liked that they ran efficient, well-organized sales, and I liked that they enunciated clearly. I disliked their way of occasionally sounding haughty and treating the audience like party crashers. I wanted to create a really friendly place, and as the owner and head auctioneer, it was up to me to set the tone. For example, unlike the majors in New York who *take* the bid, I *ask* for the bid. The auctioneer will say, "I have $800, $800, I have $800," while he waits for someone to raise her paddle indicating a bid, to which he then says, "I have $850, $850. The bid is at $850." In other words, he has accepted an $850 bid.

That method assumes that audience members understand about bid increments, but in a fast-paced auction, where numbers are ricocheting around the room, people can easily become confused. That's why an auctioneer *asks* for the next bid. "Do I have $800?" I ask the audience. "Do I have $800?" Once someone bids the $800, I ask for the next bid: "Do I have $850?" This way the audience knows what the bid is. There's no confusion. It takes some of the fear out of bidding.

Interspersed with the bids I talk to the audience, try to be funny, make them laugh. I have even given out football scores, especially on winter Sundays when Chicagoans are obsessing over the Bears. I think this sort of casualness helps people feel relaxed and comfortable. Once my attempt at humor really backfired, however. A lovely older gentleman, very dignified, used to come to every one of my auctions, always by himself, and he always sat right in the front row where I could see him. He was a collector who bought often and paid high prices, just the kind of customer we loved. One night, though, for the first time ever, he brought his wife with him. During the auction I could see her leaning over to him, whispering something in his ear, even once gently holding down his hand to stop him from bidding. Overall he wasn't bidding much and when he was, he was stopping before he was successful. Finally I couldn't take it anymore and I looked at him and said, "You shouldn't have brought your wife tonight!" I thought it was hilarious, but she got very offended, not being aware of my style, and stormed out of the salesroom. He followed right behind. And although he came back to future auctions, he never again brought his wife.

I think that my greatest strength as an auctioneer, developed over many years, is my ability to just *know* when someone is going to bid. That may sound silly—an auctioneer with ESP—but I can't tell you how many times all of the bidding was on my right but something tugged my gaze to the left just as someone made a bid. I am not the only auctioneer who has this instinct. Many others do, as well. "I know whether a person will or will not bid," says Terry Dunning, of Butterfields. "I can tell by the look in their eyes, before they raise their bid card, and I know whether they'll keep bidding."

Not all auctioneers have that ability, but they all do have their own style. To be a successful bidder it helps to familiarize yourself with the different ways in which auctioneers work. To do that the most important thing you can do—bar none—is listen to the auctioneer.

Auctioneers have to say something between the numbers and many use a sort of chant, which is merely filler, held over from old-time cattle auctions. It sets a rhythm, a pace. It gives potential buyers time to think about their next move. And it keeps your attention (and hopefully doesn't lull you to sleep). The words the auctioneer uses between bids—whether they're little asides, jokes, or cajoling—are meant to carry the action from one bid to the next in a way that everyone can understand.

I've warned you that auctions often move very fast. This happens not because the auctioneer is trying to fool you or confuse you, but because auctions are theater. Each lot is a minidrama waiting to play itself out. As in any good play, the action has to keep moving forward. Tobacco auctions, for instance, can move at a rate of 500 lots an hour! Most arts and antiques auctions, however, move at a rough pace of 100 lots an hour. Sometimes they move faster, sometimes slower, so it can be a mistake to rely too heavily on the auctioneer's pace at any given moment.

There are many ways to coax bids from an audience. One of my favorite descriptions of the various styles comes from a book written over a quarter of a century ago by L. J. Hewitt. He describes six different styles that I believe still exist today. First, he says, there's the self-deprecating approach, where the auctioneer gazes over the audience at a slow moment and says something like "You're all a lot smarter than I am," implying that he has no idea how high the price will go. He's just the auctioneer, after all, not an expert like you. Next, there's the personal plea. "If I don't get more than $1,000 for this silver porringer Mrs. Fancypants will kill me!"

There's also the demanding auctioneer. "This is a top-quality chest of drawers!" he bellows, letting the audience know who's boss and who isn't. Another type of auctioneer will take the audience into his confidence, as if they are old friends having lunch at a favorite restaurant. "Between you and me," he'll coo, "this is worth twice as much."

The last two styles—flattery and insults—are opposites. The flatterer does just that. "You all know how much this millefiori glass bowl is worth," he will say, even though no one may in fact even know that millefiori is a type of glass decorated from within the glass itself. The last style of auctioneer can be amusing to watch but off-putting to experience. "Is this an auction or not?" he might sneer when the bidding slows to a snail's pace. "Should we all just fold up and go home?"

All of these auctioneers have the same goal, of course: to get you to part with as much of your money as possible. These styles have evolved because they work. Try not to get taken in by any of them.

At the start of each lot the auctioneer will announce the lot number and identify the object for sale. To pique the crowd's interest, he may describe it, as well, and maybe even point out the difference between its style, say Louis XIV, and another similar style, like Louis XV.

But no matter what the auctioneer says, don't change your bidding strategy because of it. The auctioneer, while perhaps an expert in a specific field, is probably not that familiar with the specific objects being sold. His spontaneous references to the object are just that: spontaneous, off-the-cuff, ad lib. He might say it's a piece of beautiful Meissen porcelain when in fact that moment is the first time he's laid eyes on it and it's not Meissen at all but Limoges instead—an easy mistake to make and a potentially expensive one.

In addition to how the auctioneer does his job, pay attention to the order in which lots are sold. It's not done randomly. There are always peaks and valleys in the order. I liked to start sales with something that had a lot of appeal but that also carried a low estimate so that I knew it would sell. Starting that way sets a good tone and gets the momentum going. I would sell progressively more expensive lots, then go down again and up again once more. I rarely put important things in the last thirty minutes, though if someone really wants something, she will usually stick around. With the increasing number of absentee bids, the order of the auction matters less and less, but I still believe in putting on a good show for those in the room.

Why should you care about the order? Because such knowledge can enhance your ability to make a good purchase. If, for instance, there are four similar chests of drawers in a sale, the auctioneer usually sells the least important one first. People will often wait to bid on the higher-quality chests, which means that the bargain of the day might be that first chest offered. I think that bargains can be found at the beginning of any auction, when people are still getting juiced up and ready to go and at the end, after the crowd has thinned out, lessening the competition.

First Bids and Increments

Where does the auctioneer get that first bid? Who decides what it will be, the auctioneer or the consignor? And what if no one in the audience accepts it?

The answers to these questions vary from auction to auction and from one auctioneer to another. At high-end auctions the first bid is often one-fourth to one-third of what the auctioneer thinks the object should ultimately fetch. At other auctions the first bid is often uncannily close to the actual final bid. She'll start out at $400 and quickly drop to $300, then $250, $200, $150, $100, and when she gets a taker, the bidding shoots right back up, ending near her original $400 offer. Some auctioneers start high because they're hoping for a sop in the audience, or maybe they think a request for a high opening bid enhances the value of the offering.

These auctioneers are the ones to watch out for. In the beginning of an auction, keep track for a few lots of the relationship between the auctioneer's opening bid offer and the final bid; then place your own bidding accordingly.

At Leslie Hindman Auctioneers, I almost always started the bidding at just over half of the low estimate. So if I was selling a gilt-bronze Tiffany clock that had a presale estimate of $1,500 to $2,000, I would have started the bidding at $800. I started low because I believe a low first bid gives people the permission they need to enter the fray. If I had started at $1,400, a lot of potential bidders would have sat it out completely, assuming that it was going to go high. Starting lower, at $800, tells people, however subliminally, that they have a chance to bid successfully, maybe even to get a great bargain. Part of an auctioneer's responsibility to the consignor is to encourage a lot of people to bid. Excitement over a work of art or decorative object generates more excitement for the auction as a whole, making the event more fun for the auctiongoer, and the going a lot easier for the auctioneer.

Once the first bid is accepted, the proceedings usually move very quickly. There is no universal auction house increment standard. Often the bidding increments will be listed in the catalog, but at an auction in which there is no catalog, you have to pick up the structure as you go along.

At Sotheby's, for instance, the bids increase by $10 until the bid reaches $200, then the increments increase to $25; after the lot reaches $500, the increments rise to $50 a bid and above $1,000 by $100, and so on. Let's say you are bidding on a Hitchcock chair, a mid-nineteenth-century open-back American side chair, and the bidding goes from $180 to $190 to $200. At that point it will jump to $225 and continue to do so in $25 increments until the bidding reaches $500, at which point the increments jump again, to $50 each. You really have to stay focused. Otherwise, you'll expect to hear a lower amount. Then you might bid on autopilot and spend more for that chair than you had intended. One bidder kept on reading the catalog in anticipation of upcoming lots while holding his paddle aloft continually. In a world of his own, he failed to notice that the increments had increased from $50 to $100. When he ended up in an unintentional bidding war with another person and won, he wasn't too happy.

In general, a good rule of thumb is that bidding goes up in 10 percent increments. Some auctioneers use different increments, but they use the same ones over and over. You'll get each auctioneer's pattern as you watch and listen.

An audience member will sometimes indicate to the auctioneer, usually by moving his hand horizontally across his throat or by crossing one index finger over the other, that he wants to cut the increment in half. Although I rarely accepted such a request, I do remember we were offering a lovely pair of American folk paintings of cats with a reserve of $750. I had a bid of $700, but was stalled as I asked for the next bid. Finally, one of the gentlemen indicated that he was willing to bid $725, or half the increment. I took it and asked for $775, which the other man accepted.

As a bidder you have nothing to lose by trying, but don't be surprised or insulted if the auctioneer doesn't agree.

Bidding Strategies

The best way to bid at auction is the way that makes you feel most comfortable. There are all sorts of contradictory theories about where you should sit and when you should enter the fray, but I advise you to try different ways of bidding until you find the one that fits you best, just as you would try on several suits before making a purchase.

Some people say that where you sit in the auction room matters. To the auctioneer, I assure you, it makes no difference. Some people like to sit up front; others prefer the back. If you sit up front, the theory goes, you can see better what is being auctioned. True, perhaps, but by the time of the auction, you should already be familiar with the objects at hand. Seeing them should just be a matter of making sure of which lot you are bidding on. The auctioneer will be able to see you if you sit up front, but since auctioneers are good at scanning the room, this should not be a concern.

Don't think you're being ignored if the auctioneer doesn't take your bid. It might just be that there's no point in accepting a new bid until one of the two bidders he's focusing on drops out. If your bid is definitely missed, just wave your paddle more aggressively. If necessary, you can even shout, "I'm in."

It may be tempting to sit next to a column so you can lean against it, but that can get awfully claustrophobic. Likewise, sitting next to a column can make it more difficult for the auctioneer to see you. Some people like to stand throughout the entire auction, leaning against a column or wall. There was a darling lady, a collector of Tiffany glass, who used to come by train from New York to all our twentieth-century decorative arts sales. She always stood behind a column in our salesroom and peeked out whenever she wanted to bid.

Personally, I like to stand in the back of the room because I want to see my competition. Not everyone cares whom they bid against, but I think it's interesting to know. If you can keep track of who's bidding against you, then you have a little more control. If you are bidding against a dealer, for example, you know you can bid a little more than he does and still get a pretty good deal compared to how much you would get it for at retail.

Once the auction begins, some people jump into the action right away for two reasons: to let the auctioneer know they are interested, and to scare off some of the competition. While the auctioneer is aware of all the bidders in the salesroom, he may concentrate on the two most committed bidders. So the early bidder is likely to be one of those two people, and that would be an obvious advantage. Some people start early, then bow out and let others bid, only to return at the end. They think it alerts the auctioneer to their interest but also indicates that they are not desperate.

It isn't a good idea to let the auctioneer, or others in the audience, believe that you are so determined to own something that money is no object. Holding your paddle in the air like a protest sign gives that impression. Others may claim, conversely, that holding your paddle up in the air will simply make you seem determined, which can scare off the competition and let the auctioneer know you are serious. Another warning about bidding early is that a lot of interest in the beginning of a lot may alert some fence-sitters that the object is worth bidding on.

Waiting until the very end to jump into the fray, however, creates its own problems—although of course you have to be there at the very end to be successful. Still, by waiting, you risk not getting into the bidding at all. Entering fresh at the end will also encourage even more new bidders. It wakes people up and then you are really in trouble. I attended an auction with my friend Debbie, a late-bidding type, who was interested in a lovely pair of Staffordshire figures. With an upper limit of $200 in her head, she watched the other bidders. When the bid got to $190 one of the two bidders dropped out and the auctioneer looked around for another bid. Perfect timing, she thought, and up went her paddle at $200. Her surprise entrance, however, encouraged two other bidders to enter. One bid $210 and the other $220. Her only choice was to stop or to keep going and bid $230, three bids beyond her limit. Had she been one of the original two bidders she might have been successful at $200. Instead, she went home empty-handed.

Of course, had circumstances been different, Debbie could have entered into the game late and stunned the competition by bidding three increments more than what was being asked. If the bidding was at $190 she could have shouted out a bid of $220. Others might not have entered the bidding; her obvious determination might have cost them more than they were willing to spend. But obviously this approach is useful only when you want an object badly.

Maybe it is best to start bidding when you feel comfortable, not first, but not last. Keep in mind that this entire process takes, on average, all of 45 seconds, and once you start, be deliberate. The auctioneer will surely keep his eye on you and your body language. If you look away or look hesitant, he might think you have hit your limit and accept a bid from someone else.

Bid decisively. There's nothing worse, from an auctioneer's point of view, than someone who sort of pokes her paddle tentatively into the air, unsure if she really wants to bid. Countless times, when someone's paddle was bobbing up and down like a buoy, I have had to ask, "Are you bidding, ma'am?"

Don't be surprised, as the bidding winds down, to hear the auctioneer say "Fair warning" or "Are you all through?" instead of "Going, going, gone." In fact, I have never heard a real live auctioneer use that last phrase. It's just too long to say.

Ultimately, you want to bid with what the writer Michael de Forrest calls "casual unconcern"—that is, not too eagerly, but not too complacently, not necessarily being the first one in, but not necessarily late in the game, either. You want the auctioneer to know you want the object but not so much that you'll pay more than it is worth.

Secret Signals

On some occasions a buyer may arrange with the auctioneer to use a secret signal to preserve his anonymity. Why would a person want no one to know who he is or that he is bidding? There are numerous reasons, but they all come down to money. After all, if a celebrity is seen bidding on a work of art, and half of the audience knows she has just earned $20 million for her last movie, or if a well-known dealer is bidding, other bidders might not think anything of running up the bids just to make that person pay more. That is why so many well-known people bid by telephone or have agents bid on their behalf.

A couple of years ago I was retained to sell the contents of a decades-old Chicago watering hole called Harry's, which had been a popular singles hangout. To add to the excitement, we decided to hold the auction in the bar itself. It was an incredibly crowded, loud, raucous event, but lots of fun. Just as I was about to begin, a gentleman came up to me and said that he planned to bid often throughout the auction, but that he preferred not to have everyone know it was he who was bidding. Because we were just about to begin, without giving it too much thought I agreed to what he suggested: that he would stand behind me and kick me gently whenever he wanted to bid. And, boy, did he ever bid a lot that night! I had the bruises to prove it!

A couple of years ago I sold some bronzes from the estate of Arthur Rubloff, an important Chicago real estate developer who had amassed a fine collection. A prominent local dealer was interested in bidding, but like the man at Harry's, he wanted to do so without his competitors' knowledge. He approached me before the auction began and told me that if he took off his glasses he was bidding. If he put them on again, he wasn't. That seemed pretty straightforward and I agreed.

Sometimes secret bidding can misfire, however. At Christie's there were two dealers both of whom thought they were the only person in the salesroom bidding by secret signal for a picture by Paul Cézanne. Unfortunately, each of them concluded that he had been the successful bidder. David Bathurst of Christie's decided the only remedy was to reauction the picture. But the two dealers refused to allow that. Bathurst felt he was backed into a corner. If the dealers refused to let him reopen the bidding, he was going to have to decide himself who got the painting. One of those dealers went home very happy that night. One didn't. Don't let that happen to you.

Absentee Bidding

One of the most convenient and popular ways to bid at auction is to stay home—that is, to be an absentee bidder. To do this you fill out and submit an order bid. Forms for these bids are usually printed in the back of the catalog, or they will be available at the auction house or by telephone. When you have placed an order bid, an auction house employee or the auctioneer will bid on your behalf up to your top bid.

Absentee bidding has become so widespread that at Leslie Hindman Auctioneers we would occasionally have *only* absentee bids for some items. Tom Porter, who owns Garth's, an auction house in Delaware, Ohio, says that for a sale of 600 objects he might have as many as 1,500 absentee bids. "It makes the job of auctioneer much harder," he admits, "but the auction more exciting." Most auctioneers welcome absentee bidding. It lets more people participate, which is good for them as well as the consignor, who reaps the benefits of increased competition.

Absentee bidding, for which the auction house does not charge a fee, is used by clients for various reasons. The most obvious is that you can't attend the auction. But some people use absentee bids because they know that the only way they can keep their bidding under control is by using order bids.

When you fill out the absentee bid form, be very careful—and very particular. With so many absentee bids being processed, sometimes very quickly and sometimes in the frenzy just before an auction begins, the neatness and specificity with which you fill out your form will be greatly appreciated and will go a long way to avoiding errors.

The bid form asks for the sale number, listed in the catalog, the lot number of the work, and a description of the lot. Don't just write "chair." Write "George I silver gilt side chair." This will help if there's any question later about which lot you intended to buy. You will also be asked for the amount of your top bid for the object. This means that if you write down $400, the auction house will bid on your behalf up to and including that amount.

Absentee bidding works only if you trust the auction house to treat your absentee bid fairly—in other words, not to bid the $400 just because it knows you are willing to go that high. Absentee bidders who win a piece at auction for their top bid sometimes call and question us about the bidding in the room. On the one hand I believe they trust us to bid fairly for them; on the other it seemed too oddly coincidental to them that their top bid should just so happen to be the winning bid. All I can tell you is that as often as this happens, it happens far more often that absentee bidders are successful at much less than they were willing to spend.

Remember that when you tell them what your top bid is, it doesn't include the buyer's premium or other charges, like state and city taxes. A winning bid of $400 is at least $460 once you include a 15 percent buyers' premium. Some absentee bids, like the one Butterfields uses, ask you to check a box if you want it to bid one more increment higher than your maximum bid. That's because if two bids for the same amount are left before the auction, should there be a tie the first one would be the successful bid. But if the later bidder had added "plus one," he would have been the successful bidder. It's a good idea.

Sometimes you will be asking for the auction house to bid on your behalf on more than one object, and perhaps you want the second object only if you don't get the first. Or maybe you're willing to pay more for the second if you get the first for considerably less than what you're willing to pay. There are ways to note this on the absentee bid form. Different methods of indicating your wishes are usually explained in the catalog. But in general, you write the word "or" between lot numbers to alert the auction house that if you are the successful bidder on your first lot, they should ignore your bid for the other lot when it comes up for sale. If you are unsuccessful on the first lot, the auction house will bid on your second choice.

When more than one absentee bid includes the same top bids, most auction houses give priority to the first one they received. In the salesroom during the auction, if someone bids $400 in person and that was your top bid on your absentee form, most auction houses give consideration to the person in the house.

You can also make an absentee bid by telephone. This is a good way to be at the auction and not be at the auction at the same time. Again, different auction houses have different rules when this is allowable, but in general they allow it when the low estimate is at least $500. If you arrange to bid this way, a client service representative will call you several lots before yours comes up. When your lot is offered for sale, the client rep will talk you through the bidding and will bid for you as the action proceeds. A few years ago we worked with a client who wanted to surprise his daughter with a very special birthday present. He took her for dinner at Sardi's. At a certain time a waiter brought over a telephone (this was in the days before cell phones) and right then and there the man bid on a pair of beautiful pearls for his daughter. He was successful, too, not only at buying the pearls but also at creating a very special memory that he and his daughter will always treasure.

With telephone bids, I always try to make sure that the client service representative and the bidder know each other, often from a previous bidding experience. The bidder tends to be more relaxed, as does the person at the auction house, which works to everyone's advantage. If you bid by phone, request that you work with the same person each time.

Sotheby's and Christie's take the idea of being there at the auction and not being there at the auction at the same time one step further with private viewing rooms. These are like skyboxes that surround the salesroom from which special clients can watch and hear the auction below but bid by telephone anonymously.

The entire auction experience is really what you make of it. If you are well prepared and self-disciplined, it can be fun, rewarding, and error-free. But the opposite is true, as well. Because auctions allow you to be in control of a lot more than in a retail store, the weight of responsibility shifts, as well. You have more control, so you have to take more control.

ON THE INTERNET

BIDDING STRATEGIES

Traditional auctions may last for hours, but any one lot usually sells in a minute or less. As mentioned earlier, within that time frame all sorts of decisions about bidding strategy have to be made. Bid early or late (late meaning forty-five seconds into the action); bid way over the current bid or just increment by increment. Or maybe skip in-person bidding altogether and bid as an absentee, on the phone, or via the Internet.

Online auctions, on the other hand, are composed of only one lot each and may last ten or more *days*. Many of the same decisions have to be made, but you have a lot more time to think about what you are doing.

Instead of wondering where in the salesroom to sit so as to psych out the competition, the online bidder doesn't have to worry about the competition at all. Bidding is a far easier, though no less responsible, act online than it is at an auction house. And like bidding at a live auction, there is no one way that suits each person and situation best.

For those who see the Internet as a way to avoid the discipline and strategy of the auction house, the method of bidding is simply to check the action a lot—every day, usually—and to bid as necessary. It's not the least time-consuming or most organized way of doing it, but it is entertaining.

But there are better ways.

Most people bid online by proxy. This is similar to absentee bidding in that you declare a maximum and the auction site automatically bids on your behalf up to that amount. Proxy bidding is the most useful way to ensure that you never have to pay more for a work of art or decorative object than what it's worth.

Say you're interested in bidding on a pair of mint-condition divided-core swirl marbles. After a bit of research you decide that you are willing to pay up to $35, even though the current bid might be only $15. Your current actual bid, however, would be only one increment above $15, or $15.50. If another bidder has by proxy bid $20, the site will bid on behalf of both of you, and the bid will rise to $20.50, which is your competitor's high bid plus one increment. As you can see, what matters most is the current high bid and the new bid, not your maximum bid, or anyone else's for that matter.

Proxy bidding is the most organized way to bid. It saves you the hassle—assuming you think it's a hassle—of checking and rechecking the auctions in which you're bidding. Proxy bidding allows you to forget about shills, snipers, and everyone else. In most cases if you are outbid, you get an e-mail alert from the site. That way if you are still interested you can revisit the auction and bid again.

On some sites, if you are bidding in a reserve auction and you place a bid that at least meets the reserve, your bid will automatically be bid up to the reserve price, making you the high bidder. In other words, say the reserve is $10; the current high bid is $6, and your proxy is $12. Your bid would be $10 and not $6.50, which in a no-reserve auction would have been the case.

A collector I know has recently become an online auction addict. He was bidding on eBay on a copper-and-gilt bronze jardiniere, which he felt was worth $700. He bid $770, and he was the successful bidder at $740. Did he pay more than he should have? He'd say no, and here's why. Once he decides what he thinks an object is worth, he automatically adds 10 percent. That way, if he is outbid by only a dollar he doesn't feel that the successful bidder got a bargain or that he missed out on one. If he really can't live without the object, he adds 20 percent to what he thinks would be a fair market price for that object. "Whether I ultimately win or lose an auction," he said, "by adding 10 or 20 percent to my upper limit, I never feel like kicking myself afterward for not bidding high enough."

Since online auctions may last anywhere from a few hours to, at the far end of the spectrum, a month, when to bid becomes an issue. If you are bidding by proxy, in theory timing is irrelevant, since whether you bid on the first day of an auction or the last, the amount you bid should be the same.

But bidding early may have the same advantage online as in a traditional salesroom: it might scare off some of the competition. If the collector I just mentioned had bid $770 on the jardiniere on the first day of the auction, subsequent bidders would continually and immediately have been outbid as the site bid against them on his behalf. Other bidders might not have bothered to keep bidding, or they might have fallen along the wayside as they began to feel that someone out there—that is, you—has bid so much there is no point in competing. Another advantage of early bidding is that in the case of two proxy bids of the same amount, the first bidder becomes the successful bidder.

A different strategy is to bid early and then one more time at the end. After all, the theory goes, if you continually bid throughout the auction you are only raising the price, in essence bidding against yourself. I collect gavels. In a recent auction for a beautiful Victorian walnut gavel I at first bid $12. Someone bid against me so the bid was $12.50. I bid $13, she bid $13.50. This went on until the gavel was at $18. I was the successful bidder at $18.50. But had I not continued to bid throughout the auction, but just once at $12 in the beginning and once again at the end, my final bid might have been less than hers, since I might have had to counter the competing bid only once, at $13.

Some people bid only at the end, believing that this calls the least amount of attention to you and to the auction. This may be true, too, but it means that you have to keep track of the closing dates and times, to the minute, of each auction in which you plan to bid. (See pages 32–33 for a discussion of sniping.) That may take a lot of time and organization.

YOU ARE THE SUCCESSFUL BIDDER! NOW WHAT?

Congratulations!

At a traditional auction the winning bidder ambles over to the cashier, pays with a check or, if the auction house accepts it, a credit card. If the object cannot be carried off, the buyer arranges for shipping at the shipping desk. Then he goes home.

Online, however, there is still work to do once the auction is over. Almost immediately upon the close of an online auction in which you are the successful bidder, the auction site notifies you and the seller by e-mail. When I receive that e-mail, I always e-mail the seller right then and there. I like to say hello, tell them I was the successful bidder, and give them my mailing address so they can begin packing my object. I also ask for their mailing address and what the final amount will be, including shipping and handling. You may prefer to e-mail the seller to inquire about the total amount you owe. If the amount comes as a surprise to you, that's an indication you didn't read the seller's sales policy closely enough before you bid, and perhaps you also failed to follow up with any questions you might have had.

Communication is always the key to a mutually beneficial transaction. Respond to the seller's e-mails quickly, as he should to yours. When you have mailed your payment, e-mail and tell the seller. Likewise, the seller should e-mail and tell you he received payment, and should e-mail again once he has shipped your package.

Remember that by bidding in their auction you have entered into an agreement with the seller to abide by his rules regarding payment and any other restrictions he might have stipulated. That means, for instance, that if the seller said "no checks," it is up to you to arrange for alternative payment.

PAYING BY CASH

Never pay in cash unless you have arranged to pick up your purchase in person. While it may be easy to pick a couple of bills out of your wallet, pop them into an envelope, and drop them in the mail, using cash is the riskiest form of payment. You will have no proof that you actually sent it, and the buyer will have no way to prove that he didn't receive it. There is no paper trail with cash, no record it ever existed. If the object arrives and it's damaged, or if it's not what was described in the auction listing, having sent cash makes it hardest to dispute.

CHECKS

Online this is probably the most common form of payment, and certainly the easiest after cash. Its only real drawback is that most sellers will wait until the check clears before they ship your object. That means there might be a week's lag between the day you send your check and the time they receive it. Depending on how soon they deposit the check into their account and your bank clears it, there might be another fifteen days of waiting, and then another week for the package to arrive on your doorstep. That's twenty-nine days of waiting. Even if you don't mind the wait, you need to be aware of it so you won't start suspecting that something has gone wrong because two or three weeks have gone by and you have nothing to show for it.

If you pay by check, be sure to note on the check the object for which you are paying, as well as the auction item number. Many sellers receive payment for numerous auction sales at the same time, and there is less chance of a mix-up if they know which check corresponds with which auction.

CASHIER'S CHECKS AND MONEY ORDERS

Most sellers prefer money orders or cashier's checks rather than personal checks. These two payment methods are safe, from the seller's standpoint, because they are already paid for. For you as the buyer, however, cashier's checks and money orders are not so easy, since they require you to stand in line at the bank or post office. The fees involved add to the overall cost of the object, too. The advantage is that the seller will ship your package the minute the check arrives, without having to wait for it to clear. If you send a cashier's check or money order, the same advice applies in terms of providing the object and auction number to which the check should be applied.

CREDIT CARDS

More and more individual sellers are accepting credit card payment. Auction sites are now acting as middlemen for the transaction, which frees sellers from having to get merchant accounts with heavy fees attached. Like using your credit card anywhere, it is fast and easy, and better yet, you can easily stop payment if you have a problem later on. Credit cards also often provide insurance on your purchase (it may not be applicable for interstate purchases, however, so check the fine print).

ESCROW

Paying by escrow is, from the buyer's standpoint, the most secure payment method, though it requires the buyer to pay a fee. As the buyer, you would send payment to the escrow service, which would inform the seller that you have paid. The seller would then ship the package. As soon as you have received and approved it, the escrow service would release the payment to the seller.

When you receive the object, if you're satisfied with it, e-mail the seller one last time and let him know it arrived safely and that all is well.

4

Selling at
Auction

12

Where Does the Stuff Come From?

I am curious about everything and everyone. If I get into the elevator at my office and a stranger is in there, I always introduce myself. I like to know who they are, what they do, where they work. And I want them to know the same about me. At parties I like to sit at a table of strangers. I figure that it will present a chance for me to learn something new.

That's why the auction business has been such a fascinating one: there is always something new. More than 3,000 things a week—ranging from fine Impressionist paintings to Civil War–era stamps to sofas designed in the 1930s by Jean-Michel Frank—are brought into Sotheby's in New York. It's the same at Christie's and, to a lesser degree, at auction houses across the country.

While an individual may bring in one or two objects to sell, others choose to auction entire households and collections built up over years and years. Most sellers have particular reasons for parting with their much-loved things, although Barbra Streisand did decide on a whim to sell her entire collection of Art Deco art and furnishings. Ms. Streisand surely did not need the money, the publicity, or the space; she probably had just lost interest in what she owned.

Many auction houses, especially the bigger ones, have business development specialists and attorneys whose main job is to procure consignments. As a trust-and-estates specialist at an auction house here in Chicago said, "My job is to schmooze bankers and other lawyers. I eat lunch for a living." During those lunches he explains the services his auction house provides and persuades the banker or lawyer to consider his auction house when the time comes to dispose of an estate.

So why do people sell? It usually comes down to the three *d*'s: divorce, debt, and death. And I would add a few others, including disease and disillusionment.

The first *d*—divorce—is an auction house's least favorite way of procuring a consignment. Under different, and happier, circumstances, married people are selling their belongings; they both have the same goal, which is pretty much the same for any consignor: to set reasonable reserves and estimates and to get the highest price possible. With many divorcing couples, however, *her* agenda can be quite different from *his*. He may insist on relatively high appraisals to increase his half of the estate; she may want just the opposite. Divorcing couples fight. Divorcing couples disagree and delay things. Divorcing couples can be maddening to work with!

A prominent Chicagoan once called to tell me that he had been transferred by his job, and that he and his wife of several years were vacating their beautiful pre-war Lake Shore Drive apartment and moving to Europe. They were looking for a fresh start; everything they owned, he said, was to be sold. Wonderful, I thought. Quality goods. Decent, smart consignors. I should have suspected something was wrong when he said he wanted to ship his belongings to us before receiving the usual presale estimates. He wanted me to send over a truck, load it up, and put it all on the auction block—which is exactly what we started to do.

We unloaded the items. We researched each one. We wrote catalog listings. We photographed objects. We thought long and hard about each high and low estimate. Then, as I was sitting at my desk one day going over paperwork, I got a call from the man's wife. "Do you have my stuff?" she asked, sobbing. "I just came home from abroad, and my entire apartment is empty!" As it turned out, her husband wasn't being transferred to Europe at all—they were in the midst of a divorce and he was trying to sell their belongings without her knowledge. We ended up having to stop the sale, trash the catalog, and return all of their possessions. I was so angry at him that I never even asked what eventually happened to the two of them, or to their art and antiques.

And then there is the next *d*: debt. A now-deceased financier, Jack Dick, lived on an estate in Greenwich, Connecticut, that eventually became the home of Leona Helmsley, the besieged New York real estate and hotel magnate. Dick took his company, Blackwatch Farms, public, making millions of dollars. As recounted by the now-deceased auctioneer Robert Wooley in his memoir, *Going Once,* he used his new-found wealth to fill out his collection of fine English furniture and sporting paintings. But like so many fast-buck success stories, Dick's company eventually went bankrupt and he owed the IRS between $7 million and $8 million. He was forced to sell many of his belongings, through Sotheby's in New York. Unfortunately the day after Sotheby's dropped the first check to him in the mail Dick died of a heart attack.

The third *d* stands for death. I know this is going to sound macabre, but auction house staff members often say that the best consignor is a dead consignor—or, as one of my colleagues once said, "a dead consignor with heirs who have no idea what they're doing" and who aren't there for endless discussions about reserves and estimates and all the other details that go into arranging for an item to be sold at auction.

In fact, about 75 percent of the household property sold at auctions comes from estates. The works of art and decorative objects in most estates runs the gamut from maybe great to maybe useless. At Leslie Hindman Auctioneers we didn't care. We sold the good furniture and works of art in our regular sales and the rest in our marketplace sales. Some estates, however, are incredibly good both in quality and in quantity.

A number of years ago Christie's was consigned the estate of the widow of an executive at a huge insurance company. Her husband had died several years before and she and her adult children were estranged. She lived alone in a three-story maisonette in one of New York's most exclusive buildings, complete with curved grand staircases and incredible views of the East River. Rumor had it that it was one of the last remaining private residences in New York with a chapel. She had left her entire estate to charity. Not surprisingly, her children were furious.

The lady had been a great collector of, among other things, miniature furniture, some designed as children's toys, some as salesmen's samples. Small Chippendale chairs, tiny Federal-style tables, diminutive French fauteuils, and miniature armchairs completely filled a huge ballroom, even obscuring the views out the window. It was eerie, to say the least, but the auction was a great success and all of the money went to charity.

In 1993 Leslie Hindman Auctioneers sold a similarly big estate, that of a prominent woman named Mrs. Ruth K. Flower, whose family's money had come primarily from hardwoods. She lived in a large Georgian-style house in Winnetka, one of Chicago's most beautiful suburbs. Talk about your consummate collector! She had spent her days buying, buying, buying. She collected enormous quantities of eighteenth- and nineteenth-century American and English furniture and English Staffordshire pottery. Taking inventory of the estate occupied half our employees for weeks. We sold everything—all 300 quilts, 22 silver tea services, 20 flatware services, 10 tall case clocks, 60 American portraits, 7 slant-front desks, and thousands of other objects and works of art. It was an incredible sale that brought in more than $1.5 million.

An offshoot of death is disease. It's always sad when someone dies, whether it's from old age, an accident, or illness. But for a number of years during the 1980s and 1990s, we in the auction business very much felt the ravages of AIDS. Clients, both private collectors and dealers, with whom we had worked for years, were dying at an alarming rate. Objects we had sold to them only shortly before were turning up back at the auction house for sale again, this time as part of an estate or to pay for their health care.

To our relief, as well as everyone else's, deaths from AIDS seem to have slowed down. Nevertheless, we still see objects coming through the auction houses that are on the block due to a person's illness or death from illness, whether it's AIDS, cancer, or old age. This kind of sale is always heartbreaking, and pushes us harder to treat and sell their belongings with respect.

Finally, the last *d* is disillusionment. Another growing reason for selling off stuff is a major life change. As one collector said to me, "Sometimes you wake up one day and you look at a collection you have built over a lifetime, and you just think, 'blah.'" In other words, he said, "You just decide you have had enough. It is time for a new look." This particular collector sold an entire cache of Civil War memorabilia, which he had spent thirty years amassing. Did it cure him of the collecting bug? No, not at all, but it did clear out a lot of space, not only in his house but in his head as well. Now there was room to think about a new interest, a new collection. I ran into him not too long ago at a presale exhibition. He was lying on his back looking at the underside of a Federal-style chair. "I've moved on," he said, looking up at me.

As the parents of baby boomers move from four-bedroom colonials, modern split-levels, and sprawling ranch houses in the suburbs to condos in the city, they are selling their belongings in droves. While they are not always consigning fine antiques, their good-quality furniture is perfect for those just starting out to furnish their houses.

Of course, it is not just individuals and estates who sell. Sometimes museums sell their holdings, and corporations occasionally sell their collections. Corporations have the same comfort level with auctioneers as estates, since usually no one has intense emotional ties to the objects. We worked hard to get those consignments and were often successful. Sometimes, though, we literally had to campaign to get them.

A large corporation outside Cleveland, Ohio, had gone bankrupt in the early nineties and needed to sell off its corporate collection. Our competitors for the opportunity included both Sotheby's and Christie's. We thought of ourselves as a big fish in a little pond, and we kept trying to impress this fact—which we considered a point in our favor—upon the corporate decision-makers. When it was time to make our presentation, we flew to Dayton complete with a goldfish and a bowl to make our point. Unfortunately, the fish died en route. But we were determined, so on the way from the airport to their office, we stopped and bought another fish. It worked out beautifully. When they walked into the giant conference room, there was our little goldfish swimming around lazily in his bowl, with a big sign next to it that read: Would You Rather Be a Big Fish in a Little Pond or a Little Fish in a Big Pond?

They loved it, and while we didn't handle the entire collection, we did get a pretty big chunk of it to sell.

Sometimes, acquiring consignments was more a matter of speed, luck, or audacity than anything else. We would meet with clients on Thanksgiving if that was what they wanted. We'd stay up all night preparing a proposal for an estate that had given us just twenty-four hours' notice, as did one client in Grosse Point Farms, Michigan. Our business development specialists would scan the obituaries for the names of prominent people, and then contact the estate lawyer. Once I read in the paper that a woman had died. From the obituary it appeared that she might have been a collector, but I had never heard of her, and I didn't know anyone who had. So I looked her up in the phone book and called each of the four people with her last name. I wasn't exactly sure what to say when someone answered the phone, since I knew she was dead. Anyway, I just asked for her and if I got her, well, I knew that wasn't the right house. The last number I called was answered by a housekeeper. "Missus is dead," she said, and offered the number of the lady's lawyer— exactly what I wanted. We not only did the estate appraisal for tax purposes but later sold her million-dollar estate, too.

"Madam, if it doesn't have a pulse," said one specialist at a West Coast auction house, "we'll sell it." In other words, if you have goods you want to sell, for whatever reason, an auction house can probably help you sell them.

13

Choosing an Auction House

Selling at auction is much easier than buying at auction. Buying requires a lot of homework, a competitive spirit, and an acquisitive nature. Buying is something you have to go out and do; selling, at least at a traditional auction house, is something that is done for you. From my perspective, the most difficult tasks are, first, deciding to part with what may be meaningful family heirlooms and, second, choosing an auction house.

The first consideration is beyond my professional scope, but I can help you find the right auction house.

Because selling at auction is an emotional as much as a financial transaction, you must feel comfortable with your choice. Tom Porter of Garth's auction house in Delaware, Ohio, told me, "we're not dealing with a person's desk as much as we are with a person's emotions. We try to remember that from beginning to end."

Don't assume that the biggest auction houses are necessarily the best. Christie's, Sotheby's, and Phillips are terrific auction houses, but they are not for everyone and not for every sale. One of the problems with these big leaguers is simply their size. They may know how to market and sell a picture by Mark Rothko or, as one Sotheby's catalog said, "an important George II mahogany cabinet on chest by William Hallet, mid eighteenth century," which sold not too long ago for $233,500, but your relatively modest Sheraton tray-top tea table, worth about $1,200, might very well get lost. In other words, although they might consent to sell it, understandably, they will devote less time and energy to it than they do to more expensive objects.

"Very few homes have the Mona Lisa hanging in the living room," says Tom Porter, "so it's baloney to think you have to send everything to New York. Most things do very well at any reputable auction house. The key is trust and marketing."

We might not have been the biggest auction house in the country, but Leslie Hindman Auctioneers could make as big a splash as anyone when necessary. We sold a 17.5-carat yellow diamond ring after we demonstrated to the consignors what we would do to advertise and sell it versus what the bigger houses would do. We had postcards made, we advertised it, and we put it on the cover of our catalog. It sold for more than $100,000.

Talk to more than one auction house if you can, and find out what each will do for you. Don't be afraid to play one off the other, either. You have nothing to lose and everything to gain. If they want your business—and they will—they will be happy to talk. Your objective should be to find an auction house that will not raise your expectations to get the consignment and then fail to fulfill them once it does.

As you ask questions and consider each house, bear in mind that you are hiring an auction house to do a specific job. "Don't negotiate every little thing to the point where you're not letting the auction house have a fair profit," says Robin Kimball Eisenbeis, who worked with me at Leslie Hindman Auctioneers as our director of trust and estate services. "After all, you have to work with them, and they have to want to work with you to do a good job."

A couple of years ago we were really excited about an estate in Indiana that was filled with wonderful works of art and decorative objects. It would have been very profitable for everyone involved, but as we started to negotiate, the consignor began to nickel-and-dime every point in the contract. Finally, our staff and I decided that the process was just too painful and that the profit would not be worth the effort, so we turned the consignor down. The lesson, I think, is don't be greedy. You and the auction house have the same goal: to get the best price possible for your belongings.

Remember, too, that you can expect an auction house to do only so much and give so much attention to a $500 object versus a $5,000 object. The latter will obviously mean more to them, and they will be more likely to work with you on it.

Now to the basics for sellers.

Commissions

Auction houses usually make money on both ends of a transaction. Some auction houses charge the buyer a 15 percent commission—the so-called buyers' premium—and this is never negotiable. Auction houses charge sellers a commission, too, and while this commission is not always negotiable—at Christie's and Sotheby's, for example—sometimes it is. Traditionally, a Christie's or Sotheby's will charge the seller a 20 percent fee for lots that sell for less than $2,000, 15 percent for lots that sell for $2,000 to $7,500, and 10 percent for lots that sell for more than $7,500.

These fees can really take a bite out of your profit. If you sell a 1950s mohair teddy bear for $900, you will pay a $180 commission and net only $720. Sell it for $2,300 and you take home only $1,955. Think about these numbers when you discuss commission with the auction house. If they really want your business, they might be willing to charge less overall or less for certain big-ticket objects or works of art. If they will not negotiate, you may do better using an Internet auction.

Some auction houses have different commission structures than the major leaguers. Weschler's, in Washington, D.C., for instance, charges sellers a 10 percent commission for lots sold for more than $2,000, then 15 percent for lots selling between $500 and $2,000, and 20 percent for lots sold for less than $500. On a $900 teddy bear, then, you'll pay a $135 commission—a bit better price than you would get at Christie's.

Commissions are necessary because running an auction house, like any business, entails expenses, including overhead, staff salaries, promotion, catalogs, and so on.

Auction Formats

Many houses have different types of auctions. At Leslie Hindman Auctioneers we had auctions that sold fine art, silver, and other decorative arts and collectibles, and our marketplace sales. At the latter types of auctions we would sell that part of an estate that wasn't really worth cataloging or marketing heavily. The advantage of having these different types of auctions is that an auction house can sell the contents of an entire estate.

As Tom Weschler explains, your mother's estate is a large four-bedroom home on four acres of rolling hills and manicured lawns. She had filled it with beautiful objects and furnishings. Weschler's will empty the house completely, placing each object in a sale format appropriate to its value. The fine collections of English sporting paintings and fine eighteenth- and nineteenth-century American furniture belong in a more heavily promoted sale because a full description and color photograph will help fetch a better price. Her very good reproduction furniture—sofas, a dining room table, armoires—however, will go into the weekly Tuesday afternoon sale, where it will sell well without the additional time and expense.

When an estate like that is offered to Sotheby's, most likely they pick through and accept the cream of the crop, leaving you with the rest of the estate's contents to sell elsewhere. "We get a lot of references from the New York houses, because they want only the really important stuff," one auction house owner told me.

Catalogs, Advertising, and Marketing

Many opportunities exist for an auction house to market your belongings, and you should be aware of them. The house's regular audience is important, but the more new people, or the more people who come specifically to look at your object alone, the better for you. Take my word for it: advertising works. If it didn't, *In Style* wouldn't be so thick, commercials during the Super Bowl wouldn't cost millions of dollars a minute, and movies wouldn't have $20 million advertising budgets.

The more overall and targeted exposure your consignment gets, the better. A photograph in the catalog is better than no photograph. A color photo is better than a black-and-white. Being on the catalog cover is better yet. A listing in an ad in *Maine Antiques Digest* is good. Assuring that the auction house will include your object in a national ad targeted to the market in which your object would be most interesting is better yet.

As you consider auction houses, be sure to ask what the house is willing to do for you specifically. At Leslie Hindman Auctioneers our marketing team met as a group long before each sale and discussed the possibilities for each lot. That's right—each lot. Sometimes there wasn't much to be said: an early-twentieth-century reproduction Chippendale wing chair might have been lovely, but there was nothing particularly special about it. That was the exception more often than the rule, though. Most things did have something special or unique about them, or we knew of a collector or a dealer who might be interested in just such an object.

If we were selling a collection of wonderful American duck decoys, for instance, we might have sent postcards to every member of the Minnesota Duck Decoy Collectors Club. We might have taken an advertisement in *Decoy Magazine* and, if it was a truly important collection, maybe even have thrown a reception in the collection's honor. Maybe the *Chicago Tribune* would have published an interesting article about the consignor. Maybe a local television station would have done a feature on it. As far as I am concerned, all presale publicity is positive.

When Christie's sold the remaining stock of a well-respected old-line antiques store in Raleigh, North Carolina, after its owners retired, the auction house decided to hold the sale at the store itself. The furniture and decorative objects were mostly of southern origin, and it was felt that bringing it all up to New York—taking it away from its natural surroundings and away from the people who collected southern antiques—just didn't make sense. The local press made a fuss over the army of Christie's staff members who descended on Raleigh for the week. Every newspaper in the area, from as far away as Atlanta, featured articles about the sale. My favorite bit of publicity, however, was provided when a local morning news show did the weather report live from the presale exhibit!

At Leslie Hindman Auctioneers we were lucky enough to get a consignment of magnificent paperweights from the collection of the Bergstrum-Mahler Museum, in Neenah, Wisconsin. A whole world of paperweight collectors exists, with clubs, publications, and Web sites. After researching clubs and collectors, and learning about paperweights, we sold all of the paperweights for $200 to $20,000 each, with collectors from around the world (literally) attending. Not every object or even every collection receives such attention, but this should give you an indication of the lengths to which an auction house can go to advertise and market your consignments.

When discussing the catalog, ask how your object will be featured. Will it be photographed? Who is going to pay for it? (In most cases you will be charged for the photography. Some auction houses absorb that cost as part of their overall marketing budget.) What criteria do they use when deciding what will be photographed in color or black-and-white?

All auction houses maintain extensive mailing lists, but it would be wise to ask about that if you're not sure. More than anything else, I think, catalogs are your best source of marketing. Not too long ago Tom Porter of Garth's was selling a clock for which they'd received an absentee bid of $80,000 from a man living in Hong Kong. He wasn't a regular client and Tom had a lot of trouble getting in touch with his bank to verify his references. About an hour before the sale Tom and the gentleman spoke by phone. The man understood Tom's dilemma and asked that even if Garth's wouldn't accept his bid for the clock this time, to please keep trying to verify the information for the future. Tom then went to the clock's owner and told her about the situation. The man didn't appear suspicious, so they decided to accept his bid, and in fact he was the successful bidder at $77,000.

Later, Tom asked the man how he had learned about the clock. After all, it's 8,007 miles as the crow flies from Hong Kong to Delaware, Ohio. The man said he'd been in London on business and had seen the catalog there. "We only have eight catalog subscribers in England, so that was good luck on our part and his," Tom recalled. Clearly even eight subscribers, if they are the right eight, are better than none at all.

Reserves

Once you have chosen an auction house, you and the house need to decide on the presale estimate and reserve. Whether even to have a reserve is an important consideration. The big auction houses require reserves, but many other auction houses do not. Reserves, though, can protect sellers from unexpected circumstances.

Some auctioneers believe that reserves muddle the sellers' opinion of the success of a sale. A seller in Cleveland was offering numerous pieces from her collection of nineteenth-century American furniture, including a secretary with an estimate of around $15,000 and a mirror with an estimate of around $5,000. The secretary sold for $12,000 and the mirror for $17,000. After the sale the consignor called, upset that her secretary had sold for so much less than the estimate. The auctioneer told her how well the mirror had done, but she wasn't satisfied. Fine, he replied, but think about it this way: I'll switch the estimates. It took a minute for the consignor to reply, but once she understood his point—that you need to think about the grand total and not the amount for each individual piece in a collection—she felt much better.

I believe that every object ultimately sells for what it is worth. If the walnut secretaire was meant to sell for $2,500, it will.

Depending on the auction house, you can choose to have a reserve placed upon your consignment, or you can choose not to. Some auction houses offer a third choice, "discretion," which means that the auctioneer will sell your lot at 10 percent to 25 percent less than the reserve at his discretion.

Finally, a global reserve takes into account all of the objects you have in a sale. Let's say you have a pewter soup tureen and a pewter jardiniere to be sold as separate lots. You assign a global reserve of $1,000 for the two lots. The tureen then sells for $650. The reserve of the jardiniere, which was $500, decreases to $350, which increases its chances of selling.

✕➤⌣➤✕

Finally, before you turn over your possessions, remember to ask about insurance, storage fees, and even parking facilities and food.

Once you have chosen an auction house, the details are out of your hands until—with luck—a check is placed in them after the sale, usually twenty to thirty-five calendar days later.

ON THE INTERNET

SELLING BASICS

The listing and digital images posted on an online auction site reveal a lot about the sellers. A listing that is thoughtful, informative, and complete usually indicates that the transaction as a whole will be, as well. By contrast, a listing that is vague, sloppy, and cursory is a red flag signaling possible complications and a lot of effort on the buyer's part to complete the transaction.

One of the most important lessons I've learned in business is the extent to which appearance matters. How you present yourself, or in this case, how your listing represents you to the outside world, is the number one factor in determining whether your online auction will be successful, smooth, and profitable.

I like what an experienced online auction seller wrote recently on the Web: "Words bring traffic to a Web site, but pictures sell. Text conveys information, photos convey emotion. Text can tell you about a product, but a photo can make you fall in love with it."

The first thing any seller has to write is a title, or headline, for the object. The reason the headline is important is that the site's search engine will allow visitors to find your offering by typing in one or more of the headline words. In this respect, traditional auction houses have it easy: "A pair of Biedermeier cherrywood side chairs" or "A needlepoint carpet" is often sufficient in a catalog. For online sellers, however, it's more complicated because the title is the main means by which millions of potential buyers will find what is being sold. In addition, experts at traditional auction houses can create as long a title as they wish, such as this from a recent Sotheby's sale: "A Victorian silver plate knife holder fitted with a set of twelve mother-of-pearl handled knives." Online auctions, however, allow only so many characters in a title.

Titles should be broad enough to capture anyone who might be interested in the object but narrow enough to attract collectors. Buyers searching for objects online use key words, which then capture all the titles that include them. For instance, I entered "porcelain dish" into eBay's search engine and captured 269 auctions. If I narrow that to "Wedgwood porcelain dish," I get 104 auctions. If I narrow it further to "blue Wedgwood porcelain dish," I see 22 auctions, and if I narrow it even more, to "round blue Wedgwood porcelain dish," my search finds only a single auction that meets my needs.

You can see how important and meaningful every word can be, and why you should think hard about every word you choose.

Look at various auction sites to see how other people's listings of similar objects are titled. Are most people selling a vase or an urn, a plate or a dish, a cup or a mug? Many people try to cover all bases, and it's not uncommon to see people selling a "vase urn," "plate dish," or "cup mug." I think you should choose one word, however, and be confident of what you're selling. A vase is a vase; an urn is an urn.

One of the biggest mistakes is not to do research before selling an object. Auction houses, of course, employ experts in various fields who identify objects and research their history before writing catalog copy. For better or for worse, the online seller is the expert. At the very least the research should include a review of prices for comparable objects on the Internet and through price guides, or through an online appraisal. These are all good foundations for writing a confident and informative heading.

By confident I mean straightforward, honest, and informative. In fact, your confidence should be apparent in every word. Titles that start "Another blue flow vase," a remarkably common occurrence, will turn more people off than on. Avoid meaningless modifiers like "wonderful," "awesome," and "stunning." They take up valuable room in your title and don't really add much. More than even those words, skip the exclamatory "Wow!!!," "LQQK," or "Rare!" Because they are now online clichés, these nonwords will not attract attention anyway. Instead, accurately describe what you're selling, and use words with heft. If a pitcher is majolica, include "majolica" in the title. If the collectible first day cover (a stamped envelope the post office issues on the day a new stamp is issued) bears an image of Woodrow Wilson, then your title should be broader than merely "presidential FDC"; it should include "President Woodrow Wilson" to capture collectors not only of FDCs but of Wilson memorabilia and presidential ephemera as well.

When you can, include whatever is unique or special about what you are selling. Colors, materials, brand names, and manufacturers are often used as key words. I think the word "genuine" or "authentic" is acceptable to differentiate an original item from a reproduction. The word "new" or "old" can be helpful as well.

Depending on what you are selling, you might be able to squeeze in some practical information, too. Some buyers choose to ignore reserve auctions, so if yours is a no-reserve auction, you might add "No Res" or "N/R" to your title. If the auction is near a major holiday, consider including "Great gift."

Next, compose the main text. Professing your ignorance is annoying and not likely to attract buyers—for example, "I am not sure what this is. I assume it is a creamer but it might be a large cup or even a vase." No traditional auction house would ever include copy like that in its catalog, and online sellers should avoid it too.

There are buyers who want just the facts about the Montblanc fountain pen you are selling. Others would like to know that your grandmother bought it in Paris for your grandfather while she was a nurse during World War I, and that he used it to write love letters to her throughout their sixty-year marriage. If you think the story behind the object is meaningful, by all means include it.

But more than anything else, include the facts! Explain what the object is and what it looks like, even if there are accompanying pictures. Your prospective buyers have computers of varying quality and speed, and what you think is a well-presented image may not appear that way to everyone. Describe the color, material, age, and manufacturer, if you have not already listed it in the title. Mention any signatures, hallmarks, or other distinguishing features that serve to authenticate the object's identity and age.

If you find that you are unsure of something, you need to do a little more research. Vagueness makes people think you don't know what you are talking about or that you are concealing something, which erodes your credibility.

Most people search for key words in an auction site's titles, but auction sites generally also allow users to search for the key words in the full text of every listing. The more specific and descriptive your listing, the greater the number of potentially interested people who will see your auction. Don't, however, try to appeal to everybody by throwing in common but tangentially appropriate words. Doing that is referred to as spamming, and it's as annoying to most people as regular e-mail spam.

It may seem counterintuitive, but try to be honest about any damage or defects in the object without dwelling on them. Note, point out, and describe exactly where the defect is. "There is a very minor crack at the base of the bowl which does not go through the bowl," wrote one seller. "You can see it in the lower right of the picture." Wrote another, "On the underside of one corner there is a small chip off the side of one point. As it's on the inside, it's not noticeable at all unless you're feeling for it." Either of these defects may not make much of a difference to some people, but not knowing about them in advance would.

Most auction listings include photographs, and auction sites provide detailed tutorials on how to include photos in your listing. Buying an object in an online auction without first seeing a picture of it is a little like going on a blind date. I want to see what I'm buying, even if it's a book and even if the seller has the descriptive powers of Tom Wolfe.

Today, with the advent of digital cameras, video cameras that can be attached to your computer, stores that develop pictures and return them via e-mail or on disk, and the availability of inexpensive scanners, there is simply no good excuse for auction listings that do not include digital images.

Consider the photograph just as carefully as you would the written listing: before you photograph the item, peruse auctions for similar objects. This is the best way to learn which angles work and which do not. Many people include way more in the photograph than is necessary. They might be selling a Tiffany crystal bud vase, but the picture shows their entire living room. This is unnecessary, and the number of shapes and surfaces in the photograph may make it very slow to download.

Many site visitors surf through scores of objects and often just move on if an auction is taking too long to load. Try to avoid anything that adds unnecessary time to the loading process, including too many pictures, music, or background patterns. Take pictures of your object against simple backgrounds that show it to its best advantage.

The number of pictures you include will depend on the kind of object you are auctioning. Some auctions have one picture and then several links—click here to see the back, click here to see the label—to other photos. This allows the buyer to download the auction quickly and then look more closely if the first glance proves promising. Photographs of defects or damage are also helpful, since what is minor to the seller might be major to the buyer, and vice versa. Some clever sellers even include an object, such as a piece of fruit or a coin, that shows the size of the object they are selling. One recent auction featured an extreme close-up of a millefiori bowl. There was no way to tell from the picture whether the bowl was 6 inches or 12 inches in diameter. Another bowl at auction, this time a white Fenton hobnail bowl, also photographed close-up, had a quarter in the picture, immediately conveying the general size of the bowl.

Although I think clear, concise, detailed, and visually uncluttered listings work best, there is a contrarian view. "I use creative ads and lots of pictures on higher-end items," wrote one seller on a chat site. "I feel if I am asking someone to pay $100 to $1,000 for an item that they have the right to see it from all angles. I use music—I eliminated it for one series of auctions and heard from my regulars how much they missed it. On better items I may use up to seven pictures—I feel any serious buyer will want to see all there is regarding a piece. Obviously this approach causes my ads to load more slowly, and flies in the face of what everyone else is saying. But it works for me."

Creating an auction listing is a time-consuming and difficult process that should be taken seriously, no matter how you choose to go about it. The online world is still in its relative infancy and whatever works for you is, ultimately, the best way to do it.

SALES POLICY

For many people, one of the most difficult concepts to grasp about selling on the Internet is that—whether they are selling belongings that have been collecting spiderwebs in the attic since the Eisenhower administration or their grandmother's prized collection of Venetian glass—the business of selling is really a business.

In other words, even if your home office is a card table set up in the corner of your bedroom and you do most of your work there in your bathrobe and scruffies while drinking your morning coffee, you have all the same responsibilities to your customers as does the local auction house down the block.

If you were to consign a circa 1958 mohair Florence Knoll sofa to Butterfields, your part in the auction transaction would be over pretty much at the same time you arranged for it to be dropped off there. There would be a contract to sign and maybe a discussion or two with the Butterfields department specialist about the reserve, but other than that, you could sit tight until a check arrived in the mail several weeks after the auction. Butterfields' business practices and policies are based on years of experience with what works to their benefit as well as to their clients' advantage.

On eBay, which happens to own Butterfields, or anywhere else on the Internet, every seller has to figure out his own personal sales policy—that is, what risks he is willing to take, what advantages he will cede to a buyer, and what rules and regulations he thinks are essential.

When I founded Leslie Hindman Auctioneers in Chicago, I was a relative newcomer to the business world. I sought out mentors and colleagues and asked their advice. I met with other businesspeople and learned which policies worked well and which didn't. Every kind of business has its own peculiarities. I had to find out what those in the art and auction world were.

One way to acquire information is to surf the Internet site. Carefully read a cross-section of sales policies, paying special attention to the voice in which each seller composes her copy. Doing this will give you a good sense of what to require of your buyers. For instance, if most sellers state that they won't ship internationally, you might find out why, and refuse to do so, as well.

As far as voice goes, be firm but gentle. Sales policies that sound like threats—do such-and-such "or else"—or lectures do not encourage buyers. For instance, I won't bid on objects, no matter how much I want them, if the seller sounds nasty. The Internet inspires little loyalty, so anything you can do to retain customers is to your advantage.

As time goes by, you'll learn what works and what does not and why. Listen to your customers, first of all. They will be the best source of advice. Internet auction clients may let you know personally about any objections they have to your customer service, or they may post a comment in your feedback profile. Don't dismiss these. In most circumstances one comment is really representative of ten or more similar ones.

Sales policies, which are part of your auction listing, should more than anything else be straightforward, complete, confident-sounding, and clearly written. Buyers should be able to read your sales policy and know what you expect from them and what they can expect from you. Fudging or omitting information in the hope that a person won't notice is just asking for trouble. If you compose a well-thought-out sales policy, your sales will be high and the number of customer inquiries will be low.

Deciding what kind of payment you are willing to accept is probably the most important decision. What's easiest for your customer—usually a personal check—isn't necessarily easiest for you. And what's easiest for you—credit cards, money orders, and cashier's checks—may be inconvenient for your customer. As a seller, your choices include cash, checks, cashier's checks and money orders, and credit cards. You can also work with an escrow service. See pages 114–116 for a discussion of these methods.

ATTRACTING A CLIENTELE

Traditional auction houses have marketing departments. As an individual or small business, you probably don't. Your resources—which in many cases are time and energy—must be spent wisely. The easiest way to attract clients is to keep the ones you have. Make these your rules of operation:

Write professional and well-organized listings.

Take good photographs that show what you're selling to its best advantage.

Institute a fair and complete sales policy.

Answer all questions as accurately and quickly as possible. This will go a long way toward building a reputation for caring about what you sell and to whom you sell.

Deal with people fairly and generously and provide excellent customer service throughout the transaction, if there is one.

Build loyalty by providing fair and accurate feedback as soon as possible.

"I pamper new bidders," someone recently wrote in an auction chat room. "I e-mail them when I receive payment and let them know when item is shipped. I let them know when I left feedback and ask that they let me know when the item gets there. I think it helps toward preventing any fears the buyer might have with an online sale. I've had pretty good success with this approach."

Many people dislike receiving unsolicited e-mail, so a mass e-mailing announcing a sale might not be well received. But when you have sold an object, you might ask the successful bidder if she would like to be alerted to your future sales. Eventually you will have a list of truly interested customers.

Lastly, there are news groups, bulletin boards, and chat rooms for every type of work of art, decorative object, and collectible. If you can think of it, there's a group of people somewhere talking about it. Find them. Get involved. You'll be surprised at how quickly you become part of a community of interested and like-minded people.

RESERVES AND OPENING BIDS

Once again, Internet auctions present sellers with a challenge that traditional auctions don't face. At an auction house the consignor might suggest a reserve, but ultimately the house will decide, and opening bids are at the auctioneer's discretion.

On the Internet, however, most sellers have to make these decisions for themselves. In addition, sellers have the choice, on most sites, of whether even to set a reserve or to offer a minimum opening bid only.

As I've said before, some Internet auction shoppers will simply not bid on auctions with a reserve, assuming that the seller wants to make an unfair profit or doesn't know what the object is worth. Since the goods in many traditional auctions have reserves, people who were auctiongoers before the advent of online sites are probably less skittish about them. The barrier seems to be most common among recent online visitors.

There is a reason for this concern, however. In traditional auctions, bidders are guaranteed to at least meet the reserve if they bid the low estimate. In most online auctions, there is no estimate to use as a gauge. Potential buyers therefore have no way to judge the reserve other than to bid and bid again to see if they are meeting or exceeding the seller's reserve. Many people find the frustration that accompanies this kind of bidding reason enough to skip reserve auctions.

Some sellers choose to set a reserve on expensive objects only. "I always use reserves on anything over $50," said one user recently in a chat room. "I am not willing to offer a $400 item with a starting bid of $25 and let it rip with no reserve."

Another difference between traditional and online auctions is that at a live auction house the reserve is always kept secret. Online, however, with no history of anything "just not being done," before the close of an auction buyers sometimes ask what the reserve is and sellers just as often reveal it. "I don't see the downside to telling the reserve," said one seller. "Either the bidder is going to make the reserve or he's not. I figure that if he knows a few days in advance what the reserve is, perhaps he'll talk himself up to it. I have never had a reserve item that didn't sell."

One seller reveals the reserve if asked and then e-mails the other bidders to tell them. "It isn't fair, in my opinion, for one person to know what the reserve is, when other bidders who would never think of asking for a reserve price might be willing to bid a little more if their high bid is close to the reserve," he said.

If you don't want to reveal the reserve, try this stock answer from another seller: "When I didn't feel like going through all that hassle, I would say something like, 'Thank you very much for your interest. Unfortunately, my policy is not to disclose my reserve before the auction ends, since it can put bidders who do not know the reserve at a disadvantage. I can assure you, however, that the reserve is reasonable and I believe a fair price for the item." That seems fair enough. But to avoid even having to go that far, include such a statement in your sales policy. Some people may ask anyhow, but in those instances you can refer them back to your policy.

Even if you do decide to set a reserve, you still have to settle on a minimum opening bid. Both can be a challenge, so many people avoid reserves altogether and only set a minimum opening bid, which acts like a reserve anyway.

Of course, another advantage of setting a reserve is that it allows the seller to place a low minimum opening bid without worrying about losing money. Just as at traditional auctions, low opening bids attract attention, and attention begets attention. Sales where there are one or two bids, whether in the salesroom or online, are never as exciting as sales that attract ten or more bidders. Exciting auctions give people a sense that they are a part of something and that maybe they can get a bargain. Even if they can't get a bargain, they have at least seen the price climb, so they know that others thought the higher cost was reasonable. People don't mind bidding high; they just hate starting high.

A perfect example of a low opener was an eBay auction of a Crown Ducal peony chintz morning set, composed of a teapot, sugar and creamer, two cups and three dishes, with an opening bid of $50.00. The auction attracted thirty-seven bids, with the successful bidder taking the set home for $2,425.01.

Setting a low minimum bid in a no-reserve auction is, I believe, an equally good idea for the same reason as it is in reserve auctions. I know of people who start everything at a dollar. Others use $9.99 as their usual opener. The chat rooms don't have a lot of complaints about selling too low, even if once in a while a buyer does get a terrific bargain.

In a chat room recently I liked one seller's excellent method for determining opening bids. "I first looked at completed transactions to see what the object fetched," she said. "That gave me an idea of how much to expect my auction to close at. Then I checked out like items that did not sell, to see if I could figure out why." Frequently, she found, it came down to the minimum opening bids the seller had chosen. "Items that didn't sell had opening bids about one-third higher than the average closing price," she said. "And then I worked out how much the item would cost, in purchase price and eBay fees, if it sold at a price close to what other items were going for. Finally, I worked out how much I had to list the item for as an opening bid, to cover my costs and make a fair profit for my trouble. Therefore, I would have been happy to sell at the opening bid price, even if the auction never went close to the other completed auctions at final bid."

Another way to set a minimum is to check out similar objects in local antique shops, to ensure that your auction will fetch as much as an ad in a local newspaper. Finally, don't ignore your gut feeling of what you think the object is worth. Sometimes you can do pretty well that way, as one seller often does. "If I feel that there may be only one person out there who will recognize what I'm selling, I price it two or three times higher than what I might otherwise ask," he said. "So far my instincts have always paid off. In these instances I've sold to a single bidder, and each time I have profited very well."

Ultimately you have to decide which type of auction—reserve or no-reserve—you are most comfortable with. Try each type a few times. You'll soon learn which works best for the category of objects you sell and the type of buyers you attract.

FEEDBACK

Buying and selling at auction is risky business. From the seller's point of view, some of the risk stems from putting too low a minimum opening bid on an object. It may then sell for less than it's actually worth. Sellers have to deal with the occasional deadbeat—the guy who bids high, is the successful bidder, and never follows through with payment.

And yet, if a seller puts too low an opening bid on an object and ultimately loses some money on it, she has at least learned a lesson. She has learned to do more research before deciding upon an opening bid, and she has learned that auctions are fickle marketplaces. Deadbeat buyers are a drag, but more than anything they are an inconvenience. Encountering one means a seller has to e-mail and phone and try to finagle the buyer to follow through with his or her obligation. At worst, the seller has to list the object again. In the end, though, she hasn't lost money.

I think buyers are more at risk than sellers in online auctions. Why? Because in the end, after he has offered the successful bid, the buyer has to send his money—whether by personal check, money order, cashier's check, or credit card—to a complete stranger. He does this based on the assumption that this stranger will complete her end of the transaction and send the object. Fortunately, considering the number of auctions in action at any one time, and the number of sales on any one day, serious problems are relatively few. Unfortunately, they do happen. I know it. You know it. And the online auction sites know it. That is why they've gone out of their way to create as safe and honest an environment as possible in which to buy and sell. Their most potent weapon against dishonest sellers and buyers is the feedback system. Basically an honor system, feedback is a way for buyers and sellers to comment on each other's performance.

Sounds scary, doesn't it? The idea that someone you don't know, whose expectations you can't always decipher, is in a position to judge you and then post an opinion of you on the Internet for everyone *in the entire world* to see. But then, you are in the same position to judge them. Feedback is the most important way consumers have to protect themselves and to help create the kind of online atmosphere that works to everyone's best advantage. That is why leaving feedback must be done with care and precision.

Positive feedback, of course, builds your credibility. "Great service, item better than described. A real pleasure!" wrote one satisfied customer. "An excellent eBay experience. Will buy more stuff from this seller," wrote another. But feedback can also be negative. When you provide feedback, it's important to remember one thing: assume innocence. Sometimes the check really *is* in the mail. We are all so busy that we want to do everything as fast and as easily as possible. Sometimes we don't have time to stop and think. It's easy to assume that someone has intentionally done something wrong, but I urge you to fight that feeling. Instead of assuming wrongdoing, try to assume "rightdoing." Most online disputes are due more to miscommunication than to miscreant behavior. In the end, if you assume innocence instead of guilt, even if no one else does, you will have an easier time of it, smoother transactions, and far less pressure in your online life.

That said, knowing how and when to leave proper feedback is imperative. "As a seller," wrote one woman in a chat room not too long ago, "my policy has been to post feedback upon receipt of payment [before the buyer receives the object], which I've done for every customer. My reciprocal feedback is pitiful, just over 100, for thirteen months of selling."

But she has been giving her policy some thought since having to file insurance for a damaged item. The object was metal and glass, shipped double-boxed with four layers of bubble wrap and peanuts. There was no movement within either box. "The glass— my biggest concern—was intact, but the buyer said a metal piece was broken," she wrote. "I offered my apologies on behalf of the post office and had the buyer start the paperwork. I offered to wait for reimbursement from the P.O. and promptly refunded the $185 to him. In light of this, I am very disappointed that the buyer, who himself has high feedback, didn't take the time to post reciprocal positive feedback in my file. I was under no obligation to refund the money to him at the start. This was just the last of many feedback disappointments for what I think is excellent customer service."

She has every right to be annoyed. Sellers are encouraged to do the right thing when buyers show their appreciation, and vice versa. "I'm sick and tired of posting positive feedback for people, and not having it returned," wrote a frequent seller. "Furthermore, in checking my buyers, I find that many of them do not participate in the feedback program at all. That is, of course, their business. But why should I post for them? As a seller, I say to the buyer, 'If you're satisfied with your purchase, I would be happy to exchange feedback with you.' I let them take it from there. As a buyer, I post feedback upon receipt of the item, and notify the seller that I have done so."

Leaving constructive negative feedback is not easy. First, of course, you have to decide to leave it in the first place. As I noted above, take the responsibility of leaving negative feedback seriously. Selling and buying online is fun, but it's not fun and games. For many people it's a livelihood; it puts food on the table and clothes on their backs.

Additionally, on most sites, once you leave feedback of any sort it cannot be edited or retracted. Think twice before you click "send," because what you say will affect your reputation, too. On some sites, you can add to previously posted feedback, allowing you to amend a negative feedback. Don't forget to do so if the dispute is resolved to your satisfaction. Before you leave negative feedback in a person's file, try to resolve the dispute. E-mail is great, but in many cases, a phone call can work wonders. On the phone, you are more apt to think clearly, to take into account the other person's feelings, and to understand her motivation. If ultimately you feel you have no choice but to leave negative feedback, tell the other party what you are going to do. Don't threaten, don't warn. Just explain, as dispassionately as possible, what you feel has gone wrong and why. Tell the person you believe that you have done everything you could to resolve the dispute amicably, that you think you have behaved fairly and properly, and that your feedback will make that clear.

"A phone call to the other party prior to posting the negative feedback can sometimes lead to a satisfactory settlement," wrote one woman in an online forum. "I have over a thousand feedbacks and only two negatives."

Then there is the two-way street: "I recently had a sale that went bad because of the buyer's refusal to respond or even to acknowledge that he was the high bidder. To be more accurate, he was the only bidder," wrote one person in a chat room. "Well, after finally receiving payment, I made a deal with him and suggested that because it was not a pleasant transaction for me and it was probably not pleasant for him, either, why don't we just forget about the feedback, good or bad, altogether. This way I won't be troubled with negative feedback, giving or receiving."

That man made an interesting point at the end. He would be "troubled" leaving negative feedback. In fact, although you certainly want to avoid having to give negative feedback, it is sometimes not only necessary but responsible. "I do not for the life of me understand why someone would *not* leave negative feedback for another if they felt it was deserved," wrote another person. "As eBay says, its the whole record that counts not just the negatives. I have a few negatives, and that is because I'm not afraid to leave them. I for one can tell you it has not affected my sales one little bit."

Before you leave a negative comment, review the other person's file. Is your complaint similar to what others have experienced? If so, you will feel better about leaving your comment. If your experience seems to be an anomaly, give it some more thought. And once again: assume innocence!

One more thought about leaving negative feedback: watch out for those who retaliate with follow-up negatives. You can find out if someone is prone to this behavior by looking at the kind of feedback the person has left in the past. When she receives a negative comment, does she immediately shoot back with a negative of her own? One way to avoid being retaliated against is to leave feedback in the final hours of the permitted sixty days after the transaction. By the time it is discovered, the person for whom you left negative feedback will be unable to leave a retaliatory negative.

There are several good reasons for a buyer to leave negative feedback:

- When a seller refuses to honor his obligation to sell the object after you were the high bidder in a minimum-bid auction or when the reserve has been met in a reserve auction.
- If you receive the object but it's not what was described, or it is significantly different from what was described.
- If you're dissatisfied with what you bought and have legitimate reasons to want to return it and get a refund, but the seller refuses to accommodate you.

As a seller, consider leaving negative feedback when the successful bidder refuses to pay after repeated requests to do so.

When composing the feedback, be straightforward. Say what happened in as few words as possible. Boil the issue down to its essence.

Don't let your emotions rule. Don't make threats. Don't complain about side issues. And don't overstate the obvious.

"Never received my Baccarat vase. Seller refuses to respond to e-mails or phone calls." That comment would have been more effective than this one that I recently read in someone's file, which seems more histrionic than serious: "I sent the jerk $200 and he never sent me my gold rose. No one should ever buy from him again!!!!" You can, however, be too terse. For instance, when the sale of a bronze Tiffany inkwell went sour, all the buyer wrote was "Seller did not honor deal agreed upon." A more specific comment, such as "Seller guaranteed satisfaction and refused refund when asked," would have been more helpful.

Should you receive negative feedback, there are several things you can do—and one thing you should not do. You can respond with your own neutral feedback in your file. If you do, keep it short and simple. In the above example, the seller might have responded by saying, "Guarantee was for merchandise damaged during shipping only, as my sales policy states." If you have received unfair feedback, you can also try to contact the other party and come to a settlement. What you should not do is retaliate. In some instances you will start what's known as a bombing war, where two people retaliate against each other and it becomes more about their own anger than anything else. No one wins in that situation.

Feedback only works when everyone participates. It is one more step, one more thing you have to do. But in the end, everyone benefits.

FRAUD AND SETTLING DISPUTES

I have been lucky online. I have bought and sold many times, and all of my transactions have gone smoothly. I got what I paid for and was paid for what I sold. I have been satisfied with what I bought, and as far as I know those to whom I sold have been equally satisfied. But that is not always the case. In fact, according to the National Consumer League Internet Fraud Watch, auctions were the source of 68 percent of the complaints about online scams in 1998; most scams occur on person-to-person auctions. Most involve the seller not sending the object or the buyer not paying for an object for which he was the successful bidder. Other types of fraud include the use of shills to inflate prices, false credit cards, bounced checks, sending counterfeit goods, or falsely describing objects being sold.

None of these are pleasant, but there are ways to protect yourself. First, bid only in auctions that make you feel comfortable. If anything you read or see in a listing arouses your suspicion, move on. During the auction, get to know the seller. Ask a question or two and judge the response on its timeliness and accuracy. If, for example, you e-mail to point out an error in the seller's listing, watch to see if she corrects it promptly. And last but not least, check the seller's feedback. If there is negative feedback, the explanation for which is not clear, e-mail the seller and ask for clarification. Beware of sellers who are reluctant to give out their phone numbers and mailing addresses, and avoid sellers who use only post office boxes. Although some people are nervous about sellers overseas, I have had no problems. Some international sellers request cash, however, and that is where I draw the line. If you choose to send cash, read the seller's feedback very carefully beforehand.

Keep a paper trail. In other words, print out or save to your hard drive everything having to do with a transaction. Once the seller notifies you that an object has been shipped, ask for a tracking number.

If, despite all precautions, you become a victim of fraud, take the following steps: First, before you do anything drastic, try to work out the dispute with the other person, just as you would with any other complaint about a transaction. Ask for the party's user-registration information. Many sites notify the person about whom the request was made, which often stimulates a response. Next, if you still need to make contact, be prepared with the evidence that the seller received your payment—a canceled check, a Visa statement, a copy of the money order with the seller's endorsement on it, or documentation that the buyer received the package.

If you sent your payment through the U.S. Postal Service and the seller says she never received payment, file a Lost Mail Claim. It probably won't help in tracking down the payment, but it will at least show the seller that you're taking the issue as seriously as she is. You can also lodge a complaint with the office of the postal inspector, and you'll be provided with a postage-free envelope with which to do it.

Whether the offender is a buyer or a seller, notify the auction site. Some auction sites have independent investigators who will explore the transaction, and many also have ways to disqualify a buyer from bidding on any future sales you might host. If you provide sufficient evidence and file complaints, most auction sites can suspend the seller's registration and the authorities will have what they need to file charges, obtain search warrants to obtain further evidence, and prosecute.

If these measures fail to elicit a satisfactory settlement, you can pursue criminal prosecution. Obviously this is not something to be undertaken without a great deal of thought. It can be a time-consuming, depressing, and expensive experience. But it can work. Robert J. Guest, of Orange County, California, was sentenced to fourteen months in jail and ordered to pay $101,485 to eBay users, banks that gave him credit, and a finance company that issued a check he cashed, on federal charges of accepting $36,000 from eBay bidders on his auctions but never sending any of the objects. It was the first federal prison sentence resulting from Internet auction fraud.

Even if you never resolve the dispute, be sure to leave feedback in the person's file, using the same restraint as you would for lesser complaints. As tempting as it might be, do not interfere in any way with a seller's other sales by contacting other bidders, which is probably in violation of the site's regulations. Additionally, do not post negative information about that person in forums or bulletin boards. Not only will you inflame the situation without solving the problem, but you open yourself to legal charges of libel or defamation of character.

5

Collecting

14

Introduction to Collecting

Antiques and many collectibles are old. Age is relative, though, and so is condition. A very old silver tea service with scratches, dents, and missing parts isn't necessarily more valuable than a newer tea service in excellent condition. If you are a serious collector, the condition of an object is paramount; if you are a flea market patron, only you can decide how much condition is worth. There is no substitute for handling an object, running your thumb around the rim of a Fiesta ware soup bowl and pulling out the drawer of an oak chest-on-chest to inspect its interior.

That said, however, no one thing devalues a piece. Age in furniture, as in life, should be appreciated for what it is. Lines can be those borne of wisdom, and a bit of wear and tear may be proof of an interesting history. Age is patina, and age is desirable. Patina is an important quality when you're shopping for antiques. (If it wasn't, furniture manufacturers wouldn't use complicated formulas to simulate the mellow look of age.) Dust, sunlight, human hands that rubbed, cleaned, and coaxed a mellow shine from a well-used piece of furniture or silver, all contribute to its patina.

All this is true—up to a point.

In porcelain, for instance, nicks and chips do matter, and may make the piece less valuable. Old silver that has been replated may be less valuable than if it had been left alone, even if the new plate makes the piece look better. With some silver plate, it's better to see the copper base showing through.

Whether you're interested in furniture or oil portraits or art glass, if you're troubled by a discoloration or a minor nick, a hairline fracture or a bit of repair, you might not want to buy antiques at all, and perhaps you shouldn't buy at auction.

It's impossible to turn yourself into an antiques expert overnight or even over a decade. You can study art history in college, take classes in appraising, even work in an auction house viewing objects day after week after month for years and still not know everything there is to know.

I'm what you might call a generalist—that is, I'm not an expert in any one field, but I'm well versed in many areas. I can tell you about your late-nineteenth-century highboy or your mid-twentieth-century collection of Roseville pottery. I can tell you why that Art Nouveau chair you covet is fake and why that Barcelona chair you bought for $120 at a tag sale is the real thing. But for a seriously in-depth discussion of Japanese Imari porcelain or the early paintings of Max Ernst, I would have to confer with an expert in each of those fields.

For most amateur collectors, however, being a generalist is the best thing to be. Unless you're a very serious collector of Imari or Ernst, areas in which great expertise is desirable, knowing a bit about a lot of things is probably enough. After all, as you collect you'll learn more and more, some by doing your homework, some merely by osmosis, from looking, inspecting, turning things upside down and inside out.

And yet, despite the ease with which you'll naturally pick up some knowledge, there is some information you definitely should know, should go out of your way to learn. The goal here is to develop an educated eye, a knack for seeing what's in front of you and putting it all together in context so that when you do bid on something at auction, or haggle in an antiques store, you have a basis for your purchasing decisions.

It bears repeating, however: one of the beauties of age is the appearance of age. Antiques will never look as good as new. And you wouldn't want them to, would you?

Buying at auction isn't all about the art of the deal, though getting a good deal is a lot better than understudying and overpaying. After all, a little homework before the sale can mean the difference between a purchase that's a bargain and a purchase that's a treasure.

Of course, there is no way any book could give you advice on what to look for regarding everything you might ever find at auction, from Alvar Aalto chairs to *zwischengoldglas,* and the thousands of things in between them (alphabetically speaking, of course). But you can learn to look at decorative objects and works of art with a keen and discerning eye, and then use what you know over and over again.

To help you, I've chosen a few very common objects to give you an idea of what to look for.

But always remember, the most important place to look, of course, is in the auction house, or on the Internet, and at the object as closely as possible, with all the vigor you can muster.

All photographs are courtesy Butterfields Auctioneers, an eBay Company.

Ceramics

WEDGWOOD BLUE AND WHITE JASPERWARE URN, 19TH CENTURY

Josiah Wedgwood (1730–95) the important English potter, was a scientist as well as a ceramicist. He introduced many exciting materials to the ceramic repertoire. Jasperware, which he invented in 1775, contains sulfite of barium, which produces a surface that can remain unglazed yet is nonporous. When people think of Wedgwood, they think of jasperware first. Jasperware has been in continuous production to this day, so collectors should inspect prospective pieces carefully.

Though some urns shaped like this had lids (the original urns of antiquity held funeral ashes), this one did not because it doesn't have an interior rim upon which a lid would rest, and the interior is the same cobalt blue as its exterior.

The urn has a cobalt blue dip—the most popular and collectible of Wedgwood colors. Others include a paler blue, black, lilac, and green. Wedgwood ceased making this particular color in 1939. The reliefs, most of which depict classical scenes, are almost always white.

This urn, with its classic shape and neoclassical scene, is very representative of Wedgwood's work. The shape and scenes depicted were often derived from ancient Greek vases, a popular influence in the 18th century.

The area between the body and foot of the urn is called the "socle." The socle here has been restored, which would diminish the urn's value.

Look for the incised mark on the bottom. It should say Wedgwood (no "e"!). If it says "England" it was made after 1891 and, if "Made in England," probably after 1910 or so. Some pieces made between 1860 and 1929 carry a three-letter mark, the last of which indicates the year of manufacture; a "24" or "36" does not refer to a year, but is a production code indicating size. Because this urn says Wedgwood alone, we know it was made prior to 1891. The "V" and "T" on the base of this vase are probably the craftsman's initials, impossible to identify.

Look for chips, cracks, or other damage by feeling around all the edges and the socle. Common areas of damage include the handles or anywhere there is a join, though some minor damage is acceptable on older, rarer pieces.

Firing cracks to the relief are not uncommon, particularly to older pieces, and don't seriously affect value.

Older pieces of Wedgwood are silken and smooth, almost glasslike. Later pieces have a slightly rougher feel.

Furniture

CHIPPENDALE MAPLE CHEST-ON-CHEST, DUNLAP SCHOOL, NEW HAMPSHIRE, LAST QUARTER 18TH CENTURY

Early American furniture has become extremely popular, and prominent collectors have driven prices of signed pieces from famous makers out of reach. Country furniture and case pieces from less well known makers can still be bought at auction for surprisingly reasonable prices. This chest is not actually made by the famous English cabinetmaker Thomas Chippendale, but copied from his well-known Pattern Book.

To find out if the hardware has been replaced, check for filled holes, extra holes, or a shadow from a previous set of pulls.

Many American woods are similar to those used in England. To determine precise origin, serious collectors sometimes send a tiny sliver of the wood to wood identification laboratories.

Because chest-on-chests are in two pieces, the molding around the area where the top is fitted onto the bottom is often damaged, which can lessen its value.

Look to see that the carvings, like the fan shell carving on the bottom center drawer, are clean and crisp.

Look for evidence of splicing on the legs, a difference in the wood's color between the legs and body of the piece, or stylistic differences. This S-shaped style of leg is known as "cabriole," and is typical of Chippendale.

Closely inspect the feet on all furniture of this type. Because furniture was moved or pushed across the floor, and occasionally water damaged, feet are often in poor condition or completely replaced. Modern vacuum machines have only worsened the problem.

This chest's apron, with its salamander scrolls and carving is typical of the Dunlaps, a leading furniture-making family in New Hampshire.

Glass

DAUM NANCY CAMEO GLASS LANDSCAPE VASE, CIRCA 1900

The Art Nouveau style for which Daum became famous began in the 1890s, and was best described by a man named Geoffrey Warren, when he suggested one think about it as "a sensuous line . . . which bends and turns back on itself. Think of the feminine form, rounded and curving. Think of plant forms growing and burgeoning. Think of flowers in bud, in overblown blossom . . . think of women's hair, think of twisting smoke."

Cameo glass is made by fusing one or more layers of glass together, which are then carved to show the layers below, creating a three-dimensional effect.

A vase like this should be in perfect condition, with no chips or cracks. Look especially for internal inclusions, which can be caused by ash in the glass, or if a piece has been set down roughly. Often when either scenario happens and there is drastic temperature change—heat or cold—the unstable glass can shatter, or the crack can expand.

The more layers of glass, the more desirable and valuable the piece. Multiple layers require more time and skill to produce. Cameo carving is created by hand or by the use of acid.

Any vase or piece of glass that is more than about 9 inches high—this vase is 24 inches tall—is less desirable, since it becomes harder to display or store.

Almost all Daum glass pieces are signed. This vase is signed DAUM NANCY, indicating it was made in Nancy, France, and is accompanied by the *croix de Lorraine,* which looks like an equal sign with a slash through it.

Metalwork

AMERICAN ARTS AND CRAFTS HAMMERED COPPER AND MICA LAMP, POSSIBLY DIRK VAN ERP, EARLY 20TH CENTURY

The first true electric lighting—meaning lighting that was designed with components specifically created for electricity—appeared around 1904 or 1905. This lamp may have been made by the San Francisco craftsman Dirk Van Erp, whose first lamps appeared around 1908. Van Erp is widely recognized as the consummate maker of copper and mica lamps such as this.

The earliest lamps, which are characterized by simple rims on the shade and generally bolder and simpler shapes, are the most valuable of the copper and mica lamps.

The early period is also noted for the strappings that divide the mica panels, which were riveted to the outside of the heat cap and the rim.

The conical shade is primarily made from mica, a delicate colored or transparent mineral. Ideally, the mica should be original to the lamp.

The most valuable lamps have all their original sockets—in the case of this lamp there are three—and chain pulls.

The transition from the shaft to the base is a bit clumsy, an indication that it might not in fact have been made by Van Erp.

The body of this lamp is referred to as an onion base due to its shape.

Look to see if the metal retains its original patina—on this lamp it's a deep red brown. Many people through the years have polished their lamps, inadvertently removing the patina and most of the lamp's value, not to mention beauty, as well.

Almost all of Van Erp's lamps are signed on the bottom either with his name and his first partner's, D'Arcy Gaw, or his alone, after Gaw left his studio, or with his name and the city name, San Francisco. This lamp is unsigned, which indicates it may have been made by one of Van Erp's competitors.

Quilts

UNKNOWN SAILOR'S PIECED-FELT QUILT, CIRCA 1805

Quilts, so strongly identified with history, have always been popular, not only because of the stories behind them, but also because they were made in so many different patterns and colors. The definition of quilt is that there must be two layers of cloth surrounding a layer of batting, all of which is stitched through.

Collectors seek quilts such as this one that are in good condition, which means the colors are bright and crisp, and the fabric in good shape, with no holes, tears, or deterioration.

Like a painting, a good quilt has a balance of colors and composition, as well as fine stitchery.

This quilt's pattern depicts a central red and white alternating motif of diamonds and squares within a border, all of which is flanked by barber pole honeycomb pilasters and an outer border of radiating alternating circles and cloverleaves in squares.

Typical of quilts from this period, at 96¼ inches by 86¼ inches, it's quite large, big enough to keep an entire family warm in one bed.

Close, even stitching—8 to 10 stitches per inch counted from one side—is a prime characteristic of a good quilt.

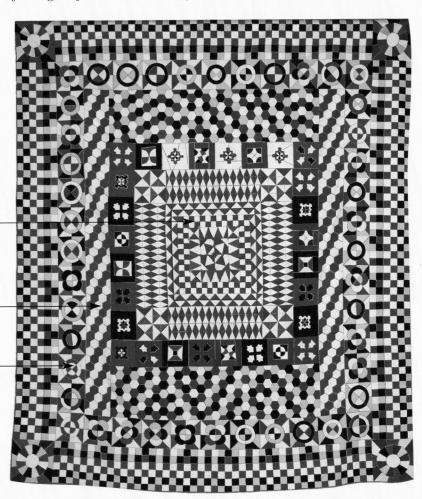

Provenance, or a proven background, always adds to authenticity and value. On the back of this quilt is a note, carefully printed in muslin, that reads: "This quilt has been in our possession for eighty years. It was made out of scraps of British Army and Navy cloth, by a convalescing British soldier. It took him twenty-two months to make it, every piece set in an overcast. This man was wounded when Admiral Nelson destroyed the fleet of Napoleon on the Mediterranean Sea about the close of the 18th Century. It was told to us that he borrowed his idea of pattern from Turkish Harem rugs."

Rugs

SERAPI CARPET, LATE 19TH CENTURY

Many "Oriental" rugs are named after the town in which they are woven. Serapi refers instead to the highest quality of Heriz (Iran) rug. Serapis were made in workshops for the European market, woven by hand from a "cartoon" from which the pattern would be copied one knot at a time, like paint-by-numbers. In the factory, there was often a man who would sing out the colors, maintaining standards and pacing, since there might have been up to a dozen of the same rugs being worked on simultaneously.

Serapis are characterized by all-wool foundations and very fine knotting.

Different types of Oriental rugs have certain design characteristics that can help identify them. Serapis, for instance, often have a "turtle" border, with the turtle separated by rosettes.

Many Serapis are large, such as this one, which is 19 by 12½ feet. Large rugs should be inspected to see that they haven't been cut down, which would greatly diminish their value.

The central medallion in Serapis, as in most other Heriz rugs, tends to be a very geometricized floral design.

Oriental rugs usually have border patterns of a wide, "main" border bounded with narrow "guard" borders. This Serapi has three guard borders on either side of the main one.

It's not uncommon for Heriz rugs, including Serapis, to be touched up with paint to hide worn or damaged areas. This is highly undesirable and should be avoided at all costs.

Serapis are distinguished by a lighter color palette than the usual Heriz carpet, often including shades of salmon, green, ivory, and sky blue.

The fringe on both ends is worn, but such wear diminishes a rug's value only if the knots themselves are worn away.

Silver

PAIR OF GEORGE II SILVER CANDLESTICKS, JOHN CAFÉ, LONDON, 1753

The style of this pair of candlesticks, made by London silversmith John Café in 1753, is called George II because their date of manufacture falls within this king's reign, and not necessarily because of any stylistic characteristics.

Often through the years the original nozzles were lost and replaced. Check to see if the replaced nozzles are a good match in both quality and design.

Look to see that the design is clean and crisp. Here, the armorial, or heraldic arms, portrayed are in excellent condition, not rubbed away as is common. This would add to the pair's value.

The heavy gadrooning is typical of mid-18th-century design.

As a primary light source, candlesticks were often used daily, so damage due to wear and tear over the years is common. Look for dents or splits along the shaft and base.

Pairs of candlesticks are very desirable. Pairs, however, aren't merely two identical candlesticks, but two candlesticks made by the same maker, typically within three years of each other.

This pair is cast, as opposed to loaded or made from sheet silver.

Candlesticks are marked on their underside with the maker's mark. In addition, their scratch-weights might be indicated. The sconces, too, might be marked, as might their nozzles.

Timepieces

CHIPPENDALE WALNUT TALL-CASE CLOCK, PENNSYLVANIA, LATE 18TH TO EARLY 19TH CENTURY

Included in the category of timepieces are all manner of watches and clocks, with "grand-father" clocks at the head of the group. This Chippendale walnut tall-case clock dates from the late 18th to early 19th century, and was made in Pennsylvania.

The broken-arch pediment is a classic Chippendale design motif.

The hood, or that part of the clock that is the facing surrounding the dial, should be easily removable. Over time, the molding upon which it rests, which is like a small drawer runner, is often damaged. A bit of repair in this area is not unusual, and if done well, will not greatly affect the clock's value.

If the pendulum appears suspiciously large in its case, that may indicate a marriage, or joining of parts from one clock to the parts or case of another. While this may not bother you from an aesthetic point of view, collectors, or true tall-case clock aficionados, will not approve.

This clock is 8 feet 1 inch tall. Longcase clocks were often reduced in height to fit into new surroundings, so collectors should inspect for truncated ornamentation or base designs that seem to end abruptly.

Finials such as the three urn-shaped ones crowning this clock are often lost and replaced or, if original, damaged. Check for new or filled holes or colors that do not match, which would indicate that the finials are not original

Serious collectors will look for repainting on the dial, which would be exposed using an ultraviolet light, just as ultraviolet light is used to expose inpainting on a work of fine art, such as an oil painting.

15

Books

Few things add warmth and beauty to a room like shelves of books. They are tangible reminders of stories read and lessons learned. They are sources of information as well as inspiration. They add a splash of color to any decorating scheme, and they are an indication to visitors of a home that is brimming with ideas and opinions.

Buying books, unlike buying, say, satinwood inlaid Pembroke tables is easy. There are, after all, billions of books in existence. *Collecting* books, however, is not at all simple. Keep in mind that what makes any object valuable—a small supply and a large demand—is true for books as well. But because they exist in such abundance, a book's condition takes on even greater significance. Book collectors also seek the earliest possible version of a particular book. This is called priority.

Unless there are extenuating circumstances, any defect, from the tiniest tear to the most subtle discoloration, can cause a book's value to drop dramatically. Books are graded on a scale with "as new"—or "very fine" or "mint"—at the top and "reading copy" on the bottom.

"As new" implies that a book is in the same condition, or very nearly so, as the day it was printed. No corners have been turned down, no words are underlined, the spine isn't broken and the dust jacket, if there is one, is in perfect shape. In other words, a book in mint condition has probably never been read.

A "fine" book is near mint, with perhaps a few slight signs of wear (someone has at least opened the book), while a "very good" book might have a few visible but not too obvious flaws.

A "good" book will show typical signs of wear and tear but would not, in most cases, be attractive to collectors unless it is highly desirable for other reasons.

A book in "fair" condition might be perfectly readable, but because of its defects, uncollectible.

A reading copy is basically worthless.

As with all collectibles, these condition ratings are subjective. Each bookseller decides on the rating a book deserves.

The concept of "priority," while more concrete, is a bit more difficult to understand. Book collectors usually want the earliest possible version of a book, the first book hot off the presses, especially in literature. If after a book goes to press an error is found—a missing comma, a misspelled word—the presses are stopped, the type is corrected, and the presses are restarted. This might happen again and again. Each time, the same stop-and-start routine occurs. These errors are called points and, for most collectors, especially when it comes to works of fiction, where facts aren't as important, the more points the better. Each printing is called an impression, state, or issue, depending on who's doing the talking. A book from that first impression, with the misplaced commas and misspelled words, is usually more valuable than a book from the third go-around, after everything has been corrected.

Remember, too, that "first edition" should not be construed to mean that a book is scarce or rare. After all, most of the thousands of books published each year *only* have a first edition.

QUESTIONS YOU'LL ALWAYS WANT TO ASK

Is the book a true first printing? Are there any points to the printing? Is it a first impression of the first edition?

ONE IMPORTANT THING: DUST JACKETS

The first dust jackets appeared on books around 1832 in England. In the United States they came into use around 1865 but didn't become standard until the early twentieth century. Even then, dust jackets, which today we take for granted as part of a book as much as the pages inside, were thought to be primarily what the name implied: a cover to keep dust from building up on the book, but not necessarily something for the owner to keep and maintain. Until about 1950 many people automatically discarded the cover before they shelved the book. Today, however, dust jackets are integral to book collecting. Any book published since the mid-twentieth century that does not have its cover intact and in excellent condition is considerably less valuable than one in which the cover exists and is as good as new. Dust jackets are important because aside from their intrinsic artistic value, they may have an author photo, words or blurbs by the author or others about the book or author, or an illustration that is important to the book but not in the book.

A dust jacket's condition is judged as harshly as the actual book—dust jackets rip and fade easily and get shelved so that their edges rip, a defect called chipping.

Sometimes a bookseller will mark a book F/VG, for instance, in which the F refers to the book and the VG to the dust jacket. In literary first editions in particular the dust jacket is far more important than the book itself. In fact, it can account for about 75 percent of the book's value.

PRACTICAL ADVICE

Any defect will lower a book's value: water stains, mold, foxing, tears to the binding, underlining or any other writing on pages, and broken bindings. Leather binding scuffs, so inspect it carefully. Former library books are rarely worth buying for the true collector; indications of one include call letters printed on the binding, library stamps, and a library envelope glued to the inside front.

Look for books signed by the author. If a book is inscribed to someone with a note of some sort, even better, and if it's inscribed to someone famous, better yet. A bookplate with a well-known name, indicating it was previously owned by that person, adds value to the book.

COLLECTOR'S CHOICE

Collecting books can be a lifelong passion that remains affordable, too, depending on your interests and the creative construct upon which you base your collection. There is no end to the type of collection you can create and no rules to go by, either. More than virtually any other collectible or antique, books can be gathered into truly imaginative collections. Here's a short list of themes around which many great collections have been built.

Particular author. This is probably the most common way to collect, and it's one of the most satisfying. Collect first editions of every book Anthony Powell ever had published, every slim volume of Anne Sexton's poetry, or the complete works of John Updike, including his novels and essays. You might choose an author you like, such as Oscar Wilde, and collect not only everything he published but also books about him and works written by friends, acquaintances, or academicians.

A related group of writers. Collecting the work of Dorothy Parker may be interesting, but it might be even more interesting to collect the work of the entire Algonquin Round Table, from Robert Benchley to Alexander Woollcott, who were part of the group of writers and bon vivants with whom she was associated in New York from about 1919 to 1929. Other groups of writers include the Bloomsbury group, from Clive Bell to Virginia Woolf; and the beat generation writers, such as Jack Kerouac, Hunter Thompson, and Allen Ginsberg.

The 100 greatest books. Many organizations and publications have sponsored lists of the 100 greatest books of one sort or another. Choose one that suits your interests and build a personal collection based on it. For instance, two of the more interesting lists include the Modern Library's top 100 novels in the English language from 1900 to 1998 and the reading list from St. John's College, in Santa Fe, New Mexico, which is known for its great-books curriculum. The Modern Library's list includes such books as *The Sound and the Fury* by William Faulkner; *The Wings of the Dove, The Ambassadors,* and *The Golden Bowl* by Henry James; and *Sons and Lovers,* by D. H. Lawrence. St. John's list is more comprehensive, including ancient as well as modern classics like Adam Smith's *Wealth of Nations,* Tolstoy's *War and Peace,* and *The Bear* by William Faulkner.

Banned books. As long as books have been published, certain books have been banned. A collection of banned books could provide an interesting way to think about books and what they mean. Some books that have been banned by various schools or libraries include Maya Angelou's *I Know Why the Caged Bird Sings,* which was said to be too sexually explicit; *A Wrinkle in Time* by Madeleine L'Engle, which was accused of undermining religious beliefs; and *The Adventures of Huckleberry Finn* by Mark Twain and *Little House in the Big Woods* by Laura Ingalls Wilder, both of which were said to be racially offensive.

People you admire. A very personal and meaningful collection can be built by making a list of people you admire, and collecting either their own writing or other authors' books about them. For instance, you might make a list that includes American heroines such as Eleanor Roosevelt, Barbara Jordan, Willa Cather, and Helen Keller, all of whom were authors as well as subjects of other books. A list of great contemporary Jewish American authors such as Saul Bellow, Cynthia Ozick, and Henry Roth would also make for an exciting collection.

Subject matter. Collections built around a particular subject that interests you can be a never-ending source of fascination. A collection comprising books about every president or a collection of books on the history of the automobile or on Cubism would provide years of challenge. You might choose a subject, such as presidents, and narrow it down to books solely about their lives during their presidency, or books solely on their personal lives instead of their political lives. If you're from Ohio, you might choose to collect books only about Ohio, such as the long-out-of-print books *Cincinnati Locomotive Builders 1845–1868* by John H. White, *Thomas Worthington: Father of Ohio Statehood* by Alfred Byron Sears, and *A History of Ohio* by Eugene Roseboom and Francis Weisenburger.

Is it true? A quirky collection can be built of biographical novels, which are largely fictional accounts of the lives of real people, such as Irving Stone's *Lust for Life,* about Vincent van Gogh; Gore Vidal's *Lincoln;* and Colleen McCullough's *Caesar.*

And the winner is . . . Many organizations present awards to books and authors and any collection based on the winners would be fascinating. The Nobel Prize for Literature comes to mind, of course, but there are many other, more specialized awards that might reflect your interests. They include the Edgar Awards for mystery books, with winners such as *Come to Grief* by Dick Francis and *The Long Goodbye* by Raymond Chandler; the Hugo Awards for science fiction, with *Foundation's Edge* by Isaac Asimov and *The Dispossessed* by Ursula K. Le Guin among its winners; and the Young Reader's Choice Awards, which has been given to Ian Fleming for *Chitty Chitty Bang Bang,* Eric Knight for *Lassie Come Home,* and Judy Blume for *Blubber.* This last could be a collection that will be cherished and added to by generations of your family.

Others. Some other themes for a collection might include imprints or printings by specific publishers; books by famous authors writing under pseudonyms, like Jane Somers (a.k.a. Doris Lessing), A. N. Roquelaure (Anne Rice), and Richard Bachman (Stephen King), among others; books you read as a child; books with errors or typos in them; or books that were pulled from print for legal reasons. You could also take a contrarian view and build a collection of books shunned by other collectors, such as Bibles (it's the most published book, and therefore unusually commonplace), textbooks, encyclopedias, book club printings, or ex–library books.

TAKING CARE OF YOUR COLLECTION

Do not store books near radiators or in attics or basements where temperatures are erratic. The ideal temperature at which to house books is 68 degrees.

Direct sunlight quickly fades book covers and yellows pages, and they will continue to fade even after they are removed from the sun.

Books are prone to mildew: make sure there's enough room on your bookshelves for air to circulate to prevent condensation.

When reaching for a book on a shelf don't grab the top of the spine, which will weaken over time; instead pull it off the shelf by the middle of the spine, even if you have to push the books on either side in slightly to get a firm grip on the book you want.

Bookends are not merely decorative objects; they also prevent warping.

Keep books out of rooms in which people smoke.

Ideally, shelve your books in glass-fronted shelves.

Try not to shelve books against exterior walls where there is any chance of water leakage.

Don't let books hang over the edge of the shelf; they need complete support.

Never leave a book open face down.

Use two hands when turning the pages of large books.

Never lick your fingers before turning the pages.

Never write in a book—or if you must, do it lightly in pencil.

Use very thin, acid-free paper bookmarks.

Do not store reviews or articles inside your books. They're often printed on acidic paper, and they can ruin the binding by their thickness.

To clean a matte cover or pages that are dirty, use a small cloth bag filled with eraser dust, available at art supply stores. Use Windex on a damp cloth to clean glossy dust jackets.

WORDS TO REMEMBER

Advance copy. A book sent out to reviewers, wholesalers, retailers, and members of the media; also called review copy.

Association copy. A book inscribed by the author and given to a person connected to the author.

Bibliophile. A lover and collector of books.

Bookplate. A label that identifies the owner of the book.

Colophon. A note at the end listing the title, author, printer, place of printing, and date.

Deckle edges. The rough, untrimmed edges of a sheet of handmade paper, highly prized by collectors; those who collect only books with deckle edges are known as deckle fetishists.

Ex–library book. A book that was at one time part of a lending library collection.

Folio. The page number.

Foxing. Rust marks on the pages.

Frontispiece. An illustration near the front of the book, often facing the title page.

Incunabula. Latin for "things in the cradle," referring, generally, to books printed before 1501.

Inscription. Anything written in the author's hand other than an autograph.

Juveniles. Children's books.

Limited edition. An edition limited in number. Perhaps because an illustration was suitable for only so many copies from the plate, the book is printed by hand, or the publisher wanted to create a scarce market.

List price. The original published price of the book.

Points. Errors and corrections in books.

16

Ceramics

Almost everyone is a collector of pottery or porcelain, whether she knows it or not. After all, the Haviland your grandmother gave you on the morning of your wedding, the everyday ware your family eats from every night, even the mugs you buy to remember a museum visit or a charity event, are pottery or porcelain of some sort.

Pottery and porcelain are both made from clay, they are relatively durable, they can be shaped and molded in extraordinary ways, and they have rich histories. Despite these similarities, however, it's easy to tell them apart.

Hold a pottery object up to the light. Its density will prevent any light from shining through. Pour water into an unglazed piece of pottery, though, and watch out. Unlike porcelain, unglazed pottery is porous. Pottery is generally thicker than porcelain, too, and has a coarser texture. Yet it's softer, less durable, and more prone to staining. Pottery cracks in a line instead of chipping. There's no "ping" when you flick it. Unlike porcelain, which is initially white, the mineral content in pottery creates color, which may range from red to yellow to green to brown, with many shades in between.

Porcelain—made from kaolin, a pure white clay, and petuntse, a type of feldspar found only in China—is almost everything pottery is not. That's because the firing process melts the petuntse, which forms a natural glass, which then fuses itself to the kaolin. The end result—porcelain—is nonporous, durable, translucent when held up to the light, colder to the touch than pottery, and likely to chip like glass. It has a sonorous "ping" when flicked gently.

There are two types of porcelain, hard-paste, often called true porcelain, and soft-paste, each with its own characteristics and collectibility.

Hard-paste porcelain, with its beautifully smooth, almost glasslike glaze, was first produced in China around two thousand years ago during the Han dynasty. Both Chinese and Japanese hard-paste porcelain was highly sought after in Europe after its introduction there in the fifteenth century, but despite many attempts, no one on the Continent was able to create it for several centuries.

While searching for the secrets of hard-paste porcelain, though, the Europeans added ground glass to clay and were able to obtain a better-quality ceramic, creamier in color than hard-paste. The finished pieces weren't as hard, dense, or nonporous as Chinese porcelain, however, and were referred to as soft-paste.

Then, in 1709, a breakthrough occurred. An alchemist named Johann Friedrich Böttger, while trying to spin gold from lead and copper, instead discovered the formula for hard-paste porcelain.

In 1710 a factory was quickly established in Meissen, Germany, and by 1713 works of hard-paste porcelain were being sold and cherished. Crossed swords are, to this day, the mark of Meissen porcelain, though they have been widely copied over the centuries. Another distinguishing feature of Meissen was the highly bronzed effect of the gilding, which was created by actually adding honey to the gilding before it was applied.

But knowing the difference between hard-paste and soft-paste is only the first thing a collector of porcelain needs to understand. Fortunately, it's relatively easy to tell them apart by comparing chips of each. You'll see that where the soft-paste appears slightly granular and porous, the hard-paste looks like opaque glass with a very thin film of glaze. In addition, on hard-paste figurines and bowls, for instance, the bottoms are left unglazed; on soft-paste the bottoms must be glazed to avoid absorbing moisture.

QUESTIONS YOU'LL ALWAYS WANT TO ASK

What is it made of?

Where and when was it made?

ONE IMPORTANT THING: MARKS

Marks are identifiers, usually underneath the glaze on the bottom or the back of a piece of pottery or porcelain. They are applied by one of four different methods: impressed into the clay by a stamp or seal, incised with a sharp tool, painted on, or printed on with engraved copper plates. None of these methods, unfortunately, is unique, and over the centuries marks have been altered, copied, faked, and erased. They are, in other words, notoriously poor determinants of authentification. So while useful to collectors, marks are not conclusions as much as they are clues.

A true mark, though, can identify an object's manufacturer and the date—sometimes down to the year and month—it was created. Sometimes it can even assign the piece to a particular maker or decorative artist.

There are many books detailing the marks on objects from hundreds of different factories throughout the world. Any collector, whether serious or casual, will want to own several, as they're the most important tool available to properly identify marks.

Once the mark is identified, you can use the object's color, style, decorative motif, and material to determine if the mark is from the right period. In other words, if a manufacturer didn't start using a pink underglaze until the late nineteenth century, but a mark on a piece with a pink underglaze indicates the object was made in the late eighteenth century, further investigation needs to be done.

By law, English ceramics were stamped "Trademark" after 1855 and "Ltd." after about 1880. United States law after 1891 stipulated that all pieces of imported pottery be marked in some way with the country of origin; the law was amended in 1914 to include the words "Made in," important tidbits to know when dating porcelain or pottery.

PRACTICAL ADVICE

The bottom of any object should show normal wear and tear in the form of minor scratches and scuff marks where it has been picked up and put down. Plates should indicate minor cutting marks from knives. Too new an appearance or too smooth a feel indicates that the object is newer than you might expect.

No porcelain "ping" indicates the object may have a crack somewhere on its surface, even if it's invisible to the naked eye.

Look for inconsistencies or unevenness in glaze and color. If either is different in tone or hue where the decorative motif indicates it shouldn't be, that's a sign that there may have been some repair in the past.

Don't depend on your eyes alone. Gently run your fingers over the entire object, especially around its edges and lip, for any change in texture. You'll feel hairline cracks or chips more easily than you'll see them.

Decoration should fit with the age in which the object was made. In other words, the figures on a piece supposedly painted in the eighteenth century would not be wearing Victorian-era clothes.

Look for stains or brown discolorations.

Poor calligraphy on Asian ceramics is an indication that a piece may be a fake.

Closely examine and feel finials, spouts, handles, and any other protrusions. On figurines, inspect arms, legs, facial features like noses and lips, and folds of clothing.

There are hundreds of manufacturers of pottery and porcelain, and collectors are attracted to each for their own reasons. Here are just a few of the more popular makers, with some information you might want to discuss with a seller.

Bauer, southern California. Creator of simply shaped, vividly colored domestic ware, Bauer was founded in 1885 in Paducah, Kentucky, where it first created redware flowerpots and vases as well as brown-glazed crocks and jugs. It relocated to California, where it became known for its green matte glaze and Ring-Ware, brightly colored concentric circles of design in reds, blues, greens, and oranges. Some Bauer is marked.

Coalport, England. Known for porcelain objects with applied flowers, called Coalbrookdale, and opulently painted floral designs, Coalport, founded in 1750, was also a major supplier of white porcelain to independent painters, meaning that not all Coalport porcelain was decorated by Coalport artists.

Delft. Known for its white glaze made from tin oxide, Delft was first made in Holland in the late seventeenth century and later in England. Usually decorated in a blue-and-white palette and often influenced by Chinese motifs, Delft made everyday ware as well as ornamental objects. English Delft is simpler in design and rarely marked; Dutch Delft is considerably more ornate. Tin glaze is soft and chips easily, so finding older objects in good condition can be a challenge.

Frankoma, Oklahoma. Founded in 1933 and utilizing the local clay deposits, Frankoma's designs are often inspired by Native American themes. Simple, durable, and rugged, it's not surprising that Frankoma's palette is composed of earth tones. Prairie Green and Desert Gold are the most desirable colors, but Frankoma can also be found in blue, brown, rose, and even orange. Sometimes the underlying clay shows through the glaze, which adds a distinctive look. Martha Stewart collects Frankoma.

Grueby, Boston. Known since its founding in 1894 for handmade objects in organic shapes, Grueby was decorated with matte glazes in greens, yellows, browns, and other colors, and with hand-tooled, applied adornments depicting leaves, flowers, and buds. Among the many objects Grueby produced, its vases and tiles are most popular. Some Tiffany lampshades have Grueby bases.

Limoges, France. Ever since kaolin deposits were found in Limoges in 1768, the area has remained a hub of fine porcelain manufacturers. Many factories are located there, but objects were not marked with the name Limoges in any great number until a century after its reputation was established. A lot of what was produced in Limoges was painted by independent artists, so while the quality of the porcelain is consistent, the decoration is not always of the same high distinction.

Meissen, Germany. The place where it all began in 1710, Meissen is still one of the most collectible and copied of all porcelains. Known for intricate and graceful figurines, its decorative motifs are often opulent, inspired by idyllic landscapes, romantic vistas, and classical subjects. Its mark of crossed swords has been widely forged for centuries; a mark with a slash through the crossed swords might indicate a piece that is less than perfect. Meissen is known for its attention to detail, even down to its mark, and poorly illustrated swords usually indicate a fake.

Minton, England. The factory at Minton made everything from elaborate majolica and ornamental objects to simple earthenware and bone china. Known for its use of the *pâte-sur-pâte* technique, Minton's best period is considered the mid- to late nineteenth century. Almost all Minton is marked.

Rookwood, Cincinnati. Impressed with the RP mark, with its letters back to back, Rookwood's sophisticated colors range from the early "Standard" glazes in dark browns, oranges, reds, and yellows to what it called iris and sea green to the later matte glazes. Since its founding in 1880, Rookwood's artists have often signed their work by incising or painting their signatures on the bottoms, making the pieces more valuable and collectible. Rookwood was hand-thrown. Look for vases, tiles, plaques, and even lamps.

Roseville, Ohio. Known for its richly hued glazes over painted, incised, or modeled decoration, Roseville pottery features hand-carved relief. Each new year's output was named after a flower—Iris, Jonquil, Sunflower, and Wisteria, among others. After the First World War, Roseville was no longer handmade, so on the inside you can often see the inverted relief pattern from the surface.

Sèvres, France. Sèvres, the national porcelain factory of France, was known for its soft blue backgrounds and fine figurines of biscuit (unglazed porcelain). Louis XV was a major shareholder in the company for two decades beginning in 1752 and actually sold Sèvres from his personal rooms at Versailles. The name Sèvres used to refer specifically to the Royal Porcelain factory, but it now refers to any porcelain from the town of Sèvres. Sèvres is often decorated with flowers, putti, cupids, shepherdesses, and nymphs.

Spode, England. Founder Josiah Spode invented bone china—hard-paste combined with calcinated bone ash. Since 1800, Spode has produced everything from everyday dinner services to parian ware to lavishly gilded ornamental objects. It is also known for its use of exotic bird themes in its decoration. Spode is still the standard for English bone china.

Van Briggle, Colorado Springs. After working for Rookwood in Cincinnati, Artus Van Briggle moved west in 1899 to found his own factory. Made of Rocky Mountain clays, Van Briggle pottery is known for languorous shapes, organic decorative motifs, and matte glazes. Van Briggle melded sculptural forms with ceramics, often creating works that seemed more ornamental than useful but were still utilitarian in nature.

Wedgwood, England. Known for its unglazed stoneware called jasperware, named after the natural stone jasper, which it resembles, Wedgwood is hugely collectible. Most jasperware designs are based on drawings by French artists of the day, who were inspired by scenes from antiquity. A nineteenth-century competitor, Wedgewood (note the second *e*), made lower-quality objects that are often mistaken for genuine Wedgwood. There are more than twenty-five authentic Wedgwood marks.

TAKING CARE OF YOUR COLLECTION

Before washing or dusting an object, cover your work area with towels or other padding. You will be surprised at how much damage even the slightest tap of a pottery or porcelain object against a counter or porcelain sink can do.

Use a soft, thick watercolor brush for dusting, and be exceptionally gentle.

Washing most pieces with a damp cotton ball is all that is necessary. Always use tepid, soapy water. Keep all of the object away from extremes in heat or cold.

Let plates air-dry. Dust very ornate pieces using a hand-held hair dryer on low.

Never pick up a piece by its spout, lid, or even handle. Always use two hands on larger objects.

Don't stack any ceramic objects except, if you must, plates. When stacking plates, always use thick layers of felt in between each one. Newspaper can rub off on objects and stain, and bubble wrap can damage the glaze. Hang cups from hooks, if possible, to avoid their chipping one another on a shelf.

Don't soak objects in water. The moisture can seep beneath the glaze.

Be very careful washing gilded edges, as the gold can scratch off easily.

Never use bleach. It will literally eat your pottery from the inside out.

Soapy detergents may damage and discolor the bright glaze of household pottery such as Bauer and Fiesta ware.

WORDS TO REMEMBER

Art pottery. A movement that began in the United States after the 1876 Centennial celebration in Philadelphia, art pottery was usually handmade, organic in shape and decoration, and functional.

Bisque, or biscuit. Porcelain purposely left unglazed.

Bone china. Porcelain containing calcinated bone, made by Spode, Minton, and Coalport, among other factories, after 1820.

Celadon. A semi-opaque glaze, usually gray-green, applied to stoneware before firing.

Chigger bite. A very thin chip no larger than a pinhead.

Chip. A chip larger than a pinhead.

Crazing. A spiderweb-like network of cracks seen in some glazed surfaces, sometimes deliberately created for decoration, sometimes not.

Gilding. Applied gold on ceramics.

Glaze. A lustrous coating used for decorative purposes and to make porous objects nonporous, or watertight, glaze can be translucent, opaque, or colored.

Hairline crack. A thin, hardly visible crack.

Lead glaze. A glaze that is colored with metal oxides.

Parian. Popular nineteenth-century material used to make inexpensive reproduction marble sculptures.

Pâte-sur-pâte. Meaning "paste on paste" in French, this ware is decorated with built-up layers of translucent white porcelain slip-carved to create a low-relief, cameo-like design.

Salt glaze. A glaze made by throwing salt into the kiln while the pottery was being fired.

Sgraffito. Scratching into the body of a ceramic object before firing to create an incised design.

Terra-cotta. Pottery purposely left unglazed.

Tin glaze. A glaze that contains tin oxide.

Transferware. A mid-eighteenth-century process that uses an inked copper plate from which a design is transferred and fixed by firing. You can identify transferware by the crosshatching caused by the tools on the copper plate.

17

Dolls

There are two kinds of people in the world: people who love dolls and people who don't. Doll collectors might disagree or shake their heads in disbelief at the idea that some people don't like dolls, given the huge crowds that attend doll shows and conventions, bid at doll auctions, read the many doll publications, and converse online in doll chat rooms and news groups. Everyone, it must seem to them, loves dolls.

For collectors, the appeal is obvious. Dolls are a gentle reminder of their childhood, a way to look back and remember and reconnect with the person they used to be. Some people collect Mortimer Snerd or Baby Snooks dolls that take them back to the 1930s. Others collect Crissy dolls, with their orange hair swirling out of their head, to remind them of their 1970s Brady Bunch childhood. Doll collecting might even be a way to extend a part of their childhood into their adulthood in an acceptable and challenging manner.

The most collectible dolls were made in Europe, primarily in England, France, and Germany, from the eighteenth through the twentieth centuries. There were as many doll makers as there were types of dolls, and doll manufacturing and production often followed technological advancement. The popularity of dolls grew as the development of steam-powered trains allowed for better distribution, for instance, while the increased availability of home sewing machines in the 1860s made it easier for individuals to create their own dolls and doll clothing.

Generally, dolls made before 1930 are considered antique, and they're often the most collectible as well. But no matter how old or new they are, most dolls share one attribute: they were meant to be played with by children. That means, of course, that the great majority of dolls are not in perfect condition. They are sometimes missing limbs, eyes, original accessories and clothing, and they are mussed up from years of tea parties. The more delicate the doll, the less chance that it survived for very long. This is the bane of the collector's existence, since the most collectible dolls are the most delicate. But of course, that's the challenge as well.

QUESTIONS YOU'LL ALWAYS WANT TO ASK

What materials are the head and body made from?

Have any features been repaired or replaced?

ONE IMPORTANT THING: EYES

They say that eyes are mirrors into the soul. That may be as true for dolls as it is for humans. Eyes are the feature, perhaps more than any other, that lend dolls the humanity through which we can imagine them real. If they're intaglio or painted on, the doll has a static look that never changes. They see the world and let the world see them in a constant state of readiness.

But many other dolls have glass eyes, and they can be very expressive. These eyes might be fixed, or they may be googly eyes, which move from side to side. They might even be sleeping eyes, with lids that shut when the doll is laid down to rest.

Glass eyes crack easily, and such damage might diminish a doll's value. Cracks in blue eyes are fairly obvious; in dark brown eyes they're not so noticeable so they must be examined closely. Paperweight eyes, glass eyes that have white threads drawn through their irises to give a depth of color and luminosity that would otherwise be absent, have crystal bulges when viewed from the side. If the eyes seem either slightly too small or too big for their sockets, they may have been replaced.

Sleeping eyes are easily damaged—any moving part is—and may have been replaced by fixed eyes. If a doll has fixed eyes yet sports two holes in the back of its head, you'll know the original eyes were replaced. Why? Because doll makers used to tie movable eyes to the holes with string to prevent their moving about or breaking during transport. The retailer would cut the string before putting the doll on display. Replaced eyes shouldn't deter your buying or spoil your enjoyment of a particular doll. That depends on how *you* see your collection.

PRACTICAL ADVICE

Save the box and all packing material of dolls you buy.

A well-known doll in an unusual size—either very big or very small—will be more valuable than a rarer doll in the size with which everyone is familiar.

A restored doll is worth less than a cracked doll in most instances.

Until about 1875 doll hair was dark.

Crazing is considered acceptable on dolls that are otherwise valuable.

Replaced heads and limbs should be of the same period as the original.

A bad original wig is better than any replacement wig.

Original clothing on a doll always adds value; the better the condition, the greater the value.

COLLECTOR'S CHOICE

Dolls are head cases. In other words, they are classified not by their clothing or the composition of their bodies but by their heads. A bisque-headed doll is considered a bisque doll even if her body is kid. A wax doll has a wax head even if her body is made from calico. Antique doll heads were made of many different materials, but these are the five types of doll heads that collectors covet:

Queen Anne. Though she died in 1714, most wooden figure dolls made from about 1690 through the 1840s are referred to as Queen Anne dolls. No one is quite sure why. Though they were manufactured for several centuries, their true heyday was the second half of the eighteenth century.

Given the monarch after whom they're named, it's not surprising that most of the earliest Queen Anne dolls were made in England by local craftsmen who hand-carved their bodies, painted their features, and even created their clothes. They were elaborately jointed, as well. Later, the dolls were lathe-turned and made in large numbers, which in addition to the fact that wood is fairly indestructible, is why once in a great while one can still be found on the market today.

The Queen Anne doll is easily recognizable, too, as the head and body are one solid piece with a high forehead, close-set features, blown-glass or carved-wood eyes, which did not have pupils, and sometimes a costume sewn directly to the body. Sometimes the wigs of these dolls, few of which have survived outside museums, were made from real hair.

China. As Queen Anne dolls began to lose their cachet, china dolls gained prominence. They were especially popular from about 1840 to 1880, though they were made until after the First World War. They were called china dolls not in reference to the country but to the material from which their heads, and sometimes their limbs as well, were made. Their heads had a particularly appealing glossy appearance due to their manufacturing method, which included being painted and heavily glazed after the first firing, then subsequently refired at a lower temperature.

For the most part made in Germany, china dolls were almost exclusively black-haired and blue-eyed; any other colors are highly sought-after by collectors. They were usually dressed in the fashions of the day and sometimes had embroidery or jewelry molded onto their shoulder plate. Like dolls that preceded and followed them, they can be dated to some extent by their hairstyles, which were contemporaneous with what women were really wearing at the time. China dolls made in the 1840s, for instance, had sausage curls on either side of their heads in what was known as the covered-wagon style. Each decade's dolls had a different hairstyle, mimicking what the girls and women who bought the dolls actually wore.

China heads were sometimes sold separately for people who wanted to make their own dolls, and while some were marked, it was done on the head's interior. This presents a conundrum for collectors, since to look for a mark they have to remove the head of a doll, which presents a real chance of damage and devalues the doll, since it is then no longer in its original condition.

Papier-mâché. The most popular of all nineteenth-century dolls, those made from molded papier-mâché—a mixture of paper, glue, and other materials—are, because of their fragility, among the most difficult to find.

After papier-mâché heads were removed from the mold and dried, they were painted and varnished or dipped in wax for a more natural appearance. Most papier-mâché dolls had molded hair painted black, some styles of which were so elaborate that they required eight to ten molds for the hair alone. Occasionally they had wigs. They usually had wooden limbs and painted eyes, though a few rare ones had glass eyes, which collectors prize.

Germany was the main producer of papier-mâché dolls, and until World War I it remained the doll-making center of Europe, though the heads were often sent to France where they were attached to bodies and clothed in ornate costumes. For much of the century bamboo teeth were used by the major German doll maker.

Papier-mâché dolls were made in France and the United States as well. In fact, the first U.S. patent taken out for any doll was by Ludwig Greiner of Philadelphia, who in 1855 patented his papier-mâché Nina doll. Nina has even more historical significance than that, however: during the Civil War her head was used as a receptacle in which medicinal morphine was smuggled across enemy lines.

Wax. No dolls were more lifelike than those made from wax. After all, wax has a translucence and a warm glow that porcelain and papier-mâché cannot match. Wax is by its very nature soft, and gave the dolls an alert and animated expression.

That very softness was also the reason the dolls' popularity waned, however. In the cold the wax cracked; in the heat it melted; and it was incredibly vulnerable to fingerprints. Nevertheless, these dolls, made from beeswax or East Indian wax, were particularly popular in England from about the 1840s until the 1870s, when bisque dolls began to be imported. The wax dolls' lifelike appearance was heightened by the use of brown or blue blown-glass eyes as well as hair and eyelashes that were inserted strand by strand into the wax using a blunt needle.

Due to their fragility, few nineteenth-century wax dolls still exist.

Poured-wax dolls, made in England from about 1850 to 1930, were an outgrowth of the Roman Catholic practice of creating religious statues from wax. Eventually, the craftsmen who created them also began to make dolls. There were also wax dolls in which a thin coat of wax was poured over doll heads and limbs made from a composite of other materials. Those that were made in England were usually marked, those in Germany were not.

Bisque. In the early nineteenth century a German doll maker noticed that the unglazed heads he was removing from the kiln had a matte finish that more resembled a girl's soft, supple skin tones than did traditional porcelain. Soon these heads, called bisque, like the unglazed porcelain used for household and ornamental objects, became immensely popular throughout Europe and the United States, especially from about 1860 to 1890, though they continued to be made until after World War I.

Though bisque heads were mass-produced, each was individually hand-decorated, a task that could take hours. Their eyebrows and eyelashes were often composed of many time-consuming and delicate brushstrokes meant to imitate real hair, and their mohair wigs were as elaborately and laboriously coiffed as the hairstyles of the upper-class women whose daughters played with the dolls.

Bisque dolls made in Paris were more ornate than those made in Germany. Typically they had almond-shaped paperweight eyes, which had a unique depth and luminescence. Scores of milliners, shoemakers, wigmakers, and seamstresses in the Choiseul area in Paris catered solely to the doll trade, while the city's most prestigious doll maker, Jumeau, employed legions of its own. French bisque dolls are particularly recognized by the sophistication of their dress.

TAKING CARE OF YOUR COLLECTION

Your collection should be displayed or stored away from direct sunlight, dust, and cigarette smoke, all of which will damage your dolls and their original packaging.

Dolls should not be stored above a radiator, air conditioner, or fireplace.

Because the lacquer used on many wooden dolls was water-soluble, any water with which it comes into contact will leave a dull, matte finish in its wake.

To clean a wax head, use a tiny bit of cold cream on a soft white cotton cloth and ever so gently wipe the doll's face; remove all the cold cream when you're finished, but do not under any circumstances use water.

Before you store or display your collection, remove rubber bands or adhesives that might have been used to hold the doll in place in its box.

Washing or even brushing a doll's hair may cause damage to the hair or disturb its original coiffure and lower its value considerably.

Periodically check wooden dolls for insect infestation.

Some modern doll clothes can be put in a pillowcase and run through the delicate cycle of your washer.

To clean a doll's cloth body, use a vacuum cleaner with a nylon over the nozzle.

Inspect dolls where their heads meet their bodies. Glue can harden and shrink, causing damage. Be sure to examine antique dolls gently.

Dolls with inset eyes should be stored face down.

WORDS TO REMEMBER

Applied ears. Ears attached to the doll's head after it has been molded.

Ball-jointed. A method of joining body parts by using little wood balls at the joints for movement.

Bonnet head. A doll that has a hat or bonnet molded to its head.

Character doll. A doll made to look like a real person.

Closed mouth. A doll sculpted so that its lips are closed.

Domed head. A head made with a closed top; also called a bald head.

Fashion doll. A French or German bisque doll made to wear the fashions of the day.

Flirty eyes. Eyes that move from side to side.

Googly eyes. Big side-glancing eyes.

Inset eyes. Eyes that are set into the doll's head and which do not move.

Intaglio eyes. Eyes molded into the head and meant to be painted.

Kid. Soft leather used to make the bodies of fashion dolls.

Mitten hands. Hands that are molded with only the thumb separated.

Molded ears. Ears that are molded right onto the doll's head.

Open-closed mouth. A mouth molded to appear open but which does not have an opening in the bisque.

Open mouth. Mouth molded open to reveal teeth or tongue.

Pate. A plate that covers the hole in an open-head doll.

Shoulder head. A doll's head and shoulders that are molded as one to attach to a kid or cloth body.

Sleep eyes. Doll eyes that are wide open when the doll is vertical but closed when the doll is lying down flat.

18

Fine Arts

When collectors speak of fine art, they're usually referring to paintings, prints, drawings, and sculptures. Sure, there may be silver that is fine, and glass that is fine, and even Barbie dolls that are fine, but they're not usually considered fine art. Neither is folk art or tramp art.

Learning about fine art means learning to see it in a new light and to embrace it instead of being intimidated by it. Walking through the Metropolitan Museum of Art in New York, for instance, with its walls of Titians and Caravaggios, its Winslow Homers and John Singer Sargents, may make people feel that collecting oil paintings is out of their league, a pastime of the rich that is unavailable to everyone else. But that is simply not true. A lot of paintings have been created through the centuries, and though many of them are expensive and out of the reach of most people, even the rich, just as many are still reasonably priced in galleries and at auctions.

What does it mean to see an oil painting in a new light? Most people see a surface image, which is really only the most obvious part of a painting. Oil paint is made up of vegetable or mineral powders mixed with oil, which binds them together. Oil paints are thick and are often applied with a brush, though some artists use a knife as if they are frosting a cake. They dry thick, too, though the actual drying process can take years, which is why most oil paintings are covered in varnish.

But before an artist can begin to paint, in most instances she has to prepare a canvas by stretching it over a frame and priming it with gesso to keep the paint from being absorbed by the canvas. Paint is then applied on top of the gesso and is really separate from the surface upon which it rests. Knowing this will heighten your enjoyment of looking at paintings and allow you to see the parts that make up the whole.

Similarly, knowing the process by which various types of prints are made (which is explained below) will help you refine your taste and enjoy collecting even more.

Prints, due to their generally lower price point, are a great way to start collecting. They have an intimate appeal that most oil pictures cannot duplicate, and they are easier to live with, more human-scaled.

Paintings and prints are treasured by many people of relatively ordinary means. The key is to understand what you're looking at, buy what you like, and appreciate the difference between collectibles that are fine and fine art that is collectible.

QUESTIONS YOU'LL ALWAYS WANT TO ASK

What medium is it?

Is it an original or a reproduction?

ONE IMPORTANT THING: DETERMINING PRICE

The price of artwork is ruled to a great extent by the laws of supply and demand. But with fine art, there are other important considerations.

Fine art is more subject to vogues and fads than many other arts. An artist or movement may be fashionable in one decade and command high prices, only to lose favor as another artist or movement gains in popularity. The prices for one artist's work may level off or decrease as collectors' demand levels off, too. Then a book or a movie or a museum exhibition may catapult him back into the public eye, spurring a critical reassessment, and once again the prices for his work may increase. This happened recently with pre-Raphaelite paintings, whose popularity and prices waned in the early twentieth century and were rekindled in the late 1990s after major retrospectives at the Metropolitan Museum of Art in New York and the Musée d'Orsay in Paris.

Prices are also sometimes based on the period during an artist's lifetime when a work was completed. A painting from the beginning of Picasso's blue period may have more cachet than one from later on, as it may seem more influential, more significant, than work from other eras of his working life.

Additionally, with fine art, size does sometimes matter. A large, complicated painting may command a higher price than another picture by the same artist in similar condition from a similar period.

Lastly, it's common for prices to spike after an artist's death. They sometimes level off later on, but occasionally they remain high. After all, from that point forward, the artist's creative output is at an end.

PRACTICAL ADVICE

Always get a receipt of the authenticity of the work, as well as a condition report, from the dealer.

By looking at an oil painting under a black light in a dark room you'll be able to inspect it for inpainting, overpainting, and surface cracks in the paint.

In an older oil painting a certain amount of restoration is acceptable, but it must be well done and not too extensive.

If a work is old and not too extensively restored, the canvas should not be too taut.

When buying an oil painting, always inspect it out of its frame to see if it's been remounted, relined, cut down from a larger picture, or otherwise cropped.

Look at the back of a canvas. Against the light you'll spot tiny holes, tears, patches, or repairs that might not show from the front.

Use a magnifying glass to examine the paint for flaking or fading.

Before you buy a painting by a dead artist, look into his catalog *raissoné*, if there is one, to authenticate the work's existence.

Before the nineteenth century, European painters rarely signed their work.

When buying works on paper, such as prints, always remove the frame and mat to examine the paper for stains or discoloring, mold damage, and foxing.

Be wary of works on paper in which the paper has remnants of adhesive tape or is brittle, folded, or torn in any way.

If old paper is bright white, smell it. If it smells like bleach, it has probably been bleached and not thoroughly rinsed, which means that damage may appear later on.

Use ultraviolet-filtering Plexiglas when framing your pictures.

Don't judge a picture in general by its frame—it makes no contribution to the picture's value.

COLLECTOR'S CHOICE

Like paintings, prints are more than just the image you see. Unlike painting, it's not the buildup of paint that lends the picture depth; it is the process *behind* the picture. Some prints, such as Japanese woodcuts, are created by the relief process, in which the line of the plate to be printed is raised; other prints are done by the intaglio process, where the line to be printed is below the surface of the plate. Finally, other prints are called planographs, in which the line to be printed isn't above or below the surface of the plate but drawn on it.

The three most popular types of prints are engravings, etchings, and lithographs.

Engravings. Engraving, first done in the mid-fifteenth century, is the oldest form of intaglio. The artist uses a sharp tool called a burin to cut into a copper or zinc plate. Burins produce clear incisions that ultimately create sharp, crisp lines, because the cut areas are polished so that they're parallel with the plate surface. Using a burin requires strength and patience. The amount of pressure on the burin causes the width of the lines to vary. They're thinnest at the ends, and they taper gradually and gracefully. Yet precisely because using a burin does require determination and strength—it scoops the metal from the plate instead of merely scratching it—the finished product is not as free-flowing or spontaneous-looking as an etching, whose lines are incised by acid, giving the artist more chance for intricacy.

Once an engraver's incisions are completed, ink is applied and a type of cloth called tarlatan is used to wipe clean the plate. The ink remains in the furrows created by the burin, the paper is placed on top of the plate, and together they're run through a press.

This is a time-consuming, laborious procedure that results in precise works of art that have been prized by collectors for centuries. Collectors seek out pictures with clear, sharp lines, sometimes with swaths of color created by nuanced lines placed in close proximity to one another.

Etchings. Invented about a century after the engraving process, etching, like engraving, is an intaglio procedure. Unlike engraving, however, it allows for a more freehand look, with thick lines and thin lines, hatching and crosshatching. An exceptionally well done etching often looks like an exceptional drawing. That's its charm and its appeal.

To create an etching, the artist first covers a copper or zinc plate with a layer of wax, called a ground. With an etching needle the artist then draws on the waxed plate, exposing the metal plate beneath the wax.

Once the design is complete, the waxed plate is dipped into an acid called a mordant, which eats away at the metal along the exposed lines drawn with the needle. Some artists say the acid "attacks" the metal, which is why the dip is referred to as a bite. There's usually more than one bite, with each creating deeper and thicker lines. After the baths are completed, the wax is wiped from the plate before the printing begins.

Collectors look for precise, distinct lines. When a copper plate is used (zinc is used, but is less common), the prints are often drawn from the first to come off the plate, because as copper, which is relatively soft, keeps going through the process for further impressions, the edges become weaker and the lines more ambiguous.

Older etchings are often recognizable by the embossed plate marks on the outermost edges of the paper, so it is common to remove a print from its frame to inspect it. This will also indicate that the etching is original and not a photographic reproduction.

Lithographs. The word lithography comes from the Greek *lithos,* meaning stone, and *graphein,* meaning to write. These words were joined together as one in Bavaria during the first years of the eighteenth century to create a process based on the simple, enduring fact that oil and water do not mix.

The process calls for an artist to use a grease pencil–like tool to draw an image on a metal plate or stone. Afterward water is washed over the surface, but it only adheres to where the greasy image *isn't* and the ink that is later used only sticks to where the greasy image is.

Since there is no incising, but only drawing on the plate or stone's surface, lithos, as they're commonly called, are planographs. The process, in which the artist draws as if she were working with a pencil and paper, allows for the most free flowing, impulsive-looking type of print (even though in reality it is as well planned beforehand as the others). In general, a good lithograph is indistinguishable from an original drawing.

Collectors check for authenticity by looking for an ever-so-slight relief of ink, and even sniff for a distinctive inky odor that often lasts for years after the lithograph's creation.

TAKING CARE OF YOUR COLLECTION

Never hang an oil painting over a fireplace. Smoke and heat will damage it.

Hang oil paintings away from direct or fluorescent light. Do not hang a painting over a radiator or air conditioner.

Avoid hanging oil paintings or prints on exterior walls that may be damp, cold, or warm.

Oil paintings are delicate works of art that only need to be dusted gently with a feather; if they really need to be cleaned, consult a professional.

Never touch the surface of watercolors, pastels, or oil paintings.

Do not smoke or use aerosol sprays near an oil picture or a print.

Store and display your pictures away from extremes of heat and cold.

Before handling a print, wash your hands. Better yet, wear white cotton gloves. The oil on your fingers can quickly and permanently damage paper.

Make sure the surface upon which you are placing a print is clean.

Spray glass cleaner on a slightly damp cloth instead of directly on the glass in a frame, as the cleaner can drip around the edges of the glass and damage your painting or print.

Dry air makes paper brittle, but damp air makes it buckle, so display your works on paper in properly humidified rooms.

WORDS TO REMEMBER

Artist's proof. The proofs an artist pulls before the final edition is created in order to check for design and detail.

Burin. An engraving tool.

Burr. The little ragged curl of metal created by incising in copper or zinc.

Contemporary art. Pictures made after World War II.

Foxing. Mold growth indicated by circular spots on the paper.

Impasto. The building up of layers of oil paint to add a three-dimensionality to a surface.

Inpainting. The precise repainting of a damaged area.

Intaglio. Any printing process in which a block or plate has been cut or bitten into, with ink then forced into the incised lines.

Mat burn. Discoloration of the area on an impression that was covered by the mat.

Medium. The material the artist uses, like oil or pastels, to create a work.

Mordant. A corroding material used in etching.

Overpainting. An addition of too much new paint, which alters the appearance of the work.

Relining. Taking a work off the frame and attaching to another support, like a board or canvas.

Restrike. An additional printing of the original plate, usually not authorized by the artist.

Scrim. The cloth used for wiping an inked plate.

Stretcher. The frame over which the canvas is stretched.

Tusche. The greasy ink used in lithography.

19

Furniture

Things are seldom what they seem,
Skim milk masquerades as cream,
Highlows pass as patent leathers,
Jackdaws strut in peacocks' feathers.
—HMS PINAFORE

Is a Queen Anne chair a Queen Anne chair only if it was made around the time Queen Anne ruled? Is a Chippendale chest-on-chest a Chippendale only if there was an engraving of it in Thomas Chippendale's 1754 opus, *The Gentleman and Cabinet Maker's Director*? The answer to both these questions is, more or less, yes.

The idea that something is Queen Anne, Chippendale, Sheraton, Victorian, or Art Deco is more than merely an idea. A genuine Queen Anne, Chippendale, Sheraton, Victorian, or Art Deco chair, for instance, has meaning beyond its mere existence as a chair, since whatever style it is was influenced by the one that came before it, and influenced those that came after it.

If the answer to the question above was no—as in no, a Chippendale chest-on-chest isn't real *only* if there was an engraving of it in Chippendale's famous opus—then authenticating furniture, and seeing furniture in the continuum of history, would be impossible.

Style doesn't exist in a vacuum, and while designers and cabinetmakers throughout history have taken objects that already existed and in some cases improved upon them, altered them, or rejiggered them to suit the times, what they produced has to be studied—stylistically, at least—in the context of the period when they were made.

That being the case, a twentieth-century machine-made chair would not be correctly identified as Queen Anne, no matter what Queen Anne–like design characteristics it possessed. It would be perfectly reasonable, however, to refer to a chair such as this as "in the Queen Anne style."

The distinction between real and unreal, authentic and inauthentic, old and new, is not relative. Those who buy or collect furniture have to decide for themselves what's acceptable, which truths they believe, and what "antique" means to them. A Hepplewhite chair made in 1802 is surely a Hepplewhite and should be judged accordingly, but how about a Hepplewhite-style chair made in 1902?

Such a chair isn't Hepplewhite, no matter how many Hepplewhite design characteristics it exemplifies. It is, after all, about more than the design. Those who collect Hepplewhite furniture expect it to have been made *during* the Hepplewhite period. Anything else—while perhaps lovely to look at and sturdy—would be considered only decorative.

QUESTIONS YOU'LL ALWAYS WANT TO ASK

Is it original to the period?

Has it been repaired or restored? If so, where?

ONE IMPORTANT THING: WORMS

You may not realize this, but in old furniture, holes burrowed by worms or beetle larvae may be desirable!

Over the decades, and in some cases, centuries, it's inevitable that furniture will come to house worms, especially if it is made from pine, walnut, oak, or maple (for some reason, worms don't care for mahogany). This is especially true of older furniture that sat for eons in environments that weren't as sanitary or as well sealed as are our interiors today. Furniture was more exposed to the elements, and sometimes those elements had worms.

It's not that the worms burrowed in; it's that they were hatched in the wood and then tunneled their way *out*. Today some owners or manufacturers actually *put* wormholes into a new piece of furniture to make it appear old. To catch these owners at their own game, administer the straight-pin test, which will help you determine if a hole is recent or not. Before you do, however, there are a couple of things you need to know. One, worms don't crawl in a straight line, but at an angle. Two, worms don't always create holes of the same depth. Armed with this information, a pin is the perfect tool with which to determine the real or fake worminess of most holes. Additionally, wormholes are often filled with a waxy buildup or dirt; a hole that is clean and smooth is yet another indication that it's man-made.

Once you know if the holes are real or fake, you can factor that information into what you are willing to pay. Fake holes don't necessarily mean you shouldn't buy a particular piece of furniture—after all, it might otherwise be the perfect piece for your front hall or den—and real holes don't necessarily mean you should. It's just one more piece of information to know, to understand, and to use in making your decision.

PRACTICAL ADVICE

Going into Ethan Allen or Bloomingdale's to look at furniture with an eye toward buying is difficult enough. Looking at antique chairs, tables, and chests is doubly so. After all, you know that the objects in retail stores are new and in good condition. Their quality is as high as it was the day they were made, which probably wasn't so long ago.

Antiques present an entirely different set of circumstances, and knowing what to look for—and what not to worry about—can mean the difference between buying an antique you'll cherish and enjoy and acquiring a piece of old furniture that will sit in the corner looking, well, merely old.

Chairs. When looking at a chair, do the easy thing first: sit in it. After all, its primary function is to support your weight comfortably and safely. Does the height of the seat allow you to rest your feet easily on the floor? Furniture makers throughout history have been remarkably consistent in maintaining the same basic dimensions, give or take an inch here or there. The seat of an armchair, for instance, should generally be 16 to 18 inches off the floor. If it is less, the legs may not be original, or perhaps they're original but they have been shortened for some reason, most likely because they were damaged. Straight-back dining chairs are usually a few inches wider than armchairs—the ones that go at the head of the table—so measuring will tell you if the arms are later additions.

You're still sitting—is the chair wobbly? Squeaky? If so, look for the source of the problem. Squeaks mean something is loose. Wobbles may derive from uneven legs, which is a sign of either damage or poor repair. Here is a wobble test: Facing the chair, put your knee where the back and seat join; then, put your hand on the top of the chairback. Now gently pull the chair toward you to see if the frame is sturdy. While you're at it, make sure that all the features are securely fitted: rungs, stretchers, spindles.

Once you've determined that the chair is complete and in good condition, look for signs of age and authenticity. Stretchers should show signs of wear on their upper side where generations of people have rested their feet. Old handmade dowels and pins—on a Windsor chair, for instance—are not uniformly round, like machine-made pieces. In general, reproduction chairs are made of cheaper material and decorated with clumsier carvings. They are often out of proportion and too ornate for the style they're attempting to imitate, as if they're trying too hard to sell themselves.

Finally, old chairs, like all old furniture, will not be pristine. Dirt and grease from long-ago hands will have stained the undersides of the seat where people grasp it to push themselves in and out from beneath the table.

Tables. Just as chair seats need to be a certain height to be comfortable, tables have to be well proportioned to be practical. The tops of dining tables are usually 27 to 30 inches off the floor, while tilt-top tables should be about 28 inches. In addition, the apron—the skirt suspended between the legs of the table—shouldn't be so deep as to make it uncomfortable (let alone impossible) to sit with the chair pulled in a reasonable distance. At the same time, note the stretchers, if any. Aside from the fact that they should be worn somewhat on the top if the piece is old, they should also be positioned in such a way as not to prevent diners from pulling their chair beneath the table. Also, like chairs, there should be appropriate signs of overall wear and patina as well as grease or dirt in the crevices. Make sure the legs are secure.

When looking at a drop-leaf table, check to see that both leaves are there! Displayed up against a wall, a drop-leaf table can be deceiving. Raise both leaves, as well; don't assume that if one works the other does too. Swing out the leaf bracket to make sure it's there and that it functions properly and supports the leaf's weight evenly. Always check leaves for warping. For tables that have separate leaves, see that their color, grain, and patina match that of the top of the table.

In the past some big tables were cut in half and refigured to make two, and some smaller tables were joined, or married, to create one larger table. Inspect the entire table for consistency: the wood grain should be similar overall, as should its color. The construction technique should be the same between two halves as well, and there should be no mismatched decoration. Unexplained holes on a table's underside indicate that legs have been removed or replaced. Saw marks near the bottom of a table's legs indicate that pieces have been added to lengthen them or even them out. This is called ending out, and if it was done well it may be hard to see.

Chests. A chest of drawers, no matter how old or beautiful it is, is no good if you can't use it as it was intended. In other words, the drawers are what is most important. Before you inspect the chest for overall condition and signs of age and authenticity, check that you can live with how the drawers pull out. Remember, too, that the chest is, presumably, old, and that the drawers will not slide out as effortlessly as they would from a new piece.

Once you're satisfied with how the drawers work, inspect them more carefully. Older drawers have thicker bottoms; newer bottoms are thin and made from plywood or fiberboard. Old chest drawer bottoms are rough to the touch.

It's always wise to look at the dovetail joints, which are the wedge-shaped pieces fit into a same-shaped space that hold the corner of a drawer together. Historically, the older the piece, the fewer and cruder the dovetail joints. Twentieth-century machine-made dovetails are small and smooth, uniform in size, and usually number between six and eight. Today, however, clever furniture makers imitate older dovetail styles, using fewer of them and less sophisticated methods. Still, at reputable shops and auction houses dovetail joints will indicate age.

The backboards of an older chest should be thick, rough to the touch, and unfinished.

If the hardware on a very old chest is not the original—and it would be surprising if it was unless the piece was of museum quality—don't worry. Hardware has always been one of the easiest things to replace, and it was done often to update the look of a chest. Plugged or unexplained holes inside the drawers are indications that the current hardware is not original.

COLLECTOR'S CHOICE

Style is a reaction to the times—to the past, to a vision for the future. Understanding the design characteristics associated with different styles will help you form a personal vision, and that will help you create a living environment in which you can live and—even better—love.

William and Mary. William, who ascended the British throne from the House of Orange in the Netherlands in 1689, inspired this Dutch-influenced style, which is characterized by turned trumpet legs, large ball feet, gold leaf, and Oriental lacquerwork. Walnut and maple were the preferred materials, though other combinations of fancy-grain veneers such as burl walnut were often used to create decorative pictures and geometric patterns. Both the flat-topped highboy, a chest of drawers atop a stand that also has drawers, and the lowboy, the stand with drawers alone, were introduced during this period, as were slant-top desks, gateleg tables, and daybeds. Chairs with horizontal curved slats and banister-backs were also popularized.

Queen Anne. A refinement of the William and Mary style, which preceded it, design of the Queen Anne period was more moderately proportioned, graceful, and refined. The enduring influence on design of Queen Anne's reign was the replacement of the turned leg with the introduction of the cabriole leg, an appendage that's been described as "curving at the knee, in toward the ankle and out again at the foot." This distinctive S-shaped leg was used on all sorts of furniture, but most notably to support chairs, beds, desks, and highboys. Its undulating lines were used on other pieces of furniture as well, including the sinuous vase-shaped back splats of Queen Anne chairs and the split-scroll pediment that topped off highboys. Walnut, maple, and cherry were the woods of choice, which were often chipped to create decorative elements such as scallop shells, sunbursts, scrolls, animals, plants, and Oriental figures. The Queen Anne style is also known for its use of veneers to create banding, marquetry, and inlay. Wing chairs came into being during this period.

Georgian. Named after three kings—George I, who was born and raised in Germany and didn't even speak English when he ascended the throne; George II, who was the last British king ever to lead troops onto the battlefield; and George III, who was the king when the British lost the American colonies—the Georgian style is a more ornate incarnation of designs created during the Queen Anne period, which preceded it. Not as refined as Queen Anne, Georgian furnishings are more striking in their use of decoration, with a varied list of motifs that include the front view of a lion's head, fan-shaped shells, masks, swags, and Greek keys. In America, Georgian furniture included the relatively new country's national emblem, the eagle. In England as well as America, Georgian designs were characterized by elaborately carved cabriole legs terminating in a pad or ball-and-claw foot, pierced back splats, and the use of gilding and heavy lacquering.

Chippendale. Finally, the first style of design not named after a king or queen! Perhaps no furniture maker or style is better known than Thomas Chippendale, whose influential book, *The Gentleman and Cabinet Maker's Director*, was published in 1754. In it he illustrated 160 furniture concepts, most of which were drawn from French, Chinese, and Gothic sources, that have remained over time the benchmark by which much furniture is still judged. Chippendale used what had come before him—primarily the Queen Anne style—and embellished it further, adding more ornamentation in the form of carved scrolls, acanthus leaves, and knotted ribbons, as well as serpentine fronts and elaborately carved ball-and-claw feet. His version of the Queen Anne broken pediment, for instance, was an ornate, outsize exaggeration of the original. New introductions during the Chippendale period include chest-on-chests, tilt-top tables, and bombé furniture.

Federal. After the American Revolution, as the fledgling country sought ways to define itself, both constitutionally and aesthetically, a renewed interest in classical forms flourished. The Federal period, influenced by George Hepplewhite's book and Thomas Sheraton's and by their emphasis on clean lines and simple design statements, was, in some ways, a reaction to the heavy ornamentation of Chippendale.

Hepplewhite's posthumously published book, *The Cabinet Maker and Upholsterers Guide*, was the foundation of what became known as the Hepplewhite style, a graceful, almost delicate look defined by its use of slender, tapered legs and spade feet, curves rather than straight lines, and contrasting veneers, often of satinwood. Hepplewhite was a proponent of inlay, japanning, and painting to ornament his works, the many decorative details of which included ribbons, rosettes, urns, festoons, chains of cornhusks, medallions, Prince of Wales feathers, and lyres. Chairbacks with shields, ovals, and interlocked hearts are Hepplewhite staples that are still highly popular today. Hepplewhite's influence crossed the Atlantic to the United States soon after his book's publication in 1788, and was widely felt by furniture makers throughout Maryland, New England, New York, Virginia, and North and South Carolina.

Delicate fluting, carving, and reeding characterize the designs of Thomas Sheraton, whose 1791 book, *The Cabinet-Maker and Upholsterer's Drawing Book*, emphasized simplicity over ornamentation, inlay over ormolu, and straight lines over curves. The Sheraton style was the most reproduced style in the United States in the decades after the country's founding. It was characterized by the use of decorative wood inlay as its ornamental foundation in place of painting and gilding. Its design motifs include the use of open latticework, fan-shaped shells, urns, lyres, and other classical objects as well as acanthus leaves, drapery swags, and stars. Sheraton-style furnishings are usually made from mahogany, cherry, or plain or curly maple.

American Empire. Though there was no definitive designer of the American Empire period, such as a Chippendale or Hepplewhite, Duncan Phyfe was the style's foremost practitioner. Influenced by the French Empire period, American Empire was known for restrained yet bold designs, often using classical forms to create a commanding presence. Design motifs include columns, animal feet, and the American eagle. The period is also known for its use of both strong colors—rich greens, deep reds, imperial purples—and softer hues, such as sage, gray, and gold. In the United States the most well known (and well done) examples of the Empire Style are the Red Room and Green Room in the White House.

Victorian. Another style named after a monarch, the Victorian period spanned the sixty-four years of Queen Victoria's reign, and so it is especially difficult to define. While drawing inspiration from many past styles, furniture makers during the Victorian era combined these influences with modern production techniques. The Gothic, Renaissance, Elizabethan, and rococo styles were among the many that influenced the Victorian era. There was a revival of interest in Sheraton, Chippendale, and Hepplewhite as well. Sometimes there would be a mishmash of styles, from Egyptian to Greek to Chippendale, all on the same piece. Victorian furnishings are today known for their heaviness in both design and ornamentation. Massive fantastic arrangements of flora and fauna highlight many Victorian creations—one writer referred to the use of such motifs as "robust excess"—as does generous gilding, mother-of-pearl inlay, and wood japanned to look like papier-mâché. Deep-tufted upholstered pieces and marble-top tables were also hallmarks of this era.

Arts and Crafts. A reaction against the mass-produced designs that became ubiquitous during the Industrial Revolution, the Arts and Crafts movement embraced a rougher craftsman style and decorative motifs based on an object's function rather than on external ornamentation. The movement represented a return to simpler design and construction methods with an emphasis on utility. Often unadorned, Arts and Crafts furnishings were straight-lined and otherwise plain, with the joinery of construction providing the main visual interest.

Art Deco. Formal, stylized, and streamlined, the Art Deco style derives its name from the Exposition Internationale des Arts Décoratifs et Industriels, held in Paris in 1925, the first exhibit of decorative arts to occur after World War I. Based on the machine age's obsession with speed, cars, trains, and fashion, Art Deco furnishings were full of geometrical decorative themes, including circles, ovals, and zigzags, and was often sharply colored in silver, black, and bright colors such as red and turquoise. Art Deco was the first truly modern style of the twentieth century, with Cubist and Modernist influences, and lasted only until the beginning of World War II, when the whimsy of Art Deco no longer fit the increasingly somber international mood.

TAKING CARE OF YOUR COLLECTION

Keep wood furniture out of direct sunlight.

When moving furniture, pick it up. Feet are fragile and can be easily damaged if you push the furniture around.

Wax your furniture no more than twice a year.

Wipe in the direction of the grain, use a soft damp cloth to remove liquid spills from wood.

To cover a scratch in a dark wood, use an eyebrow pencil or shoe polish.

Wipe lacquered wood clean, but don't wash it, as water can cause damage to the lacquer.

Musty smells in drawers or chests can be removed by sprinkling fresh ground coffee inside, and removing it twenty-four hours later.

Veneered surfaces are particularly likely to be damaged in dry environments, so be sure to maintain proper humidity—but remember that too much dampness may cause warping or lifting.

Always dust before you clean or polish a wood surface, as particles left behind can cause abrasion.

Feather dusters are fun to use, but the feathers can easily break off and their sharp tips could scratch the surface of your furniture.

Metal hardware should be dusted but not cleaned with metal polishers because you could easily damage the surrounding wood.

Gently vacuum upholstered furniture.

WORDS TO REMEMBER

Acanthus. A wild plant native to southern Europe whose leaves are popular classical design elements.

Apron. A decorative skirt hanging between furniture legs.

Banding. Strips of inlaid wood, often in a contrasting color.

Bentwood. Wood that has been steamed and bent into shape.

Bombé. A bulging, kettle-like shape often used on commodes and chests of drawers.

Boulle. After André-Charles Boulle; refers to brass and tortoiseshell inlay.

Carcase. The body of a case piece, such as a highboy or chest of drawers.

Chamfer. Smoothed-off beveled edge.

Chip carving. Geometric shapes cut into a flat surface with a flat chisel.

Cock beads. Tiny projecting half balls.

Demilune. A table shaped like half a circle.

Dowelled. Fastened with wooden pins instead of screws.

Ébéniste. French term for cabinetmaker.

Escutcheon. A cartouche-shaped ornamental plate surrounding a keyhole.

Festoon. An inlaid, carved, or painted decorative strip made to resemble ribbons or garlands loosely connecting two points.

Gadroon. An ornamental edging that resembles rope twists.

Inlay. Wood and other material such as ivory inset into timber to form decorative patterns.

Japanning. Lacquering a surface with a hard varnish, using Asian decorative motifs.

Marquetry. Inlays of various veneers, from other woods to mother-of-pearl to tortoiseshell, to create ornament.

Married. Created by joining two separate pieces, usually from the same style and period.

Ormolu. Gilded bronze, brass, or copper.

Patina. The mellow color and texture that old furniture acquires from dirt and waxy buildup over time and through use.

Reeding. Parallel convex moldings often found on columns and the legs of chairs and tables.

Splat. The central support that joins a chair's top rail to its seat and forms the section against which one's back rests.

Stretcher. Horizontal rail between the legs of a chair or a table that's used for both decoration and strength.

Turned leg. A chair or table leg turned on a lathe, plain or with shaped sections.

Veneer. A very thin layer of decorative wood glued to thicker, less expensive or less attractive timber.

20

Glass

Glass is as varied as silver or porcelain, yet because of the transparency of most glass, in some ways infinitely more fascinating. It is easy to understand how porcelain is made, for instance, but the fact that you can see through most glass, even though sand is a major component of it, never ceases to amaze many collectors. For many, that transparency is the charm of glass and the source of its beauty.

Glass objects are created by three methods.

The earliest glass objects were made by the free-blown process, in which the glassblower attached a blob of molten glass to a hollow rod, then blew through the tube as if playing a trumpet, all the while turning and shaping the piece.

The challenge for the glassblower is to make sure the glass is hot enough to be pliable, yet not so hot as to be completely liquefied. The formed glass object is transferred to a pontil rod for further shaping. The pontil rod leaves a mark on the bottom of the glass object when it's detached. Pontil marks that are polished are the sign of a quality glasshouse. They're not for decoration alone. Applied pontils, or "button" pontils, were added when the blower wanted a finished look to the glass but the glass was too thin, or the area was too small to finish.

As glass increased in importance, the demand far outpaced the supply, due to the slow process of hand-shaping each individual object. The eighteenth century saw the creation of blown molded glass, a process by which the glass is blown directly into a mold. When the glass cools the mold is opened and the imprint of the pattern remains on the outer surface of the glass. Blown molded glass is easily identifiable because, once it is removed from the mold, the object's interior is the concave version of the exterior pattern. Another feature is that mold lines where the two sides of the mold disconnect are apparent on the glass object.

Though this process allowed for increased production, the demand still outpaced the supply. The mid-nineteenth century saw the creation of yet another process: pressed glass. This material is similar to blown molded glass, but the process is considered by many to be the first truly significant innovation in glass-making in a millennium because it did away with the blowing process altogether. Instead the molten glass is shot into a mold, and a plunger pushes it into every crevice and corner. The speed with which this could occur allowed for the first time the mass production of glass, which not only satisfied but enhanced the demand.

Pressed glass can easily be distinguished from blown molded glass by its inside surface: unlike the inside of a blown molded piece, the interior of a pressed glass object does not reflect the pattern of the exterior.

QUESTIONS YOU'LL ALWAYS WANT TO ASK

What is the condition?
Is it marked or signed?
What period is it from?

ONE IMPORTANT THING: CHOICE

Glass collections are formed around a dizzying array of themes, which allow novices and experts alike to amass interesting collections. Some collections are based on the shape or the function of an object, concentrating on, say, bottles or paperweights. Others are composed of the work of certain manufacturers such as Tiffany, Swarovski, or Daum. Many people collect based on the type of glass. For these collectors, displaying quantities of carnival glass together, or ruby glass or milk glass, works well aesthetically in a way that mixing types does not.

Another theme around which people collect glass is color. Aside from the popularity of ruby glass and milk glass, collectors concentrate on cobalt blues, greens, amethysts, and even black. Any large group of similarly dark-colored glass can be a beautifully imposing image, whereas light-colored glass is gently easing.

Many glass collectors are purists who prefer to choose a theme and stick to it when displaying their collections.

PRACTICAL ADVICE

There's so much glass from which to choose that it definitely pays to shop around.

Makers' marks and artists' signatures are rarely found on antique glass.

Even a fine, barely noticeable crack will devalue a piece of glass.

Let there be light: to find damage that may not be obvious, hold a glass object up to the light and look for irregular refractions.

The most common place to find a crack is at the base of a handle, since that's where pressure can be strongest.

Cracks can often be felt with fingernails more easily than they can be seen.

Glass objects in perfect condition should have a "ping" when flicked.

Always pick up a glass object by its body until you are sure that the handles are not cracked; pick up stemware by stem and bowl.

Signs of wear on the bottom are an indication of age, though minuscule scratch marks should be spread evenly over the base, not pointed in one direction, which would indicate forged age.

Always feel the rim and bottom of every wineglass or dish in a set for rough edges.

Remember that the more elaborate the piece, the more likely it is to be damaged.

Bubbles in a glass object do not necessarily mean it's old.

COLLECTOR'S CHOICE

Glass is the third most popular collectible in the United States, after stamps and coins. That's not too surprising, given that glass has existed for more than 3,500 years. It has always been a favorite and easy thing to amass, and has often reflected the ups and downs and the joy and turmoil of American life. American brilliant cut glass, for instance, was hugely popular during the affluent Victorian era. Even its name, "brilliant," indicates the good times. Depression glass, on the other hand, was appropriately simple and inexpensive or sometimes free. Here are a few of the more popular types of glass that are collected today, each of which was made by various manufacturers.

American brilliant cut glass. There's almost nothing more resplendent than a piece of American brilliant cut glass picking up the flicker of a flame or the illumination of a chandelier or lamp. Its beauty comes from the intricate, deeply cut patterns that cover the entire surface of an object, giving it an intense sparkle and luminescence.

In vogue in the United States from about 1880 through 1916, American brilliant cut glass was initially hand blown, then cut with a stone or wheel, and finally polished by hand. In later years, to save money and time, it was mold-blown, cut, and polished using an acid wash, which created a less sharp-edged and less brilliant object. Still later it was blown into a mold with the pattern already there. Each of these developments lessened the quality of brilliant cut glass and hastened the end of its popularity.

Collectors prize American brilliant cut glass objects created by the earliest method—hand blowing and hand polishing—with larger pieces, such as punch bowls, and more complex patterns, being the most desirable. Because of the ornate decoration, small nicks are less damaging to an object's value, though cracks and fractures greatly lessen it. The best American brilliant cut glass is made from lead crystal, which has an exceptional brilliance.

Carnival glass. Made from 1905 to 1930 by various companies in the United States, England, Germany, France, Australia, and Sweden, carnival glass was produced by spraying glass before firing with a metallic salt solution. The luster and sheen that formed after it cooled so resembled its more expensive inspiration, in fact, that it became the poor man's Tiffany glass. Unfortunately, its success in attracting a wider audience was also the beginning of its end. As one collector famously noted, "When the maid could possess iridescent glass as well as her mistress, the latter promptly lost interest in it."

Today, however, carnival glass—which in some circles is referred to as taffeta glass—is as popular as ever. Noted for its prismatic play of colors that resemble a rainbow on a bubble, carnival glass was made in hundreds of shapes, sizes, and objects. Because it was created to mimic Favrile, it's usually naturalistic in style and organic in shape, with adornments designed to resemble leaves and flowers.

Dark, lustrous shades of red and purple, as well as pastel, are the most desirable hues. Orange, which collectors call marigold, and blue, as well as a high-gloss finish, are signs of contemporary carnival glass—carnival glass enthusiasts don't use the word reproduction.

Crackle glass. Crackle glass, the latest American-made glass to become a hot collectible, has an illustrious history. It was first created in sixteenth-century Venice by some of the world's greatest glassmakers. Revived several centuries later, its modern heyday lasted from the 1880s through the 1920s, though it continued to be made until the 1960s.

Also known as craquelé glass, ice glass, and overshot glass, crackle glass is made by immersing hot molten glass in cold water. The glass cracks and is then reheated and shaped into the desired object. The reheating seals the cracks. Whether intentionally or not, this process creates a crackle whose beauty masks imperfections in glass.

Vibrantly colored objects are sought-after. Older crackle glass has a delightful "ping" when flicked; newer pieces have a more thud-like sound. Older shapes are less perfect than newer pieces. Additionally, older pieces will have some expected wear and tear on the bottom as well as where a stopper might have been, as on a cruet.

Depression glass. It was made during the Great Depression, but its value as a collectible is far from depressed. In fact, Depression glass—clear or colored machine-made glass—is probably the most widely collected glass available today. In the 1930s, people couldn't afford new dishes—at least not new, *fine* dishes—so Depression glass, with its molded patterns imitating more expensive etched glass, was born.

Originally sold in five-and-dimes and department stores, Depression glass was also a popular premium given away by movie theaters, gas stations, and cereal companies. One had to redeem several coupons or buy several tickets to acquire unusual or large pieces, and today such objects are highly prized by collectors. These include serving pieces, salt-and-pepper shakers, butter dishes, covered pieces (with their covers), and pitcher-and-tumbler sets.

Unfortunately, because it was not of terribly high quality, and because it was made to be used instead of merely displayed, Depression glass is often in poor condition. When buying it, closely inspect rims and brims and edges for cracks and chips. Depression glass, which came in a wide variety of colors, was only occasionally marked, and then only with a paper label, which today would be a rare thing to see.

Mercury glass. Also called silvered glass, mercury glass was originally created as a less expensive alternative to silver objects, both utilitarian and ornamental. The process of creating mercury glass, which was first patented in England in 1849 and in the United States six years later, was actually quite easy, though maintaining it was not.

Mercury glass was made by pouring a silvered liquid into the space between two walls of glass through a hole in the bottom of an object. The liquid stuck to the walls of the interior and drained out the hole, which was then plugged with a glass or metal disk. (If there is a mark, it will be on this seal.) But the plug was often hastily or haphazardly placed, allowing air or moisture to seep in. If the seal remained tight the silver remained bright; if not, the silver faded, became cloudy, and even peeled.

The first mercury glass objects were doorknobs, which didn't require polishing! Later almost every conceivable object was made of mercury glass, from salvers to crucifixes to vases, which have often been turned into lamp bases.

Milk glass. Originally created as a substitute for a more expensive material, milk glass is yet another type of glass that has morphed over time into an expensive collectible. A white opaque glass created from tin oxide in the eighteenth century but popularized in the United States during the nineteenth and twentieth centuries as an alternative to porcelain, this is one of the most reproduced of all glass types, making it, therefore, one of the hardest to authenticate. That's because unlike other types of glass whose production methods have changed drastically over time, making newer versions easier to spot, milk glass is milk glass is milk glass, new or old.

The best way to distinguish between older and newer milk glass is to study examples of each. Some hints that a piece is older include sharp detail and a slight luminescence along its edges, noticeable when the object is held up to a strong light.

The most sought-after milk glass objects are large pieces and covered dishes shaped like animals—rabbits and chickens, in particular.

Ruby glass. Also known as cranberry glass because of its rich red color, ruby glass, which became popular after the Civil War, is made by adding gold oxide to the glass—the more gold, the redder the glass.

Both cranberry and ruby glass can be solidly colored throughout, but just as often the material is "flashed," meaning that it consists of a piece of glass with a very thin layer of another piece attached as an outer layer. This outer layer, known as flashing, is sometimes cut away in patterns to expose the colored layer underneath. This beautiful, deep-colored glass—whether you call it cranberry glass, ruby glass, or flashed glass—is highly collectible.

Older colored glass of this sort is heavier than newer reproductions, though often the color is just as intense. More than many other types of glass, except perhaps milk glass, newer ruby glass objects are hard to distinguish from older ones, but in some ways collectors worry less about age. Collectors of colored glass are usually more concerned with deep rich hues, which range from a barely transparent crimson to a light-filtering pink.

Vaseline glass. Some collectors think all glass glows with beauty, but Vaseline glass is the only type that really does glow, at least, when held beneath a black light (which makes authenticating it easy). Other types of glass may glow in ultraviolet light, but only Vaseline glass glows uniquely lemon-lime. Also called pearline, canary glass, or uranium glass—the glow comes from adding two percent uranium to the glass—this fluorescent green-yellow translucent glass was first made in England in the 1870s and got its name from its resemblance to petroleum jelly, or Vaseline.

Vaseline glass was popular in the United States until about World War II, when production stopped due to the government's need to conserve uranium. After the war ended and as the Cold War began, some Vaseline glass collectors were turned away from antiques shows for fear that the glass was radioactive. It is, actually—but so infinitesimally that it poses no real danger.

TAKING CARE OF YOUR COLLECTION

To wash most glass, use tepid water and mild dishwashing detergent; clean cut glass with softener-free dishwashing detergent.

Cover your work surface with a towel.

Newspaper is a great—and inexpensive—glass shiner for transparent glass.

To remove stickers and some stains, you can purchase specific solvents. Never try to shave off a sticker from a glass surface. You'll do more damage than you expect.

Store glass away from direct sunlight, which over time can dull its brilliance, and extremes in heat, which can cause damage.

Pick up one piece of glass at a time, as even a slight knock of one piece against another can cause damage to both objects.

When dusting, hold the object in one hand while you dust with the other.

Permanent residue may form if you allow water to evaporate from a glass vase.

Use a plastic scouring pad and silver polish to clean a cloudy glass plate.

Toothpaste can be used on iridescent glass to bring out the highlights. Simply apply with your fingers, lightly rub, and wash with water.

Hand-wash your collectible glass; reverberations may cause damage if you put it into the dishwasher.

Rinse glass objects in exceptionally clean water to avoid leaving even a faint residue, which later on will be obvious even to the naked eye.

Air-dry glass objects.

Prevent glasses and glass cups from cracking by putting a silver spoon in them before pouring in hot liquid. The spoon will absorb some of the heat.

WORDS TO REMEMBER

Annealing. Cooling glass slowly and evenly in a furnace to make it stronger than quickly cooled glass.

Art glass. To some aficionados, only glass made in the United States from about 1870 to 1930. To most, however, any ornamental glass made since the mid-nineteenth century.

Beveled glass. Glass with its edges ground in a sloping angle.

Blobbing. Decorating hot glass by dropping blobs of molten glass, often of a different color, onto its surface.

Bruise. A chip that hasn't broken away from the glass; some bruises can be polished away.

Cullet glass. Recycled glass.

Favrile. Iridescent glass produced by the exposure of hot glass to metal fumes and oxides in a process patented by Louis Comfort Tiffany in the 1880s.

Flashed glass. Glass with a thin layer of glass of a different color fused to it.

Hobnail. A popular type of pressed glass in which a regular pattern of raised knobs appear after blowing glass into a mold; sometimes called dewdrop glass.

Iridescence. A rainbow effect that changes as the object is moved in the light.

Knop. A hollow or solid bulge in the stem of a drinking glass.

Lead glass. Very heavy glass made with lead oxide instead of lime.

Nic. A chip the size of a pinhead.

Pontil rod. The rod onto which blown glass is transferred from the blowpipe for final shaping.

Silica. Silicon oxide, a mixture that is the main ingredient in glass, the most common type of which is sand.

21

Jewelry

Jewelry is a unique decorative object in that you wear it. If you haul your Federal sideboard down the street, people will stare. If you carry a bracket clock or two at a cocktail party, you may not get invited back. But when you wear an Edwardian brooch or a fiery opal ring to a wedding, or a beautiful gold locket for a night out on the town, people will admire you not only from afar but from close-up, too.

You can collect jewelry in an infinite number of ways, from type (such as bracelets, chokers, or tiaras) to period (Victorian, contemporary, or Art Nouveau) to material (gold, Bakelite, or tortoiseshell) to type of gemstone (diamonds, rubies, or sapphires). Then again, you might collect jewelry eclectically and with no theme whatsoever, based solely on whether you like individual pieces.

But no matter what or how you collect, you need to know what a carat is to fully understand gems. When someone speaks of a one-carat diamond, for instance, she is referring not to its size but to its weight. The same is true if she is talking about an emerald, a sapphire, or any other gemstone.

The word "carat" actually comes from "carob," a bean that tastes vaguely like chocolate. In ancient times, gems of all types were weighted against the carob bean, which weighed about one carat. In 1913, carat weight was standardized internationally and adapted to the metric system. One carat equals 200 milligrams or 0.2 grams, or a little more than one-fifth of a gram—visualize it however it's easiest for you. In other words, it takes 142 carats to equal one ounce.

Sometimes gems are also referred to by points, with one carat equaling 100 points. A half-carat diamond, for instance, would be referred to as 50 points. This is particularly useful when you're talking about small diamonds. A 5-point diamond is one weighing 5/100 of a carat.

With gold, however, the term is "karat"—note the spelling. This is a different word with a different meaning. Instead of weight, "karat" refers to purity. Pure gold is 24 karats, but because gold is a soft metal, it is usually combined with other alloys to increase its hardness and durability. That's why you'll hear of 18-karat gold, for example, which is 18 parts gold and 6 parts other base metals. The most common gold used in American jewelry today is 14 karat. These other alloys also affect gold's color. Yellow gold is created by alloying the metal with copper and silver; using only copper creates rose gold; white gold contains silver, nickel, and zinc, and occasionally palladium; green gold contains silver, copper, and zinc.

This is a very serious business: in fact, the Federal Trade Commission rules require that all jewelry sold in the United States as gold be described by "a correct designation of the karat fineness of the alloy." No jewelry of less than 10 karats, or 10k, may be sold in the United States as gold jewelry.

If you remember what carats are and what karats are not, collecting jewelry will be easier and more enjoyable.

QUESTIONS YOU'LL ALWAYS WANT TO ASK

Are these the original stones?

Has the piece been repaired?

ONE IMPORTANT THING: TREATED, SYNTHETIC, AND SIMULATED STONES

Most gemstones are naturally beautiful, and many stones are treated to enhance their beauty. This isn't necessarily a bad thing—it's too commonly done for it to affect quality or value that much. Gems that are treated are still authentic gems, formed over millennia. Synthetic gems, however, are altogether different. Created in laboratories, they imitate natural stones in chemical composition, physical properties, and appearance.

Rubies and sapphires are routinely heated at the mine site to enhance their color; most tourmalines are not treated. Pearls, too, may be bleached or even dyed. Other stones, such as diamonds, may be treated to improve their clarity. Many emeralds are oiled with colorless oils to make their natural inclusions, or flaws, less obvious. If colored oils are used, however, the real color of the stone cannot be determined properly, and this affects the value.

Another type of treatment is fracture filling, in which stones are filled with opticon, or wax, to make their inclusions less obvious. This is done with poorer quality diamonds and emeralds.

Other enhancements include drilling holes with a laser in order to bleach out black inclusions inside a stone; infusing a plastic bonding agent into the stone to stabilize the color already there; and diffusion, which is the combination of chemicals and high temperatures that result in a shallow subsurface layer of color.

A synthetic stone is an artificially fabricated stone. It is less pricey than its natural counterpart, and usually only an expert can tell the difference. Simulated stones, however, are complete fakes, usually glass made to resemble the real McCoy. Their colors are invariably dull, and they are easily scratched. They should be easily avoided.

PRACTICAL ADVICE

Feel a stone: you'll often feel damage you can't see.

If a piece is in its original case, and fits perfectly into it, that's a good indication of its authenticity.

Small errors in the placement of facets, such as extra facets or off-center facets, decrease the value of a gem, making it duller than it would otherwise have been.

Inspect the reverse side of a piece of jewelry for damage or repairs before you purchase it.

COLLECTOR'S CHOICE

Whether you're interested in earrings, necklaces, bracelets, rings, or stickpins, the stones used to adorn them are a key element. There's no reason to prefer one type of gem over another beyond their aesthetic appeal to you. But knowing what the gems are, and what to look for in them, will go a long way toward ensuring that you will make the best purchases possible and look your best when you wear and enjoy them.

Diamonds. Diamonds are more than just a girl's best friend, they're everyone's best friend. That's because there's virtually no one on whom a diamond doesn't look good, no setting in which a diamond doesn't shine, no time at which a diamond isn't a cherished gift. Yet, there are diamonds and there are *diamonds*. You want to buy the latter, of course.

Diamonds do not have the most glamorous ancestry. After all, a diamond is a mineral composed of pure carbon, which is really just coal. Still, it is the hardest natural substance known to man. Diamonds can be colorless to black, transparent to translucent to opaque. They're highly refractive, which accounts for their brilliance—remember, reflection is white light bouncing off surfaces that gives a stone brilliance, while refraction is white light being broken up into its spectral colors, lending a prism-like effect.

Diamonds are judged on the four Cs: carat, cut, clarity, and color. Run each of these through your mind as you look at the diamonds in a piece of jewelry and you can't go wrong. Carat, as already noted, refers to the stone's weight, not its size. Cut refers to shape and proportion, both of which are important to consider and affect price. The stone's shape—which may be round, square-cut, oval, pear-shaped, or various other shapes—should relate to its proportions, symmetry, and polish. A beautifully cut stone emits maximum brilliance as the light is internally reflected from facet to facet, and then refracted out through the top. If a diamond is too deep or too shallow the light won't be reflected so much within the stone and will ultimately be reflected out through the bottom, creating a dull appearance. Clarity is just that: how clear the stone appears. You should examine a stone from all angles—front, back, top, and bottom, if possible, in natural light.

To really examine a stone, you should buy a ten-power loupe, a small device that magnifies the object ten times. With it you'll be able to easily see various imperfections and blemishes, the existence of which should be expected. Such defects shouldn't necessarily rule out a stone, but they should at least be taken into account. Look for small hollow specks, called bubbles; clusters of white inclusions, called clouds; milky flake formations, called feathers; fractures or chips in the stone; small chips caused by careless mounting; and scratches. The more imperfections a stone has, the less the light can ricochet from facet to facet, and the duller the diamond will look. In a high-quality stone, there will be no inclusions visible to the naked eye.

Color is probably the easiest characteristic to understand. Colored diamonds are expensive and rare, but most diamonds will range from white to slightly yellowish in tint. This is normal; only you can decide how yellow a tint is tolerable. Too distinctive a yellow is not terribly desirable, however, and should be avoided, as should brown and gray, which are also common.

Emeralds. More than any other stone, perhaps, an emerald should be judged by its color first. Not for nothing are emeralds, one of the most popular colored gemstones in the United States, referred to as "green fire." Too dark a green, however, may appear black and is not desirable. Too light a green will appear glassy. A somewhat darker green might make up in richness what it lacks in brightness, and the opposite is true, as well. You'll know the right green—a saturated, lush green reminiscent of grass after a rainfall—when you see it.

Emeralds are found in black calcium-rich shale in countries as diverse as Colombia, Brazil, and Zambia, and each country's gemstones have a unique hue. The Brazilian stones are darker, like a pine green, Zambian are a bright blue-green, and those from Colombia are known for a good balance of medium-dark rich color with a touch of blue.

A perfect emerald with no inclusions is almost unheard of, so inclusions are acceptable up to the point at which they become harmful to the stone's looks or durability. Inclusions should not be so deep that they might cause the stone to crack or break the stone if it is hit.

Emeralds are usually cut in what is commonly referred to as an emerald cut, which is rectangular, though they can occasionally be found cut into ovals and several other shapes.

Opals. With opals, it's all about the fire. Whether the background is black, gray, or white, the fiery, kaleidoscopic play of color that dances across an opal's surface is its most important characteristic. Because black shows off this play of color best, black opals are the most coveted. White, the most common, are beautiful as well, though because of the lighter background the colors may not seem as robust as they might be on a darker stone.

Opals have been described as jelly-like masses that formed cracks as they hardened. It is the light reflected from these tiny cracks that gives the opal its multicolored appearance. They're composed of water and silicon oxide, which really does form a gel that seeps into the cracks in rocks and petrified trees and, over eons, hardens into what we know as opals.

The beauty of opals is in the surface play of the color, which does not emanate from within, as happens with other stones. Opals are therefore not facet-cut but more often are flat or cabochon. When you look at an opal, take special note not only of the background color but of the colors that sparkle across the surface as the stone moves. Reds and oranges are rare and highly prized, while greens and blues, though beautiful, are more common. Also study the patterns. The colors may reflect off the surface in tiny squares, triangles, or rectangles, the more symmetrical the better.

Pearls. Antique pearls are a popular collectible. Beautiful and interesting in origin, they're used in a wide variety of designs, from a single pearl on a lapel pin to hundreds on an extra-long, or opera-length, necklace. And you won't need special equipment to see a pearl's fine qualities or flaws. Good eyesight will do it!

Pearls are formed when an irritant gets inside an oyster shell. With natural pearls, this happens, well, naturally. Cultured pearls, made by a process developed in 1918, are those in which the irritant is introduced by man. Either way, the oyster covers the irritant with nacre, or mother-of-pearl, a combination of protein and calcium carbonate, which eventually forms the pearl. The thicker the nacre, the more lustrous the pearl.

Luster and color are the two most important characteristics to look for when buying antique pearl jewelry. When a pearl has a good luster—a bright, even, shiny surface—it's said to have a fine orient. No one really knows what determines a pearl's color. White is most common, though there are radiant pearls in pale pink and blue and even black. Whichever color you prefer, the goal is to have the same color throughout a piece of jewelry.

Though pearls are organic, they're not likely to dry out or flake unless exposed to chemicals, such as harsh detergents, perfume, or hairspray. Collectors should pay special attention to a pearl's shape and smoothness. The rounder and smoother the pearl, the more costly.

Rubies. The best rubies glow red, due to fluorescence. They're a bright velvety red, some with undertones of pink, orange, or purple. But no matter what secondary color supports the red, ultimately the stone is judged on how red it is. The best red, known in rubyspeak as pigeon-blood red, is very rare. The closer a stone comes to it, the greater will be its value to collectors.

Rubies, which were Jacqueline Kennedy's favorite gemstone, are a transparent variety of corundum, an aluminum oxide material, with a tiny amount of chromium that gives them their color. Pigeon-blood red rubies, as well as all the other best rubies, have traditionally come from the golden triangle of ruby-producing countries—the area where Laos, Myanmar, and Thailand meet. Myanmar (formerly Burma), perhaps more than any other spot on earth, is the true center of the ruby world, home of the famous Mogok rubies, known throughout the jewelry world for their spectacular color.

The shade of a ruby can indicate the gem's country of origin. Stones from Thailand tend to be a little browner, those from Sri Lanka a little more purple. Rubies that are too brown or even gray, or too pale, are far less desirable. Be sure, as well, always to look at pieces of jewelry in both artificial and natural light, as, depending on the type of stone, the color will glow brighter or seem dull.

Sapphires. Sapphires are actually rubies, but because of a slightly different chemical composition—a small amount of iron and titanium—they're blue. In fact, sapphires come in many colors, from pink to salmon to purple, even to yellow. Any sapphire other than blue is called a fancy sapphire. But if a sapphire is red, of course, it's a ruby.

Like rubies, sapphires are all about color. Blue is the most common, the standard against which all other sapphires are judged. Search for sapphires with electric-blue tones, a blue that is hot and icy at the same time. Sapphires, when seen in different kinds of light, from bright sun to subtle candlelight, should always retain their intense color and sparkle. Green or gray overtones mixed in with the blue lessen a stone's colors and therefore its value. A pastel blue is less desirable as well.

Sapphires have a long, rich history. The ancient Persians believed the earth rested on a giant sapphire and its reflection colored the sky. Sapphires have always been associated with faithfulness and sincerity, and many engagement rings to this day are sapphire rings because of that association.

The best sapphires are a cornflower blue and come from the Kashmir region of northern India. As with rubies, the color can indicate a stone's country of origin. Sapphires from Myanmar tend to be a deeper blue, while the Sri Lankan sapphires have violet undertones. Sapphires can also be found in Australia, Kenya, China, and even the United States, as well as several other countries.

TAKING CARE OF YOUR COLLECTION

Store pearls away from heat or sunlight, both of which can dry them out.

Never clean pearls with detergent, bleach, or ammonia. Just rub them gently with a damp cloth.

Don't put on pearls until after you have applied perfume, makeup, and hairspray, all of which over time will damage them.

With diamonds it's not the stone but the setting you need to worry about: soak the jewelry in warm water and an ammonia-based window cleaner. Then gently scrub each piece with a toothbrush, rinse it, and let it dry. This will remove grease and oils and make the diamond sparkle again like new.

Avoid mixing more than one type of jewelry in a jewelry box; they jumble and can damage one another.

Don't clean emeralds with hot soapy water or steam or with an ultrasonic cleaner, each of which may remove the oil in their inclusions and make fissures more apt to cause the stone to crack.

WORDS TO REMEMBER

Baguette. A narrow rectangular cut stone.

Bangle. A stiff design with no links.

Bezel. A type of setting in which the metal completely surrounds the stone; it also refers to the part of a watch that holds the crystal in place.

Bleaching. A process that lightens or whitens pearls.

Brilliant. A standard round cut for diamonds, with 57 or 58 facets.

Cabochon. A stone cut so the top has a convex surface with no facets.

Cameo. Layered stones with a design carved in relief on the top.

Cleavage. The tendency of stones to split along one or more directions.

Crown. The facets between the table and the girdle of the stone.

Culet. The bottom point of a faceted stone.

Doublet. A common process in which a nongem material is cemented to the top or bottom of a gem to build up thickness and permit the gem to be used in a particular setting.

Emerald cut. A square or rectangular step-cut shape, meaning that the facets resemble steps instead of the facets found on round, pear, marquise, or oval stones.

Facet. The small polished surface areas of a gemstone cut to enhance the refraction of light.

Fisheye. A diamond that because of bad faceting has a dull center due to poor cutting proportions.

Flawless. Any jewelry that has no flaws, cracks, inclusions, internal lasering, or other imperfections.

Girdle. The center line of a diamond between the upper crown and the lower pavilion.

Inclusion. Internal flaws in a gemstone, usually a foreign substance like other minerals, gas bubbles, or liquids.

Luster. An effect produced when light is reflected from the surface of the gemstone.

Orient. The luster on the surface of a pearl.

Paste. An imitation stone made from lead glass.

Pavé. Style of gem setting where stones are set very close together with hardly any metal showing between them.

Pavilion. The facets or cuts below the girdle.

Table. The large facet at the top of a gemstone.

22

Metalwork

Metal has been a part of everyday life since before recorded history. The first-ever metal weapons made by man were fashioned from copper. The use of pewter dates back more than two millennia. Bronze dates back at least four millennia. In the Bible, the words for bronze and brass were used interchangeably to refer to the same thing.

Almost from their inception, people have valued not only the metals themselves—bronze, brass, copper, and pewter—but objects fashioned from them. They're heavy and durable, often utilitarian by yesterday's standards, unusually decorative by today's.

Despite what the Bible says, however, brass and bronze are not interchangeable, nor are any other two metals. Though they may share certain qualities, each metal has its own properties. Bronze, for instance, is an alloy—a mixture—of copper and tin. The tin adds strength to the copper, forming a harder, more durable material. Despite its strength, however, bronze is highly malleable and easily shaped into decorative objects, from the rough-and-tumble western frontier images of Frederic Remington to the contemplative and introspective work of Auguste Rodin to the novel, almost decadent Art Deco figural sculptures by Bruno Zach, Jeanne Robert Colinet, and Edgar Brandt. Bronze has also been used to make extraordinary (and extraordinarily heavy) tables, ormolu furniture mounts, and candelabra, among other objects.

Sculptors in particular are attracted to bronze as a medium because it can be forged in great detail. It doesn't rust or pit, and isn't expensive in and of itself. Instead, its value springs from the degree of finishing an object requires. It can be engraved, hammered, gilded, melted, chiseled, or cast. Bronze can have a particularly satisfying range of patinas, from a dark and warm brown to blue to green, that add depth and richness to any object created from it.

Authentic period bronze sculptures are highly collectible and are prized possessions of many museums. Collectors, however, need to be on the watch for contemporary reproductions, called *surmoulage,* made from the original nineteenth-century casts, which lack the sharp definition of the original.

Where the properties of bronze make it an excellent metal from which to create sculptures, brass has been used chiefly for decorative everyday objects such as buttons, gelatin molds, door knockers, and clock dials, among many other things. An alloy of copper and zinc, in its molten state brass is so free-flowing that complex creations can easily be made from it. Its bright glint adds warmth to any setting. Like bronze, though, brass yields well to many types of decorative finishing, including stamping, chasing, engraving, pickling, and lacquering. Look for brass that has a ripe coppery hue.

Copper, the base of both bronze and brass, is itself a highly collected metal distinguished by its earthy reddish tone. It's easily shaped by hammering, chasing, engraving, gilding, enameling, or applying precious stones. It is not, however, easily castable like bronze. While copper is used extensively as a decorative natural resource, it is also the foundation of most silver plate.

If silver plate, with its copper base, is often called the poor man's silver, then pewter is the *poorer* man's silver. A mixture, in varying degrees, of lead, tin, and other metals, pewter can be shiny like silver or a dull, restful gray, like the sky on a late winter afternoon. In its solidity, it is associated with Colonial America, where it was often fashioned into plates, flagons, and foot warmers. It has been said that pewter was to the eighteenth century what plastic was to the late twentieth century.

Pewter was used extensively to create utilitarian household objects, and because it has a low melting point, it was recycled over and over again through the centuries, making old pewter rather hard to find. (Its low melting point also made pewter a poor material to use for cooking utensils.) It was produced in great quantities, especially in the United States after the Revolutionary War, the conclusion of which saw the end of the embargo on raw tin, allowing the pewter industry to thrive. Still, though pewter was favored in both America and Europe, the demand for it waned as porcelain and earthenware became more easily available. Contemporary pewter objects appear thinner, even brittle, to the touch, and have what pewter collectors call a soapy feel.

QUESTIONS YOU'LL ALWAYS WANT TO ASK

What type of metal is this?

Is it pure or plate?

ONE IMPORTANT THING: METAL AND FOOD

Metal and food have a love-hate relationship. On the one hand, some metal is the perfect material from which to fashion cooking vessels. On the other hand, lead, which is a component of pewter, is poisonous (it's said that Nero was poisoned from drinking out of pewter cups, which contain lead) and copper leaves a metallic taste on some food. So pay special attention to the type of metal and the quality of the object you're considering when you set out to buy any metalware to use with food.

Copper cookware is highly recommended by many great chefs for its excellent heat conductivity—about ten times that of glass or stainless steel—but they will tell you that it must be properly tinned to be truly useful. This means that the interior of copper cooking vessels is covered with a thin layer of tin to prevent the food from coming into contact with the copper itself. (The only good use for unlined copper is to beat egg whites; the chemical reaction between the copper and the egg makes the whites frothy and better able to resist overbeating.) Tin is nonreactive and easily refurbished, which makes it a good choice for lining. Metal utensils, however, can scratch tin, so most cooks recommend using wooden utensils with tin-lined copper pots and pans. Some of the best copper cookware comes from Villedieu les Poeles, France, known as the City of Copper.

PRACTICAL ADVICE

Repaired metalwork can be distinguished by soldering at the seams.

Authentic bronze shows the mark of the finishing file on its surface.

A magnet will not be attracted to bronze, but will be attracted to cast iron.

The facial features and other details on original bronze pieces should be well defined.

Brass was sometimes covered with lacquer to eliminate the need for polishing. The lacquer may get worn away or scratched, and the brass underneath will tarnish. But you can easily remove the lacquer, so don't pass up a bargain on a lacquered brass object.

Some copper kettles from the 1840s had colored glass handles.

American pewter is distinguished by its molded edge.

Unmarked old pewter is worth half as much as marked old pewter.

Pewter marks can be confusing because some American makers marked their wares "London."

A general rule: the thistle is the mark of Scottish pewter makers; Parisian makers used an angel with the word "Paris."

Minor scratches and dents on pewter don't affect value as much as do splits, pits, dents, and holes.

A glass-bottomed pewter mug indicates it was made during the Victorian era.

American and English pewter was usually devoid of decoration other than a molded or reeded edge or an engraved coat of arms.

Flicking a piece of good pewter should produce a gong-like sound; a thud indicates poor quality.

COLLECTOR'S CHOICE

There is no end to the types of objects created from metal. Consequently, there's no end to what collectors cherish. Over the years, however, each metal has become associated with particular objects.

Brass candlesticks. For eons candlelight was the only illumination other than the sun and the fire in the hearth, and candlesticks of one sort or another have been made for almost as long. Because of the fluidity of brass in its molten state, it was easily shaped into a wide array of candlestick designs, which usually followed the fashion of the day. Not surprisingly, then, brass became the metal of choice for candlesticks. They continue today to be as popular and collectible as ever. Pairs of identical candlesticks are the most highly sought-after.

Candlesticks can be "read" for age, as certain characteristics, while not foolproof, are indicative of the time in which they were created. Older candlesticks, for instance, were made in three separate sections—the base, stem, and sconce—and then soldered together. Since the copper used for the stem and sconce of candlesticks made before 1780 was cast in two parts, there's a vertical seam in evidence. The seam was sometimes left alone, which makes it easy to see and feel. At other times it was decorated or covered with a flange, or rim. If the seams on the stem and the sconce are not in alignment, it is very likely that repair work has been done to the candlestick. Later core-cast candlesticks don't have seams at all. Another area to look at for evidence of repair includes the junction of the base and stem, which is prone to splitting.

The dawn of the seventeenth century brought with it some new developments, including the addition of a sconce in place of the pricket, the iron spike on which the candle was impaled. Some sconces could be removed to make cleaning easier. A small sliding rod in the stem was invented, too, which adjusted the height of the candle or ejected its stump. Both the sconce and the interior rod mechanism are easily damaged and so should be inspected closely.

Older candlesticks, like any antique, should show pleasant signs of wear and tear, such as minor scratches where over the years wax has been cleaned out. To ensure that a brass candlestick is, in fact, all brass and not merely brass-plated, use a magnet. It won't be attracted to brass.

Pewter porringers. Perhaps the most famous pewter porringers in history—next to those created by Paul Revere—are the ones thrust out in desperation and hunger by the orphans in the Broadway musical *Oliver!* Their porringers were probably no more glamorous, however, than the gruel for which they were asking: "More, sir. I want some more."

Though pewter has been used to make many different objects, perhaps no object more than the porringer takes advantage of pewter's hard, gray solidity. The porringer is as humble and basic as the activity for which it was used: eating gruel. In fact, porringers—5- to 6-inch bowls from which the masses ate their soup and stew—are not glamorous at all.

But it is their modesty that collectors find beautiful. What little decoration porringers have is generally all in the handle. With a bit of study, handles also can be the key to assigning age, maker, and the maker's location.

Though some porringers had three tiny ball feet and others, made before the seventeenth century, had two handles, the porringers with which we're most familiar today were footless and made with one handle, sometimes called an ear, sometimes a tab, which was attached horizontally flush with the top rim. The handle was occasionally plain, but more often decorated with engraving, piercing, or other embellishments or shaped like a flower, fleur-de-lis, or other ornamental objects. Different design motifs were used by different makers in different places at different times in history. Sometimes a porringer will have a touchmark—a maker's mark—and if so, it too will be on the handle.

Newer porringers have thicker walls and folded-over rims, which give the bowl a thick appearance.

Bronze animal sculptures. As the Victorian era progressed and middle-class and affluent life became prim and proper, a group of artists, led by the French sculptor Antoine-Louis Barye, began to express the wilder side of life through bronze depictions of animals in their natural state, which wasn't always pretty. After all, animals hunt each other down, prey on one another for food, and can be violent in their behavior.

Bronze was the perfect medium for such artistry, as more than any other metal, it is capable of being rendered in intense detail, right down to the whiskers on a fearsome snout. The works of the animaliers, as the sculptors were called, were collected throughout the mid- to late-nineteenth century and remain popular today. The group, not surprisingly known as Les Animaliers, included such well-known artists of the day as Augustus Saint-Gaudens and the painter Rosa Bonheur.

Their works, sculptures of one or two animals, were made to sit atop a mantel or table. Some artists such as Pierre Jules Mène focused on domesticated animals like horses and camels, and on dogs, including mastiffs, deerhounds, and whippets. But most of the group's adherents sculpted untamed animals such as lions, elephants, wild bears, rams, tigers, and antelope in robust and spirited activity.

Works by the animaliers can be easily dated and attributed because they were usually attached to a plinth, or base, which was incised with the artist's signature or initials and the date. The Victorian era coincided with the era of mass production, and these animal sculptures became the first bronzes to be cast two or three times from the same mold.

Arts and Crafts copper. Because of copper's availability, affordability, and malleability, throughout history it has often been used as an expression of the times. That was never more evident than in the very late nineteenth and early twentieth century when the Arts and Crafts movement—a response to the increasing reliance on mass production—embraced oak instead of imported woods like walnut, used earthenware in place of fine porcelain, and preferred copper to precious metals such as silver.

The idea was to create handcrafted everyday household objects that looked handcrafted. No effort was made to hide tool marks or to make smooth, glowing surfaces. In fact, the most noticeable characteristic of Arts and Crafts copper is its hand-hammered mottled exterior. That the copper could be dipped into a chemical solution and immediately given a patina that lent the object an aged, pleasantly worn look only heightened its attractiveness to artists and consumers alike.

The artisans attracted to the Arts and Crafts movement were just as interested in the process of creation as in the finished product. They tried to emulate the past by setting up workshops which, unlike those that exemplified the Industrial Revolution's embrace of mass production, relied upon a guild-style system in which apprentices worked and learned alongside elder craftsmen.

Well-known designers like Tiffany and Stickley were attracted to the Arts and Crafts movement, but one of the most productive, and collected, was the Roycraft Copper Shop in East Aurora, New York, founded in 1895 by Edmund Hubbard. Thousands of objects—including ashtrays, letter openers, serving trays, bowls, bookends, inkwells, picture frames, candlesticks, and vases—were created in his metal shop, each of which bore the Roycraft mark, a capital *R* in a circle capped with a cross.

Collectors of Arts and Crafts hammered copper prize simple shapes and subtle decorative motifs, which occasionally were embellished with rivets, cabochons, enamel, or lacquer.

TAKING CARE OF YOUR COLLECTION

Never use steel wool or scouring powder to clean pewter.

Metal polish will permanently damage the patina on bronze, copper, and brass.

Old pewter has a high lead content that corrodes easily in acidic conditions, so never store it in oak furniture, which is particularly acidic. Additionally, always wrap and store pewter in acid-free material.

To clean copper: saturate a sponge with lemon juice and sprinkle on some salt. Gently rub the metal, then rinse and dry it.

To remove small scratches from copper, rub the piece with jeweler's rouge, which brings out the color in precious metals.

To clean pewter, soak the item in water using a mild soap. Then dry it with a cotton cloth.

WORDS TO REMEMBER

Antimony. A metal that when combined with other metals makes them harder and stronger.

Booge. The sloping sides of a pewter plate.

Cire perdue. The "lost wax" process of casting bronze in which a wax sculpture is covered with clay and then melted away, leaving a clay mold, which is then filled with molten bronze.

Coffeepot era. The period from 1825 to 1850, when pewter was made in shapes to imitate silver.

Eight-inch-plate era. American pewter made from 1750 to 1825.

Pontypool ware. Japanned tinplate produced in Wales at the Allgood family factory at Pontypool, mostly decorated with Chinese scenes and figures and distinguished from other tinware by its luster and durability.

Sadware. Early English and American plates, chargers, and dishes made from pewter that was hammered out of a single sheet of metal. Its makers were known as sadware men.

Touchmark. The maker's mark on pewter objects.

Trifle pewter. Pewter made from tin and antimony.

23

Quilts

Quilts seem distinctively American, but in fact they've been made in one form or another throughout the world. They are, however, highly regarded in America as representative of such values as home, community, and hard work. To many, the difficult work of making a quilt, which may take anywhere from 200 to 800 hours, is not valued for its own sake, and quilt making is seen not as a sportsmanlike challenge but as an expression of love, hope, and commitment to peace.

Home. Community. Hard work. Love. Hope. Peace. These are the rocks upon which quilters work, and perhaps that is why, in the fast, faster, fastest world in which we live, collecting objects that speak of a slower, more languorous time, has become an important endeavor. Not to mention that quilts keep us warm.

The word "quilt" comes to us from the Old French word *cuilte* via the Latin word *culcita*, which refers to a stuffed sack. And that, in fact, is pretty much what a quilt is: a layer of stuffing, usually wool or cotton, stitched between two layers of fabric. Originally, quilts were used not only as bedding but also as floor mats and even as window protection. Now, of course, collectors often hang them on walls as prominently as they might a Botero or Braque.

The history of quilting really reflects America's pioneer spirit, as the first reference to quilting in the New World comes from a Salem, Massachusetts, sea captain's late-seventeenth-century household inventory and continues west and south from there. Over the ensuing decades and centuries quilting took hold in Amish communities in Pennsylvania, Ohio, Indiana, and Illinois. It was practiced by Native Americans and by African-Americans before and after the Civil War. Quilting spanned economic classes, too—after all, the poor get cold just like the rich—with the less fortunate using rougher materials in place of the velvets, silks, and satins of the wealthy.

Collectors especially value a quilt with a strong connection to the artist and the environment and times in which she lived. Condition, of course, is important, as is artistry. But more than anything, it's the simplicity and beauty of these useful pieces that will catch—and keep—a collector.

QUESTIONS YOU'LL ALWAYS WANT TO ASK

How old is it?

Who made it? Where?

ONE IMPORTANT THING: QUILTING AND TUFTING

When we speak of a quilt, we mean the entire object. But the top and bottom pieces of fabric, whether whole-cloth or composed of many pieces sewn together in a "crazy" pattern or a distinctive design, have to be sewn together. There are traditionally two ways to do this.

"Quilting" is the stitching with which the two outer sections are held together with the stuffing in between. The quilting forms its own design, from bells to flowers to geometric patterns, aside and separate from the fabric's design. The most singular American contribution to making quilts is using the stitching to echo or relate to the fabric design.

When the top and bottom are joined together by running yarn or string through the layers at even intervals and tying them together, it is known as "tufting." This was a popular way to create novelty quilts, pieced together from old ties, hair ribbons, pieces of men's suiting, draperies, dress labels, or any number of other unusual types of cloth.

PRACTICAL ADVICE

All the parts of a quilt, including the top, appliqués or designs, quilting, bottom, and borders, should be original to the time they were made.

Inspect all parts of a quilt for wear and tear, including the binding edge and corner blocking.

If a quilt's design tells a story, is it complete? Can you interpret it?

Look for an embroidered signature or date.

Check to see if the pattern of the quilting relates to the design of the fabric.

The stitching should be even, tight, and in a straight line.

Colors should be consistent and not faded in places.

Look for stains and discoloration. Blood and rust stains especially eat away at the fabric.

When held up to the light, an old quilt will exhibit dark spots, which may in fact be cotton seeds, indicating that the quilt may have been made before the cotton gin came into use after its 1790 invention.

Eighteenth-century quilts were often used as bedspreads and are bigger than blanket-sized nineteenth-century examples.

Some eighteenth-century quilts have their corners cut to make room for bedposts.

Many early-eighteenth-century quilts had one central design motif, such as a tree or a flower basket, with no border.

Thin, all-white quilts with sophisticated designs and fine stitchery were fashionable in the late eighteenth and early nineteenth centuries.

COLLECTOR'S CHOICE

Different styles of quilts were created at different times in history, depending on the fabrics available and who was doing the sewing. Here are a few of the better-known types that you'll find. You needn't limit your collection to one or another, but knowing the differences will enhance your enjoyment of them.

Amish quilts. The Amish people produced, and still produce, quilts marked by contemporary-looking geometric patterns and radiant colors, the earliest dyes for which were made from weeds, berries, and bark.

Typically, the Amish from the Lancaster, Pennsylvania, area used one big central design motif, such as an eight-point Star of Bethlehem or a diamond, with a wide, symmetrical border.

Other Amish quilters, from Ohio and Indiana, for instance, used complex designs and intricate piecework, while still others were known for their use of jewel-like blues and golds.

They all share one particular Amish characteristic, however, and that is exquisite needlework.

Pieced and patchwork quilts. It used to be said that because of their large size, whole-cloth quilts required a large room in which to work, and for many people of moderate means that "fact" eliminated the possibility of quilt making—at least, until they began to piece together smaller scraps of fabric, which solved the problem of space and paved the way for quilters to expand their handiwork. While there may be some truth to this, in reality patchworks are already sewn together to make a complete fabric before they're quilted. Quilting is done one section at a time, either in a hoop or on a frame, with most of the quilt rolled out of the way.

In creating patchwork, various pieces of cloth were sewn together to form a larger piece to be used as the top or bottom, and then quilted. The value of such a quilt depends on its workmanship and the design created, as well as the quality of the fabric used.

A pieced quilt is really a large cloth appliquéd with many smaller pieces which, as well, form a pattern or design.

Crazy quilt. A late-nineteenth-century invention, similar to a patchwork quilt, in that it is composed of numerous pieces of fabric stitched together, though in theory, at least, not deliberately arranged in a pattern. (The best ones were, in fact, arranged deliberately, and their brilliance lies in the fact that they don't look as if any thought went into them at all.) Because crazy quilts incorporated many old silks, which were notorious for shattering, they were often more fragile than other quilts, and were used as throws instead of blankets.

Album and friendship quilts. These are quilts made by several people, usually as gifts commemorating a wedding, anniversary, birth, or community event. The top and bottom pieces were made by a few people or only one person, and a group would later have a quilting bee, where the stitching, or quilting of the two layers, would occur. These were social events as much as work, and the joy with which these women communed with one another was often evident in the joyous nature of the quilt itself.

TAKING CARE OF YOUR COLLECTION

The best and most natural way to display a quilt is on a bed.

If you hang a quilt on a wall, try to distribute the weight evenly and leave it up for only six months at a time to minimize stretching and tearing at weak points.

Never use nails, pins, or staples to hang a quilt.

Preserve quilts by airing them every six months by spreading them out for several days on a bed or on a sheet on your lawn. Hanging a quilt over a clothesline can cause irreparable damage.

To vacuum a quilt, place a nylon stocking over the nozzle of a canister vacuum and hold it several inches away from the quilt itself. Do not vacuum quilts that have beadwork or embroidery. Never beat the quilt to clean it.

Wash quilts in a large basin to minimize the number of folds. Use a mild solution; do not use bleach. Rinse thoroughly and blot dry with towels. Never squeeze or machine-dry a quilt.

Some fabrics in a patch or piecework quilt may not be colorfast—one small piece can ruin an entire quilt. Blacks and reds are especially prone to run, though other colors do as well.

Do not overwash quilts, which can stretch, distort, or weaken the fabric. Dry-cleaning can be very harsh as well.

Store quilts by folding them in white cotton or muslin sheets to prevent dirt buildup and tearing at the fold.

To fold a quilt, spread it face down on a clean white sheet and cover it with another white sheet. Then fold it, accordion-style, which will stretch the fabric the least.

WORDS TO REMEMBER

Appliqué. Fabric cutouts arranged in a decorative pattern and applied to or layered over another fabric.

Broderie perse. Individual design motifs, like shells, flowers, or birds, cut out of a piece of fabric and applied to a larger solid color fabric to form a patterned quilt (Persian embroidery).

Double wedding ring pattern. Scraps of cloth pieced together to form two interlocking circles.

Drunkard's path. Pieces of fabric in a curved design.

Grandmother's flower garden. A floral pattern formed by arranging small hexagonal pieces of fabric.

Linsey-woolsey. A strong, durable fabric made from a combination of linen and wool and used, generally, for whole-cloth quilts.

Log cabin. Narrow strips, or logs, pieced together to form a pattern.

Trapunto. A raised effect achieved by inserting stuffing, usually cotton, into certain areas outlined by stitching. A trapunto quilt can be identified by inspecting the back for tiny holes into which the stuffing was inserted.

Tumbling blocks. A three-dimensional pattern created with small fabric diamonds.

Wadding. Stuffing the top and bottom of a quilt.

24

Oriental Rugs

Though the terms associated with Oriental rugs seem complex and exotic—*ghiordes, torba, qali, mafrash, pushti,* to note only a few—the rugs themselves are really the humblest of objects. The best rugs were expertly made by hand, often intricately designed and colored, with designs of great and deeply symbolic meaning. Even so, their purpose was to cover a floor or perhaps a window, to be used as a table covering or maybe to be made into a saddlebag. Though they could cover a palace floor and be trod upon by kings and queens, they were more often small and used for prayer, a modest activity.

You can view a rug as simple and self-effacing, or you can see it as elaborate and complicated. But if you can combine these different ways of seeing rugs into one grand view, their nuance and beauty will make them more meaningful to you as a collector.

Whether they were made in central Persia or west China, rugs throughout the centuries share the same basic foundation, which is composed of warp and weft. The warp is the lengthwise element that is crossed with a widthwise element called the weft. On two sides of a rug the warp ends in fringe; on the other two sides the weft forms the selvedges, or the edges that are finished off to prevent unraveling.

A rug's pile is created by looping short pieces of yarn around two warp strands so that the ends of the yarn stick up and form the surface of the rug. This is called knotting, and an expert weaver can do a thousand knots an hour. The tighter the weave—in other words, the more knots per square inch—the more durable the pile and the rug (though not necessarily more collectible). That's why when you walk on truly good rugs your footsteps do not create lasting impressions in the pile. It's not the height of the pile that matters or gives a rug this characteristic. Instead, it's the knots, tight and taut and vertical, that spring back to life with collective energy when pressure initially tamps them down.

Flat weaves or tapestry weaves are rugs that have no pile. Instead, the warp and weft are themselves tightly woven together, with the widthwise yarns, or weft, colored to create the surface pattern. Kilims are a type of flat-weave rug.

No matter if a rug is piled or flat woven, collectors seek out certain similar attributes: hand-knotted instead of machine-made, natural dyes as opposed to chemically produced colors, and ethnographic authenticity of the rug and its weavers.

Those rugs that do reflect these characteristics are the true Oriental rugs that collectors covet. Rugs that do not may still be beautiful and they may still be desirable to some people, but to collectors they're considered decorative objects and not particularly collectible.

These decorative rugs are often what you will find in department stores or retail rug shops, and they are what most people today are referring to when they talk about Oriental rugs. Machine-made rugs aren't really Oriental at all, but Oriental style, and they often reflect modern Western decorating tastes more than the history and land of their origin.

Look for rugs you love, rugs in good repair made by hand with naturally dyed wool or silk. If you do, you will build a fine collection in which you can take pride.

QUESTIONS YOU'LL ALWAYS WANT TO ASK

Where is it from?
How was it made?

ONE IMPORTANT THING: COLOR

Together with its design, the color used in an Oriental rug is its most noticeable attribute. Two kinds of dyes are used: natural dyes made from vegetables, animals, and minerals; and synthetic dyes made from chemicals.

Chemical dyes were first introduced in Persia (now Iran) in the late nineteenth century. They were less expensive to use and make, and their vibrant—some would say crude—colors were thought to be attractive to the Western market, which was demanding an ever greater number of rugs. Yet the colors ran easily and were thought to be generally unreliable. After the First World War, however, more sophisticated methods of creating the dye produced a more stable, colorfast tone. These more complex dyes made them harder to distinguish from natural dyes, and their use increased dramatically.

It can take 325 pounds of dead insects or dried herbs to produce one pound of even the most common natural dye, but the color eventually created reflects the intensity of the process. Natural dyes have a sophisticated palette that ages and evolves over time, resulting in a mellow tone evocative of their origin.

Red comes from the roots of the madder plant and from certain insects; yellow is from the reseda plant, blue is from the indigo plant. The reds, yellows, and blues produced from these sources generate strong colors that look strong naturally. Chemically produced colors, on the other hand, are in many instances vibrant, yet somehow lifeless all the same. While chemicals may produce vivid oranges and electric greens that are unavailable naturally, these are colors that have no historic grounding in rug making, anyhow.

Depending on the area of origin, the color used in most Oriental rugs is steeped in tradition and symbolism. Because of this, it can be used to some extent to identify where a rug is from. In Muslim countries, for instance, green, the color of Muhammad's coat, is sacred and rarely used as a predominant color. It is, however, used widely in rugs made in China. There, the sacred color is yellow. Also, to the Chinese, Indians, and Persians, white represents grief. Blue symbolizes heaven in Persia and power and authority in Mongolia. Red is a widely accepted symbol of wealth and rejoicing in Muslim countries.

PRACTICAL ADVICE

Age is less important than rarity, design, and condition with most rugs.

The amount of light that filters through a rug held up to the light is an indication of the amount of damage caused by moths gnawing through the rug over the years. While a rug is held to the light, also look for holes or thinning.

Never buy a rug that hasn't been completely unfolded for your inspection; always inspect the entire rug, looking at both the front and the back.

As a general rule, the fewer decorative borders a rug has, the older it is. The presence of many borders indicates a rug made specifically to be exported to the West.

Put your ear to an old carpet and scrunch the fiber. If it sounds crunchy that's an indication the rug may have suffered from dry rot and will be easily damaged when walked upon; a good rug has soft wool and a full pile.

Repaired pile feels bumpy to the fingertips. Original pile feels smooth.

Wool is the most durable fiber with which to make a rug, silk the most luxurious.

Large carpets usually work out to be less expensive per square foot than smaller ones.

Just as some rugs are joined together to make a larger one, some large ones are cut down to increase their desirability. Avoid both of these types of rugs. To spot a cut rug, look for missing borders and truncated designs

If there has been reweaving, look to see that it was done everywhere where it was necessary, in similar shade yarn and tightness.

A design on a handmade rug will be clear on both sides. On a machine-made rug the design will be clear only on the top.

Even wear all over the rug is an indication that it was artificially worn to make it look old.

Don't assume a rug is old just because it's in poor repair.

Lay a rug on its face and look on the back to see if there are any light-colored patches that might signal mildew.

No matter how old silk is, it should always be soft and smooth, never brittle.

To check for repair, rub your hands on both the front and the back of the rug: mended areas will feel rough and bumpy. Remember, too, that not all rough areas are mended, but mended areas are almost always rough.

Check to see if the ground has been touched up with ink or paint to make worn-out areas look better.

Look for re-bound or added edges, damaged fringe, worn creases, holes, stains, repairs, washed-out or strident dyes, and ripples, all of which affect a rug's value.

Clean fringe with no wear or damage indicates a rug that is not too old or that the fringe was added later.

COLLECTOR'S CHOICE

When people speak of a Tabriz or Bidjar or Kerman rug, they're identifying the rug by its place of origin or the place from which it was imported, which are the most common ways of naming a rug. Sometimes a rug is referred to by a broad ethnic or tribal weaving group, such as Kurdish or Baluch, other times by a specific tribal group, such as Afshar.

In the broadest sense, however, rugs are broken down into five categories: Persian, Turkish, Caucasian, Turkoman, and Chinese. Each has specific design, color, and manufacturing characteristics, though because weaving tribes were often mobile, they carried these characteristics across borders, making it harder as time went on to easily identify rugs.

Persian. The earliest known Persian rug dates to the fifth century B.C. and was found by a Russian professor in 1949 in the Atlai Mountains in Siberia. Having been frozen into the tundra for over two thousand years, it was almost perfectly preserved, its deep red still brilliant, the deer and horsemen depicted on its borders still precise. The very qualities that this ancient rug possesses are what make Persian rugs so desirable. They're well known for their durability, color, and intricate, realistic design.

Persian rugs are an intrinsic part of Iranian culture. They come in a wide variety of designs, colors, sizes, and weaves, and each one is unique, so identification can be difficult. One way to understand Persian rugs, however, is through common design motifs, the most usual of which is the lushness with which flowers, other plant life, and the natural world in general are depicted. Fields of animals, birds, orchards, and flowers including tulips, roses, and narcissus are common, as are borders lined with rosettes.

Persian weavers made great use of the vase as a symbol of peace and tranquillity, and the tree of life, a historic religious and mythological symbol connecting man to the heavenly world. Pictorial scenes were common as well, illustrating human figures on horseback, scenes rooted in the history of the shahs and princes who ruled the land.

Turkish. While many think Turkish rugs lack the intricacy and sophistication of Persian rugs, their dazzling colors—canary yellow, lavender, mauve, red, and powder blue—and their well-deserved reputation for durability make up for what they may lack otherwise.

With a tradition of rug making almost as long and illustrious as that of the Persians, Turkish rug makers, who included both tribal and nomadic peoples who drew on their Turkic heritage and cultural iconography for inspiration, relied less on weaving meticulous and specific flowers and more on a stylized floral design. While some Turkish rugs have geometric motifs, human and animal motifs are rarely if ever used because the Koran's injunction against the portrayal of living things is more strictly observed by the Turkish Sunni Muslims than by the Shiites in Persia.

The Turkish are particularly known for making small rugs specifically for prayer, as well as unusually large rugs intended for libraries and dining rooms.

Caucasian. Using what have been characterized as "bold, heraldic, and violently beautiful colors," the rugs originating in this region—between the Black Sea and Caspian Sea and including parts of Russia, Iran, and Turkey—have, intentionally or not, been designed to reflect the often strife-filled lives of its population.

Most nineteenth-century Caucasian weavers were villagers using small looms, so you'll rarely come across room-size rugs, but instead many smaller prayer rugs and lengthy runners. These will be made from wool or occasionally cotton—silk wasn't much used in this region—and the designs will include crosses, anchors, ram's horns, and geometric forms, as opposed to an abundance of flowers and leaves. Floral motifs that do exist in Caucasian rugs are far stiffer and more angular than those used in Persian rug making. While Caucasian rugs sometimes include religious symbols, in some instances their meanings are indecipherable.

Turkoman. Renowned for their short, cropped pile and densely knotted, highly durable quality, Turkoman rugs were constructed from heavy wool or camel hair on a sheep or goat hair foundation. Many of these sturdy textiles weren't woven as traditional floor coverings but instead as tent decorations and trappings, such as door covers and door surrounds, as well as saddlebags and as parts of a young woman's dowry.

The Turkoman region extended from the Caspian Sea in the west to Tibet in the east and was bounded north and south by Russia and Persia. Rugs from this region, with their many rich shades of red, wine, mahogany, earthy brown, and grays, are distinguished by tones from the somber side of the color palette.

The design itself makes use of an arrangement of several medallions in geometric patterns, called guls. These are the most common decorative motif of Turkoman rugs. They are said to represent tribal emblems, each variation of which was said to be at one point the exclusive property of an individual tribe. Also common in Turkoman design are octagons, hexagons, eight-pointed stars, and some stylized animal and floral motifs.

Chinese. Unlike Persia and Turkey, where rug making was local and designs and weaving techniques were closely associated with various tribes, across China there were few regional differences in rugs made. Though rugs themselves had been used in China from at least the twelfth century, it wasn't until several centuries later that the making of rugs was imported into China from Mongolia and Turkistan.

While many Chinese rug makers stuck to classically Chinese design motifs and limited themselves to a simple color scheme, including blue and cream, others used a more vibrant rainbow of color that included bright yellows and oranges.

Chinese design motifs include many animals, from the real—elephants, horses, bats, and cranes—to the fantastic, such as dragons and the phoenix. Known for their exacting rendering of the natural world, Chinese rug makers included lotus blossoms, pomegranates, peonies, and daffodils as well as some symbols derived from religious life—for example, the conch, symbolizing the call to prayer, and the vase, which contains the water of perfect wisdom.

TAKING CARE OF YOUR COLLECTION

Instead of folding a rug, roll it with the pile on the outside, to prevent cracking or stretching the fragile backing fabric.

To avoid any trapped condensation, which can lead to mildew, don't wrap a rug in plastic, use rubber bands, or tie it too tight with string.

When storing a rug, avoid attics and basements where temperatures can swing from very hot to very cold.

Display rugs out of direct sunlight, which will fade the wool over time.

Avoid putting your rugs in high-traffic areas of your house, as such traffic may eventually strain the fibers beyond their limits.

When hanging a rug, don't stretch it too tight, as changes in humidity will cause it to shrink or expand. The rug must retain enough flexibility to account for these natural, though slight, changes in size, yet not sag, which would strain its backing.

Do not use staples, nails, or glue to hang a rug.

Shaking or beating a rug will strain its backing as well, and may cause an older rug to disintegrate.

Air your rugs outdoors occasionally, especially on damp foggy days. Do not, however, hang them over a clothesline.

Because sand and grit can grind down the pile and weaken its foundation, rugs must occasionally be vacuumed. First, place your rug face down and gently pat it to dislodge naturally as much of the dirt as possible which is caught between the loops. Then use an upholstery attachment with a piece of nylon over the nozzle and gently vacuum.

Blot, don't rub, any liquid that spills; if necessary sponge the area gently with cold water.

Never wash your rug in a machine or send it to a dry cleaner, where harsh chemicals might cause damage.

To dry a rug, roll it, pile side out, in heavy towels and then lay it flat to dry in a shaded area.

Never place an Oriental rug directly on an uncarpeted floor. Use an underlay to protect the rug from being squeezed between two hard surfaces—your foot and the floor—and to lessen the damage of such pressure.

WORDS TO REMEMBER

Abrash. An obvious change in color or tone that doesn't correspond to a change in design, caused by a weaver going to a separately dyed batch of yarn partway through making the rug.

All-over. A pattern that is repeated all over the field of the carpet.

Cartoon. The design for a tapestry or carpet.

Dry rot. A fungus that grows in conditions of heat and moisture and breaks down the cellulose in a carpet's fibers.

Field. The area of a rug enclosed by the border.

Ghiordes. The type of knot used in Turkey.

Gul. The basic design motif of Oriental carpets, usually an octagon.

Herati. In Persian carpets, an important and common·pattern consisting of a central rosette and four lanceolate leaves curving outward.

Kilim. A woven, knotless and therefore pileless, carpet.

Medallion. Any large central motif used as a focal point of a design.

Mir. A palm leaf, common in the design of Persian rugs.

Nap. The rug surface, made up of knots in the warp and weft; also called the pile.

Palmette. A flower that is a common design motif in Persian rugs.

Sine. The type of knot used in Persia.

25

Silver

Silver is easy to collect. You can start small and, if you want, stay small, yet still build an impressive collection. There are collections of beautiful silver spoons, for which the collector never paid more than a couple of dollars apiece. Wonderfully eclectic collections of flatware abound, assembled with an eye toward interesting patterns, particular makers, or certain time periods.

Silver has been used to create hundreds of different types of objects, from soup tureens to napkin rings to chocolate pots to hip flasks and, of course, flatware, tea services, candlesticks, vases, and serving pieces.

Not all silver is alike, though, and there is a lot of confusion about the differences between sterling silver and silver plate. Actually, there's even some confusion about "sterling," "silver," and "sterling silver." Many people use the terms interchangeably, and sometimes that's okay. But true aficionados know the difference, and it's more than merely a matter of semantics.

"Silver" is a generic term for objects made from any combination of silver and an alloy, whereas sterling silver is 92.5 percent silver. Pure silver alone is too soft to be used in making any sort of sturdy object. The high silver content in sterling adds not only to its value as a collector's item but also to its cost, and this has been true throughout the ages. Silver has always been expensive and was, for many years, owned only by the wealthy. By the mid-eighteenth century, however, a growing English middle class made the development of a less expensive but still decorative substitute possible.

To meet this demand, copper and other metals were covered with thin sheets of silver and hammered and fused together, lending an object the look of sterling silver without its expense. The final product could then be made into useful as well as ornamental objects. Sheffield plate, for example, was used widely for tea trays, tea and coffee pots, and candlesticks, among other household objects. Named for the place where it was first developed, Sheffield can in many instances be decorated like sterling, though the thinness of the silver makes engraving almost impossible. Sheffield silver is easy to manipulate, though, and can be inlaid with thicker pieces of silver that can be engraved with coats of arms or monograms.

Age, use, and polishing may cause some of the silver plating to wear away, allowing the reddish tinge of the copper beneath to show through. This is called bleeding and is not necessarily a cause for alarm.

By the mid-nineteenth century the process by which Sheffield plate was created was supplanted by a faster, less expensive process called electroplating, where an electric current was used to deposit a thin coat of silver on a base metal. Though most Sheffield silver was unmarked, electroplate is often stamped EP or EPNS, the latter indicating that it was electroplated with nickel instead of copper.

The differences between Sheffield and electroplate are fairly obvious once you see and feel them side by side. In natural light Sheffield has a slight bluish color, while electroplate has a somewhat harder, harsher, and shinier appearance. Both lack the truly warm glow of sterling. Additionally, because Sheffield plate starts out as sheets of silver applied to copper sheets, once it is made into objects, there are natural seams. Electroplate coating of silver is uniform.

If you're in an antique store and still stuck not being able to tell the difference between sterling and silver plate, bear in mind that most sterling tarnishes gray or brown, while silver plate tarnishes black.

QUESTIONS YOU'LL ALWAYS WANT TO ASK

Is this the best of its kind that I can afford?

Are there any repairs?

Am I paying a premium for a rare mark? Is it worth it?

ONE IMPORTANT THING: MARKS

Like marks on porcelain and pottery, silver hallmarks are less than fail-safe measures of authenticity and age. Unlike those on porcelain and pottery, however, silver hallmarks are consistent in design and meaning.

In fact, the word "hallmark" derives from Goldsmiths' Hall in London, where starting in 1478 all silver had to be assayed before it could be sold or exported. The hallmark was meant to guarantee that the object had been tested by a government testing agency and conformed to a legal standard of the proportion of actual silver to the base metal, which for sterling, as mentioned, is 92.5 percent.

Most English silver has four marks. First, there's the sterling guarantee, which may be either a leopard's head, crowned or uncrowned, a lion walking, or a lion's head, uncrowned. Second is the town mark, which indicates the town, such as Norwich or Birmingham, in which the piece was made. Next comes the date letter, unique from year to year, but always enclosed in a shield. Last is the maker's mark, which was either a symbol, a letter, or a set of initials.

Hallmarks are usually grouped together on the bottom or near an edge of an object, though over time many have worn away or been altered or even forged. It's not entirely uncommon for a mark to be transferred from one object to another. Such fakery can be detected usually by breathing on it—if it's a later addition its outline will show—or by feeling for a seam, which will be noticeable from the tarnish in its crevices.

American silver had no standard marks. Instead early silversmiths stamped it with their initial or a personal symbol to guarantee quality. They impressed the word "standard" to indicate the sterling standard. By the middle of the nineteenth century American silver was often marked with the name of the retailer or manufacturer instead of the maker. After 1907 the United States required silver to be stamped "sterling."

PRACTICAL ADVICE

When collecting, look for quality first. Age and maker's marks are meaningless if the object is of poor quality.

Repair is always detrimental to value except in rare cases where a unique style takes precedence.

Silver pieces found in the Southwest and Mexico that seem crudely made are not necessarily old; in fact, old pieces are usually very well made. High-quality craftsmanship is a distinguishing characteristic of Native American silver.

Old silver shouldn't necessarily shine brightly, as it's only modern refinery techniques and machine buffing that allow newer silver to shine.

Look to see that an object's handles are in good shape, not damaged or dented, and that feet, finials, and other protrusions are intact.

Deep tarnish may eat into silver and cause damage—it's best to avoid such pieces.

Engraved dates on silver may be the date the silver was given to someone or the date being commemorated, not the date the object was manufactured.

A shiny but smeared area on a silver object might indicate an engraving that has been buffed out.

Embossed areas should be closely inspected for wear.

Don't buy silver that is too worn. The more worn it is, the faster it will continue to wear away.

Most silver design followed the fashion of the day, so dating it that way can be easier than using the marks, which may be fake or altered.

Check to see if a piece can still do what it was intended to do, such as hold hot water or other liquids.

COLLECTOR'S CHOICE

How can you decide what theme to build your silver collection around? Some people choose a particular maker—Phipps & Robinson or Tiffany & Company, for example—or a style, pattern, or function. Here are some of the more popular types of objects people collect, along with a few things to know and some things to explore when seeking them out.

Flatware. For centuries, people treasured their spoons. Many people received them upon their baptism, and if one got wealthier through his lifetime, the type of spoon he used increased in quality, from wood to horn to pewter to brass. The lucky few ate from silver spoons (there were no forks as we know them until about 1660). It wasn't until people decided to provide their guests with eating utensils that the concept of tableware came into being; up to that time people traveled with their own. Such silver pieces were produced solely for guests, and eventually additional, more specialized pieces were created, such as fish forks and teaspoons.

Some people assemble a flatware service by picking and choosing among makers and patterns. Others collect straight sets made in the same year by the same manufacturer. Not surprisingly, these are the most valuable.

When collecting a service, first choose a pattern you like. Make sure it was made in the right size—in other words, that it wasn't manufactured only for eating dessert. Once you're ready to make a purchase, buy the dessert forks first, as they're traditionally the most expensive, but be careful that what you buy didn't start out as spoons and later get shortened and fitted with tines—a common scam. Note that knives, made from thin sheeting, tend to wear out first and are often missing or very hard to find.

Tankards. Made in great quantities when a quart or more of ale was the drink du jour, tankards became less popular to own, and therefore make, as wine and other spirits gained in popularity. In fact, by the nineteenth century they were made mostly for presentation purposes only. Today they're very collectible.

English tankards from the eighteenth century were fairly plain, often decorated with only a coat of arms. American-made tankards from the eighteenth century, especially those made in and around New York and Pennsylvania, are often elaborately decorated on their handles and around their bases. Hallmarks on American tankards usually are found to the left of the handle, while on English tankards they're to the right. Sometimes lids and handles are stamped separately from the body.

A tankard's handles are often hollow, and the weight of so much liquid inside caused some handles to pull away from, or tear, the main body, so it's important to look for damage in this area, as well as undamaged handle sockets. Additionally, the rim near the handle may have been split and repaired. The thumb rest on top of the hinge may leave a dent in the top of the handle, which can help authenticate a tankard as old, and often is a sign of use and charm.

Candlesticks. Silver candlesticks are generally either cast or made of sheet silver, the latter of which tends to be loaded so they won't tip over so easily. To see what you have, turn the candlesticks over. If they are cast or silver sheet you'll see only silver; if they are loaded, the bottom will be covered in baize (the green feltlike material used on billiard tables), wood, or a metal plate. You can further distinguish between sheet silver and cast silver by feeling the candlestick. Sheet silver is smooth and of even thickness; cast is rougher. Cast is considered the highest quality.

Candlesticks are highly collectible and many have been produced through the ages in Europe and the United States. But due to wear and tear even the highest-quality ones are easily damaged. Silver candlesticks are usually several pieces soldered together, so it's important to inspect them closely for splits and repairs before making any purchases. All of this fusing creates subtle seams. You'll be able to feel them with your fingertips.

Pairs of candlesticks are most desirable. It's important to note, however, that, strictly speaking, a pair is not merely two identical candlesticks but two candlesticks made by the same person—not just the same manufacturer—within three years of each other, and preferably closer in time than that. Marks will come in handy to determine such authenticity. Look for them on or underneath the base or in a line on the stem just above the base.

Coffee and tea services. Almost nothing looks more impressive on a dining room sideboard than a gleaming tea and coffee service. No wonder, too, since services can be very expensive and demand a fair amount of care. After all, all those handles, spouts, and feet are easily damaged.

While it seems that there's been teatime in England since time immemorial, in fact tea (and coffee) were not widely introduced there until the early seventeenth century. The first teapots were small—tea was very expensive—and egg-shaped. Their spouts had a detachable stopper to keep the leaves from being poured into the cup.

The coffeepot was taller, with the spout at least halfway up or a lip at its rim to prevent the dregs from escaping. The shape changed from cylindrical to pear-shaped to drum-like to octagonal as the fashion changed. Today there's a look to suit every taste. Complete sets, which came into being during the late eighteenth and early nineteenth centuries, are, of course, the most sought after and prized. Most people started with a teapot and assembled the rest of the service around it.

Teapots are invariably the most used pieces and therefore the most likely to be damaged or repaired. Check the body for leaks or thin spots by feeling its inside. Collectors look at hinges as well as lips, rims, spouts, and legs, which can over time push into the base and cause damage. Loose handles do not affect value as they can be easily tightened, though sometimes handles pull away from the base over time causing damage or tears.

Both teapots and coffeepots should be marked on the base or in a line near the handle, as should their lids.

TAKING CARE OF YOUR COLLECTION

Wear cotton gloves as often as possible when handling silver to prevent oils and acids from your hands touching the object.

Don't feel you have to polish silver that's tarnished before you store it; polishing it just exposes silver to the elements.

Wash dirty silver before you polish it, as dirt can scratch it.

Use a soft children's toothbrush to clean hard-to-reach spots and engraved areas.

Choose a less abrasive polish that doesn't protect as well against tarnish over a more abrasive polish that protects better. You can always polish, but an abrasive polish can cause damage.

Polish silver by hand instead of having it mechanically buffed as buffing will wear away bits of silver.

After you use any silver utensil, wash it by hand with liquid detergent. Dry it immediately with a cotton dish towel, as even water can stain silver.

Avoid putting silver in the dishwasher. The detergent and hot water are too abrasive a combination and since some silver is repaired with pitch, a low-melting cement that expands with heat, knife blades in particular may pop out of their handles.

Don't wash the hallmarks on the bottom of silver objects as they can wear away over time, lessening the piece's value.

Store silver in acid-free paper, not felt, as felt emits hydrogen sulfide, which causes silver to tarnish.

Some paints and oils used on the interior of silver storage cases can actually accelerate tarnishing, so seal the interior wood surfaces with lacquer or polyurethane.

WORDS TO REMEMBER

Alloy. A mixture of metals.

Assay. To test silver to determine its purity.

Britannia Standard. Silver with a silver content of 95.8 percent, as opposed to sterling silver's 92.5 percent.

Casting. Using molds to shape molten silver into legs, finials, and handles.

Chasing. Detailing the surface of a metal article with various hammer-struck punches.

Coin silver. Eighteenth- and nineteenth-century silver that is approximately 900 parts silver, sometimes marked "coin" or "pure coin."

Enameling. Coating a silver object with colored molten glass.

Hammering. Beating a sheet of metal to give it a particular shape.

Hollowware. Silver pieces—teapots, vases, cups—in which you can put things, as opposed to flatware.

Presentation silver. Silver objects such as loving cups, trophies, and medals, created for commemorative purposes.

Repoussé. Emboss from the back or inside and then push back on the outside—in other words, *repoussé,* or *repush* in French.

Vermeil. Gilded silver gilt, used to lend silver hollowware the appearance of a more precious metal.

26

Timepieces

Clocks and watches have a language all their own. Their internal mechanisms work in concert with one another to keep track of time and of our lives. Inside their gold or wooden cases the parts are complicated, fragile, small. They talk to one another in a way, following orders, doing what comes next and next and next, ceaselessly, as time continues to pass.

Most timepieces, in their most simple incarnation, whether six-foot-high tallcases or bejeweled wristwatches, are based on the same fundamental principle. They're pieces of equipment performing regular movements in equal intervals of time linked to counting mechanisms that record the number of movements. It has pretty much been that way since the beginning of mechanical timekeeping.

The earliest known public clock was erected in Milan in 1335; the oldest extant clock has been at Salisbury Cathedral in England since 1386. More than 250 years after this clock's construction, in 1637, Galileo noted the characteristic timekeeping property of the pendulum. He found it to be reliable since the time required for a complete swing depends only on the length of the pendulum and is almost independent of the arc. But this observation was made by Christiaan Huygens, as well, and in 1657 Huygens, not Galileo, made the first pendulum-regulated clock. This understanding ushered in the modern era of timekeeping, and in many ways has changed little to this day.

To those who collect timepieces, a clock's interior life is as important as its exterior case. Clocks and watches are judged on both, and to most collectors both the interior workings and exterior casing must be of the same high quality. A timepiece is a kind of machine and a piece of furniture as well, and neither the machine nor the furniture has a lot of meaning by itself.

Because timepieces have this dual personality they can be more challenging to collect than many other objects. Which question do you ask first: is it attractive or does it work? Both are important to a timepiece's desirability, and both need to be answered, though one is more subjective than the other, of course. To have value, a clock should work, have its original parts, including the glass, and be in good condition. To be considered an antique, a clock must be at least one hundred years old.

Once these things have been established, collectors look at various other aspects of a timepiece, including, of course, age and rarity (clocks were designed according to the fashions of the day) and condition (moving parts often mean missing parts). If there's a label on a clock, so much the better. Most clocks in America were produced with labels, so the absence of one should be considered in light of its overall value, and the presence of one should be looked at with a bit of skepticism, as they can be faked or changed by unscrupulous sellers. A watch with its original packaging can indicate a piece's history and lend a note of authenticity as well.

QUESTIONS YOU'LL ALWAYS WANT TO ASK

How old is it?

Does it run?

What repairs have been made?

What parts are not original?

ONE IMPORTANT THING: COMPLICATIONS

Complications are a watch's functions other than those that tell time. They are key components of a watch's value. The more complications a watch has, the more valuable it is.

The most common complications include indications of the day, date, and month. Others include a minute repeater, perpetual calendar, alarm, split-second chronograph, lunar phases, and registers that indicate the passage of a given period of time. Another desirable complication is the tourbillion, a device in a mechanical watch that eliminates timekeeping errors produced by the slight differences caused when it is in a horizontal or vertical position. A self-winding or automatic device in a watch is considered a complication, as well.

PRACTICAL ADVICE

Collections can be based on certain makers, dial styles, mechanical aspects of the watch's movement, or the intricacy of the mechanisms—for example, with chimes, calendars, and so forth.

Second hands have been used on watches since 1780 and on clocks since about the same time.

Inexplicable holes on a clock dial indicate that it is not that movement's original dial.

Replaced hands aren't bad if they at least match the style and material of the originals.

Look for a watch marriage, in which the movement of one watch was joined with the case of another.

Restoring a clock is very expensive so you're better off buying one that is not in need of repair.

Eight-day clocks are more desirable, and therefore often more expensive, than clocks that need to be wound every day.

Clocks taller than eight feet may be impressive to look at, but they are not so collectible, as they will not fit easily into most homes.

Clock hoods are easily bashed and clock feet rot and are easily destroyed, so inspect these parts—the top and the bottom—carefully.

Inspect all moldings carefully to ensure that they are sturdy, original, and all there.

Check painted dials for flaking.

Areas most likely to be worn on a watch include the bezel, the lugs, and the crystal.

The letters GF on a watch mean "gold-filled."

Women's watches are less collectible than men's watches, because the latter are considered less like jewelry.

COLLECTOR'S CHOICE

Grandfather clocks. Originally called long-case or tall case clocks, the current name came into use around 1875 due to the popularity of a song called "My Grandfather's Clock," which began, "My grandfather's clock was too tall for the shelf. . . ." Today, of course, grandfather clocks, which are called long-case clocks in England, are beloved additions to many homes, not only for keeping time but for keeping watch over generations of families as they lead their daily lives.

Tall case clocks are weight-driven and were made possible by the invention of the pendulum in 1657. They're really just clocks atop a base in which the weights are housed, crowned by the framework of the actual movement and clock face. In other words, sort of like a table clock mounted on a pedestal. They also have longer pendulums, which among other things, makes them good timekeepers.

The earliest tall case clocks had square or round dials. Around 1715 the arched dial was designed. Basically a square with a semicircle on top, like a hat, this allowed for more decoration or information, such as the maker's name. Before the arch dial came into being, if there was a signature, it was usually found on the bottom of the dial. Within a few years, the decorations became quite a bit more extravagant, with images of ships, animals, and, appropriately enough, Father Time, among many others.

The cases reflected the fashions of the day and were made from woods that were popular at the time, including cherry, mahogany, and oak.

A pendulum that appears suspiciously large for its case may indicate a marriage, or joining, of parts from one clock to the parts or case of another. While this may not bother you from an aesthetic point of view, collectors and true grandfather clock aficionados will not approve.

Watches. Like jewelry, a watch is something that can be both collected and worn, so its appearance is important. From a collector's standpoint, the more unusual the watch, the more desirable. A watch with moving figures on its face, one that has an alarm or plays music, a watch in an elaborate gold case—these are the kinds of unique pieces that collectors often seek.

Particularly in the twentieth century, watch design has changed. In the 1920s watch faces went from being round and plain to being square, rectangular, oval, and octagonal. During the 1930s watch faces began to be somewhat abstract and exaggerated. It was also during these decades that manufacturers such as Tiffany, Rolex, Patek Philippe, Cartier, and Jaeger le Coultre, among others, made what are today the most sought-after watches. By the 1940s watches had become very jewel-like, with precious gems and gold used extravagantly in their design. In the 1950s they took on the futuristic look that was characteristic of much of the design then.

When looking at a watch, of course, you need to be concerned with more than its look. You'll want to know about its mechanism, if it works, if the parts are original, what repairs have been made, and what repairs might have to be made in the future. If there are functions such as a chronograph, a calendar, or a repeater, are they in good working condition. For every no you get, the value of the watch is considerably lower than it would otherwise be.

Pocket watches. The more effort that has been put into the manufacture of a pocket watch, all else being equal, the more highly prized it will be by today's collector. Pocket watches have been made for several centuries, though it is rare to find particularly old ones dating from, say, the eighteenth century. Those that do date from before this time are heavy, thick, and not too easily portable.

After about 1800, however, watchmakers in Continental Europe started to make slimmer pocket watches with fancy enameled cases, sometimes shaped like hearts or violins. Dials from this era also often included minor dials with moon phases or calendars, which make the watch more collectible today. By the mid-nineteenth century the keyless watch was introduced which precluded the need of a separate key to wind it.

There are two types of pocket watches, those with hunt cases, which have a cover that closes over the face, and open-face watches, which do not have a cover. Hunt cases are more desirable, partly because there's more gold in the case, as are repeating watches, which sound out the time on demand when a lever or button is pressed.

Collectors look for crack- and chip-free dials, easy-to-read numbers, straight hands, cases free of dents and scratches, and hinges and latches that are in good working order. The presence of the original box adds value and helps to authenticate the watch as well, especially if the serial number on the box and on the watch match. If they don't, the watch and box may be a sort of marriage and should be questioned.

Bracket clocks. Bracket or mantel clocks have been made since the seventeenth century and derive their name from their placement on wall brackets for display purposes. They're similar to long-case clocks, without the long case and with a shorter pendulum. Chimes appeared relatively late in the history of this form. Bracket clocks became popular in the last half of the nineteenth century, and many styles were manufactured. European bracket clocks are typically housed in elaborate, fanciful cases, while Victorian-era clocks were heavily carved.

Clocks in this form were produced in Germany and England; it can be difficult to identify their country of origin when they are not marked. Many were marked, or signed, however, and such signatures can be used to help date and authenticate the clock. Early clocks, dating before the eighteenth century, often had the signature on the bottom of the dial plate. As time went on, the signature was within the chapter ring, the part of the dial on which the hour numbers are engraved, attached, or painted. Sometimes the signature was in the arch of the dial. After about 1830 the name that appeared there was sometimes that of the retailer rather than the maker.

To detect a fake painted signature, feel it. The fake ones feel rough while genuine signatures are smoother.

In America, especially during the nineteenth century, bracket clocks were particularly popular. They were affordable, with little brass and white painted dials. Again, however, they were altered as the fashions changed, and you should inspect them carefully, looking for replaced or missing feet and finials.

Carriage clocks. First developed in the late eighteenth century in France by Abraham Louis Bréguet, and called *pendule de voyage*, these relatively small spring-driven clocks were meant to be taken on the road. They usually came in small leather boxes and in various sizes, including the smallest, called *mignonnette*, full size, and giant. Most were made in England and France, but they were very popular in the United States.

The earliest carriage clocks have brass frames cast in one piece with beveled glass panels on the front, sides, back, and top, revealing the movement. Such construction left little room for decoration. After about 1845, though, once cases began to be made from several parts, designs became more elaborate and included gilding, engraving, or enameling.

TAKING CARE OF YOUR COLLECTION

It's time to get your clock professionally cleaned and lubricated when it exhibits slow or labored chimes or begins to run slow or fast. This will occur about every five years.

Make sure that your clocks, especially grandfather clocks that sit on the floor and bracket clocks that sit on a shelf, are level.

Keep clocks away from direct sunlight and heat, especially radiators.

Dust clock cases with a feather duster, using a commercial antistatic cleaning and dusting spray.

Keep watches clean and dry, and remember that "water resistant" means only that you can get caught in the rain, not go scuba diving.

Lacquered brass or silvered dials should never be cleaned with water.

Get cracked crystals replaced as soon as possible so moisture doesn't seep in.

If you do get your watch wet, even if it is just splashed from the sink, immediately dry it off to prevent any moisture from seeping inside.

Watches that need to be wound should be wound regularly, even if you do not wear them regularly.

Never change or replace clock or watch parts on your own.

WORDS TO REMEMBER

Arch. The curved part of any clock case.

Automatic winding. Winding that occurs as the wearer moves his arm.

Bezel. The ring, often brass, that secures the glass cover to the dial of a watch.

Bob. The weight at the end of a pendulum.

Boss. The disk applied to the arch of a dial on which the maker's name appears.

Calendar aperture. The widow in some dials that displays the day and the month.

Chapter rings. The part of the dial on which the hour numbers are engraved, attached, or painted.

Chronograph. A watch with a center second hand that can be used as a stopwatch.

Crystal. The clear cover over the face of a watch.

Cut-down. A long-case clock that has been shortened.

Escapement. The mechanism that controls the transfer of energy from the power source to the counting mechanism.

Hood. The top part of a long-case clock, usually detachable to provide access to the interior.

Horology. The science of time measurement, including the art of making watches and clocks.

Lugs. The connection points for a watch strap.

Mainspring. The large flat metal spring that provides the power for the clock and drives its wheels.

Pendulum. The device that swings at a fixed rate and controls the rate of timekeeping.

Repeater. A watch that strikes the time on request.

Train. An interconnected series of wheels and pinions that transmits the power of the spring or weight to the hands of the watch or clock.

Appendixes

Appendix A

GLOSSARY OF TRADITIONAL TERMS

Absentee bid. A bid submitted in advance by a client and placed on his behalf by the auction house. Also called an order bid.

Advance. An increment by which the bid continues.

All or choice. A lot that includes more than one thing that the successful bidder can buy, if he wishes, at the same price each as his winning bid.

As is. There is no guarantee that the object is anything other than what you see.

Bid increment. The fixed amount by which bidders must increase their bid.

Bought in. When a lot fails to sell because it has not met the reserve.

Buyers' premium. A percentage of the final bid added to the total cost of the object, paid for by the high bidder.

Buyer's privilege. When the successful bidder gets to buy the remaining lots of similar items with his original high bid.

Caveat emptor. Latin for "Let the buyer beware."

Choice. In a set of five chairs, if sold "choice," the bidder can take one or more of the chairs for the high bid.

Collusion. When two or more people agree not to bid against one another to deflate the value of a particular object.

Conditions of sale. The rules and regulations set forth by an auction house that govern its sales.

Consignment. An object given over to sell on behalf of the owner by a third party, such as an auction house.

Discretion. An agreed-upon percentage below the reserve price at which the seller authorizes the auctioneer to sell the lot.

Estate sale. The sale of property left by a person at his or her death.

Fair market value. The highest price an object will bring in a competitive and open market.

Global reserve. A reserve in which the overage above the reserve from a successful lot is applied to a subsequent lot up to a pre-arranged limit.

Hammer price. The last bid recognized by the auctioneer before he bangs his gavel.

Jump bid. A bid raised by an increment higher than the standard increments.

Knocked down. Sold.

Lot. An individual object or a group of objects tagged as a single object for sale.

Open outcry auction. An English auction, or an ascending-price auction.

Pass. When an auctioneer decides to skip a lot.

Phantom bidder. In order to keep a slow auction going, the auctioneer may look into the corner of the room and acknowledge a nonexistent bid.

Presale estimate. The price range assigned to a consignment based on an estimate of what the object will sell for.

Price realized. The price achieved at the auction, usually inclusive of the buyers' premium.

Provenance. The ownership and exhibition history of an object.

Reserve. The lowest price for which an object will be sold.

Seller's commission. A percentage of the final bid charged to a consignor.

Times the money. The successful bidder must take all the items in a lot—say there are five—by multiplying the high bid times five.

Unrestricted sale. An auction in which there are no reserves or minimums.

Withdrawal. The removal of a lot from an auction.

Appendix B

GLOSSARY OF ONLINE TERMS

Alerts. E-mail from the site that tells buyers and sellers what is happening.

Auto extension. On some sites, an option for either the seller or the auction site to extend the end of an auction beyond its original time if someone places a bid near the end of the auction.

Bid cancellation. Bidders can cancel their bid if they feel uncomfortable with the seller.

Bid history. A list of those who bid on an object and the amount they bid.

Bid retraction. The legitimate cancellation of a bid on an item by a buyer in the midst of an auction.

Bid rigging. The illegitimate bidding by a seller or a friend of the seller to inflate the price of an object; also known as shilling.

Blacklisting. Some sites allow sellers to keep individual buyers from bidding on their auctions.

Closing notification. An e-mail from the auction site alerting the successful bidder and consignor that an auction has ended.

Deadbeats. Successful bidders who fail to pay.

Escrow. Money held in trust by a third party until the buyer receives the merchandise from the seller.

fdbk/fk. Feedback; users' comments about each other.

Feedback bombing war. When users retaliate with negative feedback in each other's profiles.

Feedback padding. When users post fraudulent positive feedback.

Final value fee. The amount the seller pays the auction site after his object sells.

Flaming. When someone sends abusive or threatening messages.

GIF. Graphics interchange format, or digital photo images.

Initial listing price. The lowest price a seller is willing to accept as a bid.

Insertion fee. The amount a seller pays to the auction site to list an object.

JPEG. Joint Photographic Experts Group—in other words, a digital photo.

Listing fee. The amount paid to an auction site by a seller to list an object.

Maximum bid. The highest price a buyer is willing to pay.

Minimum opening bid. The lowest first bid a seller will accept.

NARU. Stands for "not a registered user" and refers to people whose memberships have been canceled.

Net cops. Auction users who report fraud.

Opening bid. The seller's bid that sets the first price.

Outbid. When a person's maximum bid is higher than the previous person's maximum bid.

Outbid notification. An e-mail message sent to buyers when they have been outbid.

Proxy bid. A secret maximum bid automatically offered by the site on your behalf.

Registered user. A person who has registered with an auction site to use its services.

Relisting. When an object fails to meet its reserve, sellers sometimes try to resell with a lower reserve.

Retaliatory. Negative feedback against a user who posts negative feedback about you.

Shilling. Fraudulent bidding by a seller or his associates in order to pad the auction. Also called a shill bid.

Sniping. Entering a high bid just as an auction closes.

Appendix C

INTERNET ABBREVIATIONS

BBW: buyer beware
BTW: by the way
CIA: cash in advance
CYE: check your e-mail
EOA: end-of-auction
FB: feedback
FVF: final value fees (sales commissions)
FWIW: for what it's worth
HTH: hope this helps
IMHO: in my humble opinion
IMO: in my opinion
LSASE: large self-addressed stamped envelope
MIB: mint in box
MIJ: made in Japan
MIOJ: made in occupied Japan
MIP: mint in package
MIU: made in USA

NARU: not a registered user
NBW: never been worn
NPB: non-paying bidder
NR: no reserve
NRFB: never removed from box
OIC: oh, I see
OOP: out of print
OTOH: on the other hand
PM: priority mail
PPD: post paid
ROFL: rolling on floor laughing
RSVP: respond, please
SASE: self-addressed stamped envelope
S&H: shipping & handling
S/S: still sealed
SW: slight wear
TIA: thanks in advance
TM: trademark
TY: thank you
USPS: United States Postal Service
WOC: writing on cover
WYSIWYG: what you see is what you get

Appendix D

Alderfer Auction Company

501 Fairgrounds Road
Hatfield, PA 19440
(215) 393-3000
www.alderfercompany.com

Bertoia Auctions

1881 Spring Road
Vineland, NJ 08361
(856) 692-1881
www.bertoiaauctions.com

Frank H. Boos Gallery

420 Enterprise Court
Bloomfield Hills, MI 48302
(248) 332-1500
http://members.aol.com/
boosgallery/booscon

Butterfield & Butterfield

220 San Bruno Avenue
San Francisco, CA 94103
(415) 861-7500
www.butterfields.com

I. M. Chait Galleries Auctioneers

9330 Civic Center Drive
Beverly Hills, CA 90210
(310) 285-0182
www.chait.com

Christie's

20 Rockefeller Plaza
New York, NY 10020
(212) 546-1000

Christie's East

219 East 67th Street
New York, NY 10021
(212) 606-0400
www.christies.com

Coeur d'Alene Art Auction

Box 310
Hayden, ID 83835
(208) 772-9909
www.cdaartauction.com

Colonial Stamp Co.

5757 Wilshire Blvd.
Los Angeles, CA 90036
(213) 933-9435
www.colonialstamps.com

Dargate Auction Galleries

5607 Baum Blvd.
Pittsburgh, PA 15206
(412) 362-3558
www.dargate.com

Dawson's Auctioneers & Appraisers

128 American Road
Morris Plains, NJ 07950
(973) 984-6900
www.dawsons.org

Defina Auctions

1591 State Route 45
Auxtonburg, OH 44010
(440) 275-6674
www.definaauctions.com

Direct Auctioneers

7232 North Western Avenue
Chicago, IL 60645
(773) 465-3300
www.directauction.com

Douglas Auctioneers

Route 5
South Deerfield, MA 01373
(413) 665-2877
www.douglasauctioneers.com

William Doyle Galleries

175 East 87th Street
New York, NY 10128
(212) 427-2730
www.doylegalleries.com

DuMouchelle Art Galleries

409 East Jefferson Avenue
Detroit, MI 48226
(313) 963-6255
www.dumouchelles.com

Eldred's

1483 Route 6A
East Dennis, MA 02641
(508) 385-3116
www.eldreds.com

Freeman/Fine Arts of Philadelphia

1810 Chestnut Street
Philadelphia, PA 19103
(215) 563-9275
www.freemansauction.com

Garth's Auctions, Art & Antiques

2690 Stratford Road
Delaware, OH 43015
(740) 362-4771
www.garths.com

Grogan & Co.

22 Harris Street
Dedham, MA 02026
(781) 461-9500
www.groganco.com

Guernsey's

108 East 73rd Street
New York, NY 10021
(212) 794-2280
www.guernseys.com

Hantman's Auctioneers

Potomac, MD 20859
(301) 770-3720
www.hantmans.com

Harris Auction Galleries

875 North Howard Street
Baltimore, MD 21201
(410) 728-7040
www.harrisauction.com

Gene Harris Antique Auction Center

203 South 18th Street
Marshalltown, IA 50158
(515) 752-0600
www.geneharrisauctions.com

Hart Galleries

2301 South Voss Road
Houston, TX 77057
(713) 266-3500
www.hartgalleries.com

Bill Hood and Sons Art & Antique Auctions

2925 South Federal Highway
Delray Beach, FL 33483
(561) 278-8996
www.hoodauction.com

Jackson & Wickliff

12232 Hancock
Carmel, IN 46032
(317) 844-7253
www.jacksonwickliff.com

Jackson's Auctioneers & Appraisers of Antiques & Fine Art

2229 Lincoln Street
Cedar Falls, IA 50613
(319) 277-2256
www.jacksonauction.com

James D. Julia, Inc.

Route 201, Skowhegan Road
Fairfield, ME 04937
(207) 453-7125
www.juliaauctions.com

Los Angeles Modern Auctions

Box 462006
Los Angeles, CA 90046
(323) 845-9456
www.lamodern.com

Joy Luke Fine Arts

300 East Grove Street
Bloomington, IL 61701
(309) 828-5533
www.joyluke.com

Luper Auction Galleries

1515 West Broad Street
Richmond, VA 23220
(804) 359-2493

Main Auction Galleries

137 West 4th Street
Cincinnati, OH 45202
(513) 621-1280

Greg Manning Auctions

775 Passaic Avenue
West Caldwell, NJ 07006
(973) 882-0004
www.gregmanning.com

Neal Auction Co.

4038 Magazine Street
New Orleans, LA 70115
(504) 899-5329
www.nealauction.com

New Orleans Auction Galleries

801 Magazine Street
New Orleans, LA 70130
(504) 566-1849
www.neworleansauction.com

Northeast Auctions

93 Pleasant Street
Portsmouth, NH 03801
(603) 433-8400
www.northeastauctions.com

Phillips New York

406 East 79th Street
New York, NY 10021
(212) 570-4830
www.phillips-auctions.com

Phillips-Selkirk

7447 Forsyth Blvd.
St. Louis, MO 63105
(314) 726-5515
www.phillips-auctions.com/
selkirk

Pook & Pook

463 East Lancaster Avenue
Downington, PA 19335
(610) 269-0695
www.pookandpookinc.com

David Rago Auctions

Lambertville Antique &
Auction Center
333 North Main Street
Lambertville, NJ 08530
www.ragoarts.com

Skinner

63 Park Plaza
Boston, MA 02116
(617) 350-5400
www.skinner.com

Sloan's Auction Galleries

4920 Wyaconda Road
North Bethesda, MD 20852
(301) 468-4911
www.sloansauction.com

Sotheby's

1334 York Avenue
New York, NY 10021
(212) 606-7000
www.sothebys.com

Superior Galleries

9478 West Olympic Blvd.
Beverly Hills, CA 90212
(310) 203-9855
www.superiorsc.com

Swann Galleries

104 East 25th Street
New York, NY 10010
(212) 254-4710
www.swanngalleries.com

Tepper Galleries

110 East 25th Street
New York, NY 10010
(212) 677-5300
www.teppergalleries.com

John Toomey Gallery

818 North Blvd.
Oak Park, IL 60301
(708) 383-5234
www.treadwaygallery.com

Treadway Gallery

2029 Madison Road
Cincinnati, OH 45208
(513) 321-6742
www.treadwaygallery.com

Weschler & Son

909 E Street NW
Washington, DC 20004
(202) 628-1281
www.weschlers.com

Wright Gallery

1140 W. Fulton Avenue
Chicago, IL 60607
(312) 563-0020
www.wright20.com

Index

Dutch auctions, 2–3, 10
Dyes, 210–211

E

eBay, x, 33
Eisenbeis, Robin Kimball, 124
Electroplating, 218
Emeralds, 190, 192–193
English auctions, 2
Engravings, 169
Escrow payments, 115–116
Estate sales, 120
Etchings, 169–170
Experts (department specialists),
    87–88, 99

F

Fashionableness of an object,
    54–55
Fayed, Mohamed al, 50
Federal furniture, 177–178
Feedback regarding Internet
    auctions, 8, 137–141,
    142
Fine arts. *See* Artworks
Flatware, 14, 220
Flower, Ruth K., 120
Frankoma ceramics, 156
Fraud problem, 8, 141–142
Friendship quilts, 207
Fun of buying at auction,
    63–64
Furniture, 172–181
    authenticity concerns,
        172–173
    bargains, 11–12, 17–18
    collector's choice, 176–179
    large-scale, 17–18
    practical advice, 174–175
    questions to ask, 173
    taking care of your collection,
        179–180
    terminology, 180–181
    upholstered, 11–12
    wormholes in, 173–174

G

Gemstones. *See* Jewelry
Georgian furniture, 177
Glass, 182–188
    collector's choice, 184–187
    manufacturing processes,
        182–183
    practical advice, 183–184
    questions to ask, 183
    taking care of your collection,
        187–188
    terminology, 188
    themes for collections, 183
Going Once (Wooley), 119
Gold, 189–190
Goncourt, Edmond de, 39–40
Grandfather clocks, 226–227
Grueby ceramics, 156
Guaranteed minimum prices, 23
Guest, Robert J., 142

H

Hamilton, Catharine, xi
Hamilton, Charles, 36–37, 39
Hepplewhite furniture, 177–178
Hewitt, L. J., 103
Hildesley, Hugh, 101
Hindman, Leslie, xi–xii
Historical significance of an
    object, 51

I

Internet auctions, x–xi
    addictive nature, 67
    answers to questions about, 8
    chat rooms at auction sites, 68
    communication between buy-
        ers and sellers, 84–85, 114
    convenience of, 67
    feedback, 8, 137–141, 142
    formats, 9–10
    higher-end merchandise, 34–35
    item numbers, 80
    myths about, 29–35
    no-fee auctions, 67–68

number of sites, 33–34
overview of, 7–10
payment procedures, 114–116
privacy issues, 8
registration procedures, 75
risks for buyers and sellers, 137
seller's location information,
    81–82
specialized sites, 7
start/end information, 81
terms of service, 8
time remaining information, 81
user agreements, 8
variety of merchandise, 66
See also Internet bidding; Inter-
    net listings; Internet selling
Internet bidding
    anonymity for bidders, 66–67
    current high bid information, 80
    early and late bidding,
        113–114
    first bids, 81, 136–137
    proxy bidding, 112
    retracting a bid, 30–32
    sniping, 32–33
    strategies for, 112–114
    success, notification of, 114
Internet listings, 75
    creative ads, 132
    defects, honesty about, 131
    descriptions of objects, 82–83
    impression made by, 129
    information provided by, 80–82
    main text, 130–131
    misspellings in, 77
    photographs for, 131–132
    reading a listing, 79–80
    search strategies, 76–79, 129,
        131
    titles (headlines), 129–130
Internet selling
    attracting a clientele, 134
    cancellation of an auction,
        29–30
    feedback, 8, 137–141, 142